Raising Equity THROUGH SEL

A Framework for Implementing
Trauma-Informed, Culturally Responsive Teaching
and Restorative Practices

JORGE VALENZUELA

FOREWORD BY SHELDON EAKINS

A Joint Publication of

Solution Tree | Press

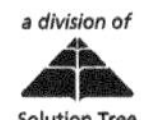

555 North Morton Street
Bloomington, IN 47404
800.733.6786 (toll free) / 812.336.7700
FAX: 812.336.7790

email: info@SolutionTree.com
SolutionTree.com

Visit **go.SolutionTree.com/diversityandequity** to download the free reproducibles in this book.

Printed in the United States of America

Library of Congress Cataloging-in-Publication Data

Names: Valenzuela, Jorge (Engineering teacher) author.
Title: Raising equity through SEL : a framework for implementing trauma-informed, culturally responsive teaching and restorative practices / Jorge Valenzuela.
Description: Bloomington, IN : Solution Tree Press, [2022] | Includes bibliographical references and index.
Identifiers: LCCN 2022007790 (print) | LCCN 2022007791 (ebook) | ISBN 9781952812910 (paperback) | ISBN 9781952812927 (ebook)
Subjects: LCSH: Affective education. | Emotional intelligence. | Psychic trauma in children. | Educational equalization. | Multicultural education. | Social justice and education.
Classification: LCC LB1072 .V37 2022 (print) | LCC LB1072 (ebook) | DDC 370.15/34--dc23/eng/20220617
LC record available at https://lccn.loc.gov/2022007790
LC ebook record available at https://lccn.loc.gov/2022007791

Solution Tree
Jeffrey C. Jones, CEO
Edmund M. Ackerman, President

Solution Tree Press
President and Publisher: Douglas M. Rife
Associate Publisher: Sarah Payne-Mills
Managing Production Editor: Kendra Slayton
Editorial Director: Todd Brakke
Art Director: Rian Anderson
Copy Chief: Jessi Finn
Production Editor: Gabriella Jones-Monserrate
Content Development Specialist: Amy Rubenstein
Copy Editor: Jessi Finn
Proofreader: Madonna Evans
Text and Cover Designer: Abigail Bowen
Associate Editor: Sarah Ludwig
Editorial Assistants: Charlotte Jones and Elijah Oates

This book is dedicated to all teachers working to develop themselves into the educators their students need.

Acknowledgments

I want to personally thank God for grace and faith, my parents, Mariam, Anisa, and Daniel.

Thank you, Tom Berger, Marva Hinton, Errol St.Clair Smith, Katrina Futrell, Michael Courtney, Marsha Granderson, Sophia Mendoza, Dominic Caguioa, Keisha Chandler, Bryan Brown, Diana Fingal, Emily Reed, Stephanie Argy, James Fester, Rich Dixon, Kendall Davies, Amber Heffner, Lindsay Zilly, Michele Dawson, Meaghan Rhame, Dr. Sarah Thomas, Dr. Marquita Blades, Amos Fodchuk, Victor Hicks, Davina Ruiz, Hedreich Nichols, Dr. William Wright, Dee Biggers, Jen Perry, Alfonso Mendoza, Yaritza Villalba, Dr. Sawsan Jaber, Alcine Mumby, and Courtney Katen for collaborating and adding to me professionally.

This book would not have been possible without Valerie Witte, Solution Tree, Hertford County Public Schools, and my terrific editors, Sarah Jubar and Gabriella Jones-Monserrate.

A Very Special Acknowledgment

It is common knowledge that no person ever succeeds alone, which is why I have to include this separate acknowledgment for Tammi Ward. She was a formative presence at the beginning of the conception of the Equity and Social-Emotional Learning (SEL) Integration Framework. She was also instrumental in helping to successfully carry out this work through various data collections and workshops. Thank you, Mrs. Ward!

Important Mentions

Equity and SEL include incredibly diverse and far-ranging topics and pedagogies, so much so that deep understanding requires learning from more than one person or organization. I want to thank and acknowledge the following scholars and entities for their fantastic contributions to these spaces: The Collaborative for Academic,

Social, and Emotional Learning (CASEL), Edutopia, Solution Tree, Association for Supervision and Curriculum Development (ACSD), the International Society for Technology in Education (ISTE), Envision Education, Corwin, PBLWorks, Dr. Sheldon Eakins, Morgan Vien, Ken Shelton, Hedreich Nichols and countless others.

I also credit the works of notable authors and life and education coaches like Eckhart Tolle, Travis Bradberry, Jay McTighe, Andrew Miller, Ava DuVernay, Ron Berger, Don Miguel Ruiz, Dr. Stephen R. Covey, Malcolm Gladwell, and Tim Grover for helping to shape my insights.

Solution Tree Press would like to thank the following reviewers:

Jennifer Carr
Instructional Coach
La Mirada Academy K–8
San Marcos, California

John D. Ewald
Education Consultant
Former Superintendent,
Principal, Teacher
Frederick, Maryland

Matt Hiefield
Teacher, District Curriculum Developer
Sunset High School

Kelly Hilliard
Math Teacher
McQueen High School
Reno, Nevada

Jessica Hochman
Educational Consultant
We Need 2 Talk
Brooklyn, New York

Shan Jorgenson-Adam
Assistant Superintendent—Learning
Battle River School Division
Camrose, Alberta, Canada

Jesse Morrill
Principal
Timnath Middle-High School
Timnath, Colorado

Mitch Nobis
Teacher
Groves High School
Beverly Hills, Michigan

Starr Sackstein
Author and Educational Consultant
The Core Collaborative
Oceanside, New York

Jennifer Steele
Assistant Director, Athletics and Activities
Northside High School
Fort Smith, Arkansas

Cecilia Wilken
Director of Teaching & Learning
Ralston Public Schools
Omaha, Nebraska

Visit **go.SolutionTree.com/diversityandequity** to download the free reproducibles in this book.

Table of Contents

Reproducibles are in italics.

About the Author

Jorge Valenzuela is an education coach, author, and advocate. He has been a classroom and online teacher since 2003, and a curriculum specialist and consultant since 2014. Using action research methodology, his work helps school leaders and teachers reach their unique success paths to innovation in school leadership, tiered instruction, project-based learning, computer science and STEM education, and social and emotional learning across the curriculum.

Jorge is an adjunct professor at Old Dominion University in Norfolk, Virginia, and the lead coach at Lifelong Learning Defined. Additionally, he facilitates workshops throughout the United States on behalf of the Association for Supervision and Curriculum Development (ASCD), Corwin, Solution Tree, and Instructional Innovation Partners. His books *Rev Up Robotics* and *Environmental Science for Grades 6–12* and his jump-start guides *Ready, Set, Robotics!* and *SEL in Action* are available from the International Society for Technology in Education. He is also an avid contributor to Edutopia and the host of the *SEL in Action* podcast on BAM Radio Network.

Jorge has a bachelor of science in management information systems from SUNY Old Westbury and a master's degree in school administration and supervision from the University of Phoenix. He is fulfilling the requirements for a doctoral degree at Old Dominion University.

To book Jorge Valenzuela for professional development, contact pd@SolutionTree.com.

Foreword

by Sheldon Eakins

As a **fellow educator**, Jorge Valenzuela and I share many commonalities. We both realize that doing the work of equity can be daunting and challenging. In facing the challenges, I began to seek opportunities to broaden my perspective of the framework of SEL or social-emotional learning. I'd previously met noteworthy individuals who contributed to this framework through my **Leading Equity podcast** and at conferences where I initially met Jorge.

At the time, I was working to become a better equity advocate and was interested in locating opportunities to expand on the issue. Attending the conference where we met was providential. I was familiar with Jorge's name; I knew he was passionate about social-emotional learning and had made many contributions to the subject. After examining the list of presenters, I decided to attend his session on the topic. It was a "marriage made in heaven," where we established a bond that to this day continues.

What impressed me most about Jorge's presentation were his strategies for implementing an SEL framework and tools that could be utilized to improve student SEL skills. I felt there had to be a connection since equity work is multileveled, and elements of SEL can be included. For instance, SEL may be considered in areas like bias, microaggression, restorative practice, and social justice – to name a few. Consequently, when it comes to the subject of SEL, I can say unequivocally Jorge IS the master who offers the best guidance on the topic I have come to know.

Once connected, the bond between Jorge and myself has extended beyond the typical working relationship. I have learned from him the importance of implementing a social-emotional framework for trauma-informed, culturally responsive teaching as well as restorative practices. His sense of urgency on the matter drives home the reason for the need to incorporate equity and SEL into lessons educators in particular develop. One of the primary reasons for incorporating equity and SEL into student lessons is the emphasis educators place on academics instead of natural student behavior.

In an era of COVID-19 and other school uncertainties, we must be even more trauma-informed regarding students. Trauma definitely impacts student behavior. Research suggests that approximately 25 percent of American children will experience at least one traumatic event by the age of sixteen. A child's trauma reaction can considerably interfere with learning and school behavior. Trauma events, as defined by the Center for Nonviolence and Social Justice, are the experiences that cause emotionally painful and distressing situations which overwhelm a person's ability to cope, thus leaving them feeling powerless.

I believe that children need space. In addition, they need to have recalibration time. While certain situations may be marginalized, a child's reaction to a traumatizing event may not be the same as that of an adult. Consequently, it is essential to ensure the child's perspective is measured to provide the necessary support. Other options for managing these kinds of events may include reciprocity and predictability. Jorge's approach to handling trauma through the SEL framework shines here.

Jorge is a well-qualified author. Not only is he an education coach and student advocate, but he also brings to the table many years as an instructor. His teaching style embraces actionable research, which he uses to facilitate his work mentoring teachers to achieve success in school leadership as well as instruction. His role as host of the podcast **SEL in Action** demonstrates the kind of wisdom this publication will impart.

To illustrate, one of the benefits of SEL involves being informed. Jorge focuses on what it means to work with students who have high needs. While some face trauma, I believe having an excellent or good working relationship with a school, guidance counselor, or assistant principal is also critical, especially in scenarios where information is proprietary.

Jorge's innovational approach to resolving this kind of challenge sets a gold standard due to the possibility of **triggers** that could occur.

In developing relationships with students, I have used Jorge's approach to identify triggers. Sometimes, we can only be informed to a certain extent, but the more information we know is helpful. My usual approach was to connect on a personal level with various activities that could later be developed as an "inside joke." In one instance, I was attempting to determine a new student's interests. With this student, I selected to play boxing.

It didn't go well.

As we were throwing air punches, he tensed up. I realized he was clearly bothered and very uncomfortable in the activity. I wasn't sure if something was wrong, but I felt a trigger had happened. I immediately discontinued the play without wanting to create a hostile environment further. Later, I approached him to talk about what had happened. He willingly shared his personal involvement in going through the justice system. The play boxing had triggered his incarceration experience.

I wish I knew more about SEL back then. It would have helped me as I reflect on my decision-making in handling the situation. Educators frequently overlook triggers and dismiss them instead of addressing them through further investigation. It takes understanding and follow-up to get to the root cause of a trigger. Emotions affect choices and behavior, and because I was mindful of this, I followed up with the student and discovered the root cause of his tension from our play boxing.

The student's reaction to the activity, followed by my further investigation, addressed the student's high need and opened the door for us to connect. It helped me understand the reason for his reaction, which helped me find a different way to improve our relationship. A lack of follow-through or disrespect for his high need could have ended disastrously or caused a profound disconnect. Of course, in situations like these, the goal is to be cognizant of the fact that since emotions affect choices and behaviors, especially in younger people, working knowledge of proprietary information is advantageous.

Jorge's work has undoubtedly had a significant impact on me. The tools and strategies recommended in this book are priceless. As stated earlier, he is a master at his craft. He doesn't limit his wisdom and knowledge to advising the educator alone. He also includes family dynamics as part of his strategy. It's imperative to consider all stakeholders in traumatic circumstances because they will process it differently. In addition to being informed, it's crucial to partner with family members as you get to know the student.

Mindfulness is a huge part of the SEL framework. For instance, in situations involving COVID 19, it helps to bear in mind student response to the condition as it happens at different levels. Student emotion and subsequent behavior toward COVID 19 in the classroom may cause them to be referred to a SPED director, as I have personally experienced.

However, being trauma-informed reduces the likelihood of referrals based on student behavior in the classroom. There may be other reasons for behavior issues, including problems associated with ADHD.

Jorge's SEL tools and strategies address ways for students to handle their behavior cognitively by teaching them how to examine personal choices that may not be physically assessable or measurable to the teacher.

According to the Collaborative for Academic, Social, and Emotional Learning (CASEL), SEL is the process through which children and adults understand and manage emotion, set and achieve positive goals, feel and show empathy for others, maintain positive relationships, and make responsible decisions.

Knowing that SEL is not an add-on but something that should be embedded within daily practices increases Jorge's credibility with me. His methods enhance my ability to build relationships that last. It can start with the type of words used and how conversations are framed in the classroom. A couple of strategies I've adopted in my SEL practices include starting the day by having students check in and being intentional about how each day starts; namely by asking students individually how they are doing.

As students see how we as educators regulate our emotions, work and collaborate, and the biases we hold, there is the opportunity to transfer those skills to them. It is also an opportunity to create an environment within the school community to have emotional intelligence skills, self-awareness, social awareness, self-management, and the empathy needed for them to succeed beyond the classroom. Instilling these skills will reduce bias and microaggressions in the generations to come!

Additionally, modeling can make a difference.

This book is a resource-based tool that all educators and other stakeholders involved in equity work, no matter where you are in your journey, will appreciate as its elements are implemented.

Introduction

> "Fight for the things that you care about,
> but do it in a way that will lead others to join you."
>
> —RUTH BADER GINSBURG, *Supreme Court justice*

At first glance, the title of this book may read to some like many buzzwords to cover in one source. Social and emotional learning (SEL) alone is a behavioral framework focusing on self and social awareness competencies and responsible decision making (CASEL, 2020b). The title includes trauma-informed, culturally responsive teaching and restorative justice, so readers know that the book is not just about SEL. Instead, it guides for assisting multiple student needs by implementing practices from these pedagogies through an equity and SEL integration framework. This book is written to either help begin or strengthen your equity journey by paying close attention to your own emotional intelligence (EQ) and the EQ of those around you.

Like past education initiatives, SEL was thrust into the national spotlight. Teachers everywhere have tried to implement it—many without adequate background in the topic, school leadership support, and while enduring political pressure. Additionally, there's been much pushback on SEL in spaces where SEL and emotional regulation are overdone and presented as a panacea for problems facing educators and students unprepared to learn (Blad, 2020).

This book is about focusing on the equity topics and SEL needs of vulnerable students. I attempt to do this by keeping research integrity (engaging in action research and citing authentic sources) and doing my best not to alienate skeptical readers. My research and work with schools informs me that teachers become frustrated when their self-efficacy is threatened by questionable policies and relentless new mandates, particularly during a pandemic like that of COVID-19 beginning in 2020. Having a set of trusted pedagogical strategies can help teachers improve SEL practice over time—even under extreme pressure.

Using what I have learned in the PhD program at Old Dominion University and in my years as an educator and curriculum consultant, I have worked with my school partners to develop a collaborative framework for equitably activating SEL across the curriculum. I say *collaborative* because equity and SEL work shouldn't alienate anyone in your school—even when some people have different core values and beliefs. The equity-based framework I introduce in this book is meant to be implemented by teams of diverse individuals who want to improve students' conditions for living and learning.

This book uplifts what I call the *Equity and SEL Integration Framework* and underscores the framework's usefulness for helping educators implement trauma-informed teaching, culturally responsive teaching, and restorative justice practices. The framework is an amalgam of insights and practices gleaned from the SEL coaching work I do with schools. It features actionable steps teachers and their coaching teams can take to make SEL a meaningful academic intervention, and not just another administrative change for educators to struggle through. The book's framework rests on emotional intelligence as its primary domain; it is designed to help us educators raise equity for those learners who need it most, including students we perceive to have privilege. Remember, equity is for all.

When I have taught this framework's principles and shared skills in workshops across the United States, some educators who were previously unsure about implementing equity and SEL in their classrooms have had their thinking transformed. Many have expressed that, instead of making them feel voiceless because of their identity, each step in the framework broadened their understanding of how to develop their own emotional intelligence skills, which then encouraged them to appropriately examine their beliefs and improve how they empathize with their students. This has led these educators to activate SEL in their daily lessons while maintaining their instructional focus. Many educators, even those who weren't initially inclined to participate, have expressed gratitude for making the process inclusive.

On the flip side, many equity enthusiasts who have participated in my sessions have appreciated the framework's method of implementing trauma-informed teaching, restorative justice, and culturally responsive teaching practices to enhance their school SEL plan. The framework in this book is not the only way to implement SEL. Still, the framework's steps create a clear pathway for building the skills and knowledge educators require to help marginalized and isolated students. My hope is that teacher teams use these practices to level the academic playing field for all students and help them succeed.

Part of the initial work was to engage leadership and teachers in learning walks to audit and glean what's happening in classrooms before investing time and resources to design professional development (PD) for SEL. Our classroom visits and discussions were very telling and helpful for informing what's needed for both teachers and students to thrive socially and academically. Classrooms will always be the incubator for what's needed in schools and education. It's challenging for instructional leaders to keep their fingers on the pulse of what's happening in their schools if they're not interacting with teachers or listening to them.

Our data discussions provided insights for recommending appropriate SEL tools and practices for empowering teachers on this new journey. Resoundingly, we found schools need to set up ways of promoting understanding and healthy discourse between adults. In turn, they could team to increase emotional regulation for staff and students, raise equity for marginalized kids, improve SEL integration in daily lessons, and maintain intellectually safe spaces for all. Moreover, we found that the steps to achieve our SEL goals require dedication to learning and practice in a straightforward process informed by data and that honors everyone's voice. I hope that this book and supporting PD through Solution Tree can provide you and your colleagues with clear guidance for achieving what equity and SEL success means in your space.

The Discovery of Social-Emotional Learning and Emotional Intelligence

As an education coach since 2014, I've spent the better part of a decade touring the United States (twenty-seven states and seventy-plus cities), working with schools to collaboratively solve instructional problems. Instructional needs I help support include tiered instruction, SEL, project-based learning, performance tasks, and science, technology, engineering, and mathematics (STEM) integration. I spent a decade cultivating the foundational knowledge for doing so as a curriculum specialist for an urban school district in Richmond, Virginia.

In addition to helping educators with multiple aspects of their instructional design practices, I assist schools in aligning and embedding key education reform initiatives across the curriculum. Some education reform initiatives I have worked with include computational thinking and computer science integration, STEM, restorative practices, SEL, project-based learning, and effective technology integration. In the ever-changing education landscape, my ability to focus on multiple areas of education is a major plus for the school systems I partner with. We work together to create viable professional learning solutions for both their staff and their students. Enhancing the teaching profession by helping educators improve teaching and learning in their schools and classrooms is important to me. It's the purpose of my work.

In my work, I've had to learn to pay close attention to my own emotions and the emotions of those around me. It's not always easy, but I have found it necessary to perform at my personal best, no matter the topic or area. So, if there is a secret to how I carry out my work, I'd say it's following my heart and refining my emotional intelligence skills. Perhaps the greatest influence for this has been my shift in focus to SEL. This shift occurred in the spring of 2016 due to a transformative professional learning I attended during a PBLWorks national faculty summit. Formerly known as the Buck Institute for Education, PBLWorks (https://www.pblworks.org) is an organization that has helped shape my pedagogical perspective in several key instructional areas. At the conference, colleagues and I learned about the effects of trauma due to racism and the deportation of many *Latinx* (a gender-neutral term for people of Latin American descent, used as an alternative to *Latina/o*) people in California. We also visited Angel Island and saw artifacts that had belonged to Chinese immigrants who were detained during World War II. It was there that I also learned about the need for equity and the importance of raising it for the students furthest from opportunity.

This experience with PBLWorks triggered many painful emotions inside me, being the son of an immigrant who was detained by law enforcement for some time, which forced me to live in the New York City foster care system. But as the adage goes, "You have to feel it to heal it," so it strengthened my journey of healing and understanding.

Since that summit in 2016, I have expanded my knowledge of emotional intelligence, educational equity, restorative justice, inclusive pedagogies, and culturally responsive teaching strategies. My previous work and life experiences, along with constant dedication to new learning, have shaped this book's advice to educators for improving their districts' SEL plans.

The Catalyst for the Equity and Social-Emotional Learning Integration Framework

The Equity and Social-Emotional Learning Integration Framework came into being because educators needed a solution to problems introduced by rapid, exponential changes in education. When the COVID-19 pandemic began in 2020, it demanded that U.S. schools suddenly figure out distance learning. Hertford County Public Schools in North Carolina and I established an instructional coaching partnership at the time to engage the school system's staff in virtual professional learning sessions. Early in that work, a Hertford County assistant superintendent introduced me to the Instructional Design Principles for Remote Teaching and Learning (see figure I.1, page 5) spearheaded by North Carolina State University and aligned with the North Carolina Department of Public Instruction. She and I had already been

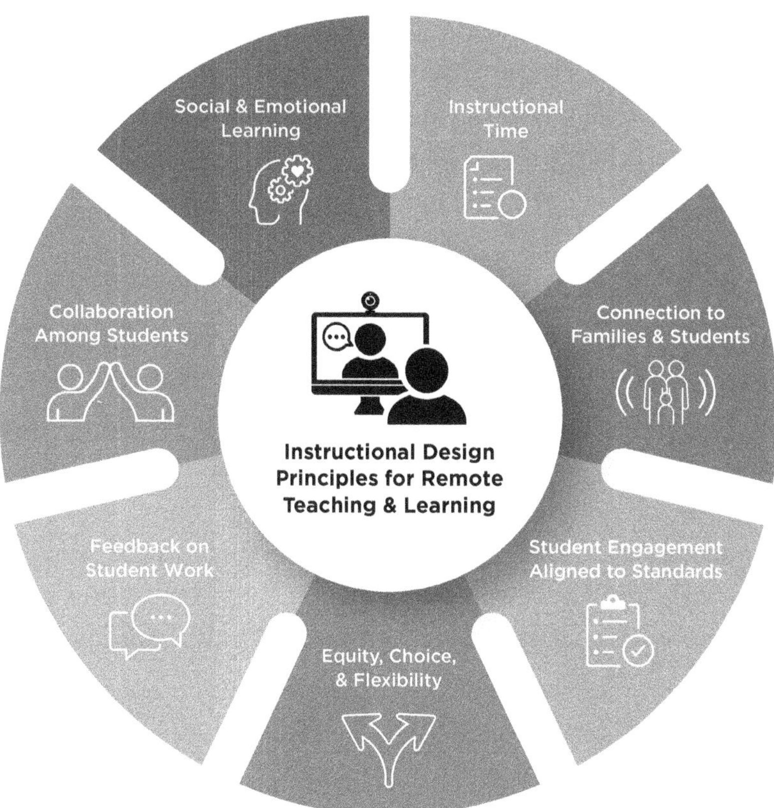

Source: North Carolina Department of Public Instruction. Used with permission.

FIGURE I.1: Instructional Design Principles for Remote Teaching and Learning framework.

working together for some time to grow teachers, and she asked me if we could align the heavy concepts that make up the framework.

After closely examining the framework, I realized how powerful it could be if we leveraged it correctly by connecting each of the targeted items—especially equity and SEL—to the teachers' practice. Together, we worked hard to create modules that would help educators integrate equity and SEL into academic and career and technical education lessons in tandem with engaging and innovative remote teaching strategies. We had many successes, including developing and refining the Equity and SEL Integration Framework for this book.

We developed the framework using data from the diverse individuals who were dedicated to uniting adults and improving student social and academic outcomes in Hertford County Public Schools. Part of the initial work of designing the framework involved engaging leadership and teachers in virtual classroom observations, where we audited and observed classrooms in session, before we invested time and resources to design professional development for SEL. Our virtual classroom visits and discussions revealed what both teachers and students need in order to thrive socially and academically. Classrooms are the incubators for what is needed in schools and education. It is challenging for instructional leaders to keep their fingers on the pulse of their schools if they're not interacting with or listening to teachers.

Our data discussions provided insights about appropriate SEL tools and practices that would empower teachers on this new journey. Resoundingly, we found schools need to set up ways of promoting understanding and healthy discourse between adults. In turn, the adults can team up to increase staff's and students' emotional regulation, raise equity for marginalized students, improve SEL integration in daily lessons, and maintain intellectually safe spaces for all. Moreover, we found that achieving our SEL goals required a dedication to learning and practice using a straightforward, data-informed process that honored everyone's voice. Beyond the workshop modules and framework for equity and SEL, this work produced several how-to blog posts and virtual conference presentations that have helped improve educators' practices in teaching with technology and focusing on equity and SEL.

This work also addresses racial equity in meaningful ways that educators who want to learn more can consider. I am proudest of that. I hope that this book gives you and your colleagues the clear guidance you need to achieve what equity and SEL success mean in your space. As a man of color as well as a parent and teacher of African American students, this is a very important topic to me, as it is for many other educators who also teach and love Black and Brown students. As an English learner who lived part of my life in poverty in the U.S. foster care system, I have seen firsthand the catastrophic effects of inequities spanning the last three generations of my family. We have been marginalized by broken family bonds, career instability, lack of opportunity, alcoholism, incarceration, and poverty. Before becoming a teacher, I was unaware of how many students of color face similar hardships. Through this book, I hope teachers will become allies who equitably use research-based SEL strategies to help teach students of color who have endured such traumas. (Data on the state of oppressions endured by people of color will appear in chapter 9, page 153. Additionally, that chapter includes recommendations for being more inclusive of students who belong to marginalized groups, such as Asian Americans and Pacific Islanders, immigrants and refugees, and the LGBTQ community.) Addressing these issues in SEL plans can be crucial to improving learning outcomes for students from underserved and historically harmed communities.

My collaboration with Hertford County Public Schools grew into multiple opportunities to refine our practice by collecting and examining data—which eventually evolved into the five-step Equity and SEL Integration Framework featured in this book. (Appendix B of this book, page 207, includes our examinations of several data collections and how the framework developed over several months if you are interested in the research aspect of this work.) Through this book, I hope to help readers align their key education reform initiatives. By bridging research and sound teaching practices with personal success stories (and challenges) from other educators and critical resources, this book can help you enhance your teaching practices with technology.

The Reason for a Framework to Incorporate Equity and SEL Into Lessons

In education, SEL advances equity and collaborative learning environments and leads students and educators to cocreate thriving schools. I developed the five-step Equity and SEL Integration Framework to help teachers seamlessly and equitably incorporate SEL into their daily and weekly lesson plans. The framework also guides them with key strategies for restoring justice, becoming trauma informed, and being culturally responsive toward the students they serve. Each step is supported by research and is grounded in sound teaching practices that are actionable and replicable in any classroom. The aim of this book is to provide teachers with strategies for beginning this work either independently or with colleagues—ideally, within a grade- or department-level team that shares students.

Not all educators teach in districts where SEL training is readily available. Even where training is available, educators don't always have a clear road map to understanding or implementing related pedagogies such as restorative justice, trauma-informed teaching, and culturally responsive teaching. Being able to combine the aforementioned pedagogies to do SEL effectively and equitably is important for educators. In SEL, we are teaching students to better understand themselves, their environment, and others. We cannot do this effectively if we lack cultural or social competence with the students we serve. Therefore, filling in our knowledge gaps and adapting sound practices are necessary for equitably activating SEL in our classrooms.

About the CASEL 5

The Collaborative for Academic, Social, and Emotional Learning (CASEL) defines five competencies that support the effort of practically applying SEL in classrooms. These competencies, known as the *CASEL 5*, are as follows.

1. Self-awareness
2. Self-management
3. Social awareness

4. Relationship skills
5. Responsible decision making

The CASEL 5 (which will be fully explained in chapter 1, page 15) is important to understanding the contents of this book, and particularly the Equity and SEL Integration Framework. These competencies are grounded in research on how educators can help students develop emotional intelligence skills for personal and social competence (CASEL, 2021c).

The five-step Equity and SEL Integration Framework uses the CASEL 5 and emotional intelligence as the foundation for developing the cultural intelligence that educators need in order to personalize SEL plans. These five steps will be fully explained in this book's first five chapters.

1. Learn the basics of the CASEL 5 and emotional intelligence.
2. Assess your unconscious biases and beliefs about students.
3. Improve your knowledge of your students.
4. Help students develop emotional intelligence skills.
5. Activate SEL in your lessons (curriculum).

Each step of the Equity and SEL Integration Framework will interact meaningfully with each competency of the CASEL 5 to ensure students gain the skills they need to become emotionally independent while in a safe, equitable space.

Who Should Read This Book

I wrote this book for K–12 teachers who are looking to develop or enhance their SEL plan but may not have experience aligning SEL with other related pedagogies, such as culturally responsive teaching, restorative justice, and trauma-informed teaching. That's where the Equity and SEL Integration Framework comes in. This book is also for district and school leaders looking to create systemic change.

Ultimately, this book is for all educators who want to raise equity for vulnerable students by becoming more inclusive in their practice and activating SEL in lessons as needed but who are unsure of where to start and how to scaffold the learning experiences of all their learners. Through lessons on the fundamentals of SEL and other equity-raising practices, both the novice and the expert can level up their SEL-infused teaching by applying the content in this book.

Whether you're an English language arts, mathematics, science, history, art, computer science, or career and technical education teacher, this book provides you the know-how for strategically engaging your learners with lessons that do not skimp on the appropriate rigor levels required for your class. Additionally, this book is for the special education support teacher and the teacher tasked to hold out-of-schooltime remote clubs of any sort (such as 21st century after-school programs).

Although this book shares strategies you can adopt on your own as an educator, you will preferably tackle this material with the support of a collaborative team or as part of a school- or districtwide collaborative team. So, whether you are teaching students in a support role, in an after-school club, or just as a fun activity, you will find strategies in this book to support you on your SEL teaching journey.

How to Navigate This Book

This book is organized into three parts, each with two or more chapters. Part 1 (chapters 1–5) defines and explores the fundamentals of the Equity and SEL Integration Framework and provides empirical evidence and lots of straightforward examples for its use as part of a comprehensive SEL plan. (The rationale and research methods employed to develop the Equity and SEL Integration Framework are found in appendix B, page 207.) Also, the intersections of educational equity, social-emotional learning, and solid strategies for becoming more socially and culturally competent are highlighted in these chapters through research, vignettes, and instructional practices. Chapters 1–5 each represent a step of the framework, respectively, and are as follows.

- **Chapter 1, "Learn the Basics of the CASEL 5 and Emotional Intelligence":** This chapter defines emotional intelligence as applied in the rest of the book and explores the elements of the Collaborative for Academic, Social, and Emotional Learning (CASEL).
- **Chapter 2, "Assess Your Unconscious Biases and Beliefs About Students":** This chapter provides tools to help us identify and unlearn our own prejudices as educators and people so we can better serve our students.
- **Chapter 3, "Improve Your Knowledge of Your Students":** This chapter explores respectful and appropriate tactics to become more familiar with students so we can begin to accommodate their unique needs in the classroom.
- **Chapter 4, "Help Students Develop Emotional Intelligence Skills":** In this chapter, we revisit some of the tools we gained in chapter 1 and apply them to our curriculum so students can develop the emotional intelligence they need to excel in their learning.

- **Chapter 5, "Activate SEL in Your Lessons":** In this chapter, we use the tools and skills we've gained from previous steps of the Equity and SEL Integration Framework to ensure our curriculum is equitable and promotes social-emotional learning.

Part 2 provides K–12 teachers with chapters dedicated to trauma-informed teaching, culturally responsive teaching, and restorative justice for improving their SEL plans. Each chapter provides an overview of an approach, empirical evidence of the approach's alignment with SEL, and strategies for adopting the approach's practices in our SEL plans. The chapters in part 2 are as follows.

- **Chapter 6, "Implement Trauma-Informed Teaching":** This chapter delves into ways in which trauma can affect students' classroom experiences, and it shares strategies for developing trauma-informed teaching practices in order to help students in need.
- **Chapter 7, "Implement Culturally Responsive Teaching":** This chapter examines culturally responsive teaching strategies and ways in which empowered educators can actively create multicultural spaces for students to engage in.
- **Chapter 8, "Implement Restorative Practices and Restorative Justice":** This chapter discusses restorative justice in the classroom and examines the large body of research on restorative practices' effectiveness in schools.

Part 3 focuses on enhancing an SEL plan with inclusive, technology-supported pedagogy and raising equity for students who are marginalized due to race, gender, sexual orientation, and immigrant or refugee status.

- **Chapter 9, "Add Inclusive Pedagogy to SEL Plans":** This chapter explores inclusive pedagogy and focuses on how inclusivity in the classroom actively improves students' lives and learning capabilities.
- **Chapter 10, "Activate SEL Through Equity and Educational Technology":** This chapter provides strategies, lessons, and advice gleaned from teachers who learned to teach remotely through the COVID-19 pandemic, and it shares tips for improving one's overall digital teaching practice. Also, it highlights technology tools and strategies for engaging students in SEL in hybrid and blended learning environments.

Finally, note that in many chapters, you will find Important Note for Teachers feature boxes that highlight unique elements of a concept or strategy. My aim is to remain on topic but supplement and clarify reader understanding throughout the book.

This book provides access to downloadable additional resources in appendix A (page 193). Readers can familiarize themselves with the rationale for and research behind the Equity and SEL Integration Framework in appendix B (page 207). Finally, this book concludes with cited references and resources.

About ISTE

The International Society for Technology in Education (ISTE) inspires the creation of solutions and connections that improve opportunities for all learners by delivering: practical guidance, evidence-based professional learning, virtual networks, thought-provoking events, and the ISTE Standards. ISTE is also the leading publisher of books focused on technology in education. For more information or to become an ISTE member, visit https://www.iste.org. Subscribe to ISTE's YouTube channel and connect with ISTE on Twitter, Facebook and LinkedIn.

This book uses the ISTE Standards as a goal metric for its pedagogical content. The ISTE Standards:

> provide the competencies for learning, teaching and leading in the digital age, providing a comprehensive roadmap for the effective use of technology in schools worldwide. Grounded in learning science research and based on practitioner experience, the ISTE Standards ensure that using technology for learning can create high-impact, sustainable, scalable and equitable learning experiences for all learners.
>
> For over 20 years, the standards have been used, researched and updated to continuously reflect the latest research-based best practices that define success in using technology to learn, teach, lead and coach. The standards have been adopted in all fifty U.S. states and many countries throughout the world. Aligned to UNESCO's Sustainable Development Goals, the standards are available in eight languages. (ISTE, n.d.b)

 Visit https://www.iste.org/iste-standards to read more about the ISTE Standards and to view the Standards in full.

Summary

I would sum up my personal story and commitment to equity and SEL as having the desire to honor students' needs and tackle them directly using good frameworks and tools. SEL and its pedagogical counterparts (trauma-informed, culturally responsive teaching and restorative practices) require adaptable people full of love and commitment who continuously evolve their practice to raise equity for all students. Given the difficulty of teaching, I've been fortunate to see many educators embody the Equity and SEL Integration Framework's five steps.

As you and your teaching team or you alone begin your journey with part 1 of this book, I hope you remember that the practices you find in the following chapters shouldn't be rigid—some may only have a season in your classroom. Therefore, ground yourself in the fundamental concepts; assume the steps in the uplifted framework with desire and openness to cocreate intellectual safety with your colleagues and students.

PART I

The Equity and SEL Integration Framework

The following five chapters offer in-depth explanations of each step of the Equity and SEL Integration Framework, notable research supporting each step, and actionable classroom implementation practices. If knowing about each step's conception and the corresponding data is valuable to you, please read appendix B (page 207).

Furthermore, this section recommends materials for some critical self-work that educators can focus on to sharpen their emotional intelligence skill sets and their equity lens prior to implementing SEL with students.

CHAPTER 1

Learn the Basics of the CASEL 5 and Emotional Intelligence

KEY CHAPTER TASKS

- Understand the five competencies in CASEL's integrated framework and how they are interrelated.
- Develop the multiple skill sets associated with the CASEL 5.
- Review research that informed CASEL's integrated framework.
- Learn the required self-work for teachers.

Understanding the CASEL 5, the five competencies uplifted in SEL, is the first step in the Equity and SEL Integration Framework because CASEL (2021c) offers rigorous research that support its integrated framework. The five competencies can help raise educational equity through coordinated efforts and intentional partnerships among schools, families, and the community. As part 2 of this book will explore (page 105), the CASEL 5 can powerfully enhance other equity-based teaching approaches, such as restorative justice and trauma-informed and culturally responsive teaching. This chapter provides the foundational knowledge required for activating SEL across the curriculum and the emotional intelligence skills needed to successfully implement the subsequent steps in the Equity and SEL Integration Framework.

The CASEL 5 can also support the implementation of equity-raising practices that schools may use to revise their diversity, equity, and inclusion (DEI) efforts. This, too, will be explored in part 3 of this book (page 151). In DEI, *diversity* refers to having perspective, representation, challenging conversations, and support of inclusion. *Inclusion* refers to creating environments that support diversity, are conducive to feedback, and are open to all. *Equity* is about being fair and appreciating both diversity and inclusion.

The goal of this chapter is to acquaint you with the theoretical goals of using SEL along with critical need-to-knows for commencing the work. This chapter will define the CASEL 5 in full, and it will provide comprehensive guidance on the research that supports the CASEL and SEL frameworks and the strategies for applying the content in this book.

The CASEL 5

CASEL (2021c), the world leader in SEL research, lists five SEL competencies through which educators can enable their students to better understand their environment, themselves, and others. Known as the *CASEL 5*, these competencies enable learners to develop the skills necessary to become better students and people.

1. **Self-awareness:** The ability to accurately recognize one's own emotions, thoughts, and values and how they influence behavior; skills for self-awareness include the following.
    - Labeling emotions accurately
    - Assessing personal assets and limitations correctly
    - Setting realistic goals
    - Possessing a strong sense of confidence and optimism
2. **Self-management:** The ability to regulate thoughts and behaviors and effectively work toward personal and academic goals; self-management includes successfully applying strategies for the following.
    - Regulating emotions
    - Managing stressful situations
    - Restraining impulses
    - Deferring gratification
    - Motivating oneself
    - Doing one's best work when completing assignments
3. **Social awareness:** The ability to empathize with others, including those belonging to diverse cultures and backgrounds, and take their perspective even when it contradicts one's own; qualities of social awareness include the following.
    - Empathizing and taking others' perspectives
    - Appreciating and respecting diversity

- Understanding and respecting social and ethical norms for appropriate behavior
- Recognizing and utilizing family, community, and school resources effectively

4. **Relationship skills:** The ability to establish and maintain healthy and fulfilling relationships with diverse individuals and groups; those who possess good relationship skills exhibit the following behaviors.
    - Providing others unconditional regard
    - Communicating effectively
    - Listening thoroughly
    - Cooperating with others
    - Resisting negative peer and social pressure
    - Negotiating conflict constructively and becoming an ally
    - Seeking help by communicating clearly and appropriately with both peers and adults
5. **Responsible decision making:** The ability to make constructive choices about personal behavior and social interactions based on ethical standards, safety concerns, and social norms; this ability includes making decisions with the following qualities.
    - Evaluating the consequences of one's actions and behavior
    - Learning to analyze information, data, and facts to make a reasoned judgment
    - Evaluating the impacts of decisions on oneself, interpersonal relationships, the community, and the overall institution (school, for example)
    - Recognizing critical-thinking skills as applicable and valuable in school, at home, and in the community
    - Demonstrating concern for one's well-being and the well-being of others
    - Exhibiting thoughtfulness of one's responsibility to behave ethically

All the five competencies are related to one another and can function concurrently; this is apparent in table 1.1 (page 18). Both self-awareness and self-management focus on skill sets related to self and appear in the same color in the framework graphic.

Social awareness and relationship skills focus on skills and attributes related to others and appear in the same category (CASEL, 2021a). Responsible decision-making skills work simultaneously with the four other skill sets. As teachers begin to implement SEL with students, it's essential that they identify and emphasize one competency's correlations with the others (see table 1.1). These are powerful concepts for learners of all ages to understand, and ones that step 4 of the Equity and SEL Integration Framework will further explore (chapter 4, page 61).

TABLE 1.1: Connections Between the CASEL 5 Competencies

CASEL 5 Competency	Example Student Action	How a Teacher Might Respond	How It Might Connect With Another Competency
Self-Awareness	A student appears upset when recess is canceled due to weather.	Have the student accurately label the emotions they are experiencing (like anger, sadness, and others).	The student can now find a strategy for emotional regulation (self-management).
Self-Management	A student shows difficulty in exercising self-control by getting frustrated easily and giving up quickly.	Have the student examine which emotions trigger frustration, and provide a system for choosing a better response.	The student can now use a strategy that is also useful for responsible decision-making.
Social Awareness	A student appears intolerant of others belonging to different backgrounds and cultures.	Have the student examine their top five cultural identities, and ask how they would feel if they had to give up any of them.	The student can now use a strategy that is also useful for relationship skills and self-management.
Relationship Skills	A student isn't mindful of airspace during group conversations and cuts others off before they finish their sentences.	Have the student examine how their peers might feel and how cutting others off impacts their rapport.	The student can now use a strategy that is also useful for self-management.
Responsible Decision Making	A student shows a lack of impulse control by grabbing things that belong to others instead of asking them first.	Have the student examine their decisions and learn a system for making better ones.	The student can now use a strategy that is also useful for social awareness and self-management.

Instilling students with the qualities of the CASEL 5, which are necessary for emotional growth, requires educators to integrate the CASEL 5 into their instruction. The following section will provide some grounding research to support you in applying the CASEL 5 integrated framework in your school.

Research That Informed the CASEL and SEL Framework

CASEL developed and informed the CASEL 5 framework through years of rigorous research. Since 1994, CASEL's research has advanced the scientific base for SEL by continuously refining and improving the original research, synthesizing other notable work in the field, and spotlighting studies from colleagues and collaborators. Early meta-analyses show that SEL is not a one-size-fits-all intervention; the highest impact (largest effect size) occurs when SEL experiences are personalized to one's context or culture (Sklad, Diekstra, de Ritter, Ben, & Gravesteijn, 2012; Taylor, Oberle, Durlak, & Weissberg, 2017; Wiglesworth et al., 2016). This is encouraging for educators who are dedicated to learning how they can adapt SEL techniques to increase diverse students' academic growth and improve their well-being. More encouraging is that over three hundred studies captured in four major meta-analyses support that SEL helps with both short- and long-term academic and emotional development (Mahoney, Durlak, & Weissberg, 2018).

A landmark meta-analysis combining data from 213 studies involving over 270,000 learners reveals that when schools include SEL in the core curriculum for multiple years, they positively impact both behavior and learning in the following ways (Durlak, Weissberg, Dymnicki, Taylor, & Schellinger, 2011).

- Schools with SEL in their core curriculum have 24 percent more students who show improved social behaviors and lower levels of distress.
- Aggression and emotional distress among students decrease.
- Helping behaviors increase in school.
- Students' attitudes toward themselves and others improve.
- Students' academic performance increases by 11 percentile points.

Approximately 27 percent more students show improved academic performance when they experience this program. The data also reveal that SEL can have long-term positive impacts on both students' academics (up to eighteen years) and their personal lives (such as emotional distress and drug use), as shown in another meta-analysis involving eighty-two studies and almost one hundred thousand students from various countries (Taylor et al., 2017).

More recent data and research show that lockdowns resulting from the COVID-19 pandemic have caused a worsening in young people's mental health (Hudson, 2022). A systematic review finds that adapting versatile SEL interventions improves social-emotional skills that reduce symptoms of depression and anxiety in youth in the short term (Clarke et al., 2021).

Knowing that SEL works and how the research informs and supports the CASEL 5 competencies is empowering. As we begin to look for ways to activate SEL in our lessons, we will quickly discover that each of the CASEL 5 has its own wide range of skills.

Working with thousands of educators has provided me with insight into their needs and anxieties. When they learn what SEL entails, they rarely push back on the importance of assisting students in developing emotional intelligence skills. Still, many are concerned that too much time on SEL will take away from their teaching of content (mathematics, English language arts, and more). Others feel they lack emotional intelligence skills themselves and wouldn't know how to go about uplifting SEL skills in daily lessons. And although table 1.1 illustrates how robust and impactful the CASEL 5 can be, it can also appear daunting with a curriculum to teach. I recommend that you treat much of this content as informative for understanding what we aim to have students accomplish with SEL using the CASEL 5. However, be sure to meet yourself where you and your class currently are on your SEL journey, and adjust as needed by focusing on relevant lessons and material. This chapter is about you, the educator or administrator, understanding the basics of the CASEL 5 and emotional intelligence.

The purpose here is to help students begin developing the emotional intelligence skills *they* require for restoring their inner peace and learning at their best. Teacher or student, it can take a lifetime to fully learn every item (or even half the items) on the skill set lists in table 1.1. We just don't have enough time with students to develop them all. Remember, students and educators are not all in the same place emotionally, but they will both do better when they're at ease in a learning environment. Psychological research shows that in order to effectively coach students through their emotions, we educators need to first fill three critical knowledge gaps as the required inward-out work: (1) understanding emotions, (2) labeling emotions, and (3) regulating (self-managing) emotions (David & Congleton, 2013).

Strategies for Understanding Your Emotions

Psychology teaches us that emotion is a complex state of feeling that impacts people's physical and psychological changes (Cherry, 2022). This, in turn, influences thoughts and behavior. Educators beginning this work must understand emotions' power over the mind, body, and behavior by focusing on the following strategies. This insight will particularly help educators understand the impact of emotions on their and their students' overall well-being and social interactions. For example, in the classroom, a student may feel anxiety due to the buildup of several stressful life situations, like a caregiver's death, encounters with a bully, and a lack of understanding of academic content. Neglecting these emotions over time may trigger excessive anxiety for students and cause apprehension, irritability, or anger (Hendel, 2018). Some students may withdraw socially or negatively engage peers as a result. This can disrupt learning and other aspects of life if the students do not receive assistance for coping with the built-up stressors and tools for working through emotional exhaustion. Unfortunately, many people never receive this assistance, and they suffer the impact of those stressors on their lives.

As an example, neglecting my own emotions caused me to avoid owning some of my previous negligence toward my students and others because I did not know how to acknowledge the way I showed up emotionally for both myself and others. If you have also behaved this way, don't linger in guilt. Emotions are not always easy to comprehend or catch in real time, but luckily, we have resources, like psychologists and the CASEL 5, to help us make better sense of it all. Furthermore, CASEL's research in the field of SEL is readily available in a neat clearinghouse of SEL background and research (CASEL, 2021c).

This chapter aims to make a lot of what the CASEL 5 encompasses more understandable and eventually more actionable in schools. The following sections include various strategies to help you recognize your emotions using Plutchik's wheel and regulate them using an emotions planner.

Recognize Your Emotions Using Plutchik's Wheel

It is imperative to accurately name emotions we experience so we can effectively manage our emotional state (David & Congleton, 2013). Psychologists call this *labeling*. To start, use Robert Plutchik's (2001) wheel of emotions to recognize your emotions in different situations. The wheel (a free, interactive, and downloadable version is available on the Six Seconds Emotional Intelligence Network website: bit.ly/3czSECq) simplifies emotions by causing us to focus on eight primary ones: (1) anger, (2) anticipation, (3) joy, (4) trust, (5) fear, (6) surprise, (7) sadness, and (8) disgust. Based on each emotion's physiological reaction, each primary emotion has a polar opposite—we call these *secondary emotions*. We observe in Plutchik's wheel that joy is the opposite of sadness, anticipation is the opposite of surprise, disgust is the opposite of trust, and fear is the opposite of anger. Furthermore, the framework shows how emotions intensify as they move from the outside to the center of the wheel—their shrinking distance from the center indicates increased intensity in the emotion. The following table 1.2 shows the primary emotions, their opposites, and some examples of their intensity-based derivatives.

TABLE 1.2: Primary and Secondary Emotions

Primary Emotion	Intensity Derivatives of Primary Emotion	Opposite Primary Emotion	Intensity Derivatives of Secondary Emotion
Anger	Rage, annoyance, aggressiveness, contempt	**Fear**	Terror, apprehension, submission
Disgust	Boredom, loathing, contempt	**Trust**	Acceptance, admiration, love
Anticipation	Vigilance, interest	**Surprise**	Amazement, distraction, awe
Joy	Ecstasy, serenity, optimism	**Sadness**	Grief, pensiveness, disapproval, remorse

Source: Adapted from Plutchik, 2001.

Restricting the wheel to the eight primary emotions helps categorize emotions and responses to them. Over time and with practice, you'll recognize that emotions we experience daily are an amalgamation of the eight basic emotions and can stem from one or more of them. This critical understanding can help us identify emotional triggers, which we must do to plan and respond with good self-regulation tactics.

Along with labeling, educators benefit from skillfully recognizing how certain emotions and the feelings they elicit can be *trauma triggers*—psychological stimuli that evoke involuntary recall of a past traumatic experience (Meyer, 2012). This recognition is especially important for the negative emotions, as they tend to cause problems for students and us. Many of us don't like to feel or lean into our negative emotions, but they are a gift because they alert us to where we need to begin our work. Emotions have the power to influence our views of the world and decisions about situations we encounter. Common situations that may trigger intense emotions and reactions for educators include the following.

- Rejection
- Unfair treatment
- Challenged beliefs and ideas
- Exclusion
- Criticism
- Betrayal

Experiencing emotions is universal, and people at any age experience trauma triggers. As a result, this critical self-work allows us to better empathize with students and determine how SEL can help them recognize emotions.

Another helpful neuroscience tidbit for demystifying emotions is that our brain creates emotions by assigning meaning to bodily sensations from our lived experiences (Zimmerman, 2019). And although they are highly related, we experience emotions and feelings in sequential order—emotions precede feelings (Meyer, 2012), and feelings precede moods and behavior (Valenzuela, 2021f). Using a tool like Plutchik's (2001) wheel of emotions to recognize the wide range of emotions that cause everyone to feel fear, anxiety, anger, sadness, joy, and love is incredibly helpful for advancing our emotional intelligence. This critical awareness can help both adults and learners *respond* more and *react* less to emotions. Although responses and reactions may appear similar, reactions happen quickly, driven by the unconscious mind's beliefs, biases, and prejudices (James, 2016). Reacting is helpful when we need to protect ourselves and we don't have much time to weigh options. On the other hand, responding requires us to be emotionally intelligent enough to tune in to our feelings and allow our emotional reactions to pass instead of meeting them with impulsive action—often to the detriment of ourselves and others. As this book progresses, you will see how continuously strengthening awareness of this can be instrumental in teachers' and students' cocreation of equitable, collaborative, and inclusive school communities.

Regulate Your Emotions Using the Emotions Planner

The more I delve into SEL and emotional intelligence, the clearer it becomes that learning to regulate oneself can take years of consistent practice, patience, and honesty. Philosopher Lao Tzu (1996) is credited with saying, "Knowing *others* is intelligence; knowing *yourself* is true wisdom. Mastering *others* is strength. Mastering *yourself* is true power." I assume he means "mastering emotions" when he references "mastering yourself." Learning to regulate emotions is the essential first step to improving our internal realities. Since we educators are also helping students with emotion management, we should take the time to become acquainted with some of the research.

Psychological research exploring emotional regulation is quite broad and informs us that we can influence our emotions (whether automatic or conscious) through labeling and regulation strategies (Psychology Today Staff, 2020). Learning to label and regulate in my personal life has assisted me in professionally helping others regulate their own emotions. For example, I previously sensed I was doing something wrong in my relationships with my two teenagers but had trouble pinpointing it. Upon discovering the book *Emotional Intelligence 2.0* (Bradberry & Greaves, 2009) and taking the emotional intelligence appraisal that accompanies it, I drilled down what I needed to do—which included learning new skills and taking new approaches during challenging conversations with my students. Before I explain how the book and appraisal helped transform my interactions with my students, let's quickly unpack how the emotional intelligence appraisal works. It uses quick and reliable methods developed by experts in psychological research and assessment to deliver individual and targeted scores for the critical components of emotional intelligence: overall emotional intelligence, self-awareness, self-management, social awareness, and relationship management (Bradberry & Greaves, 2009). All you need to do is answer the questions honestly. The assessment tool does the rest; it recommends new skills and how to bring them into action. When I first took the assessment in March 2019, my social competence score was seventy-four. This score pinpointed I needed to make a more conscious effort to regulate my emotions, especially in social interactions with my students.

My emotional intelligence scores told me that I had to revamp my method for providing feedback to my students. Learning to empathize by accepting what the students would often say about my feedback became instrumental for moving us forward. For example, they told me that my feedback was problematic for the following reasons.

- I spoke too long without interruption (twenty to thirty minutes).
- I brought up already-discussed points and veered off topic.
- I compared students to others too frequently.
- I used educational jargon.

By taking the time to apply strategies in *Emotional Intelligence 2.0* and use good common sense, I learned three things that improved my feedback to students (Bradberry & Greaves, 2009).

1. I ask students if they want my feedback before providing it. My students (and others) resent it when I don't do that.
2. I think about what I want to say and write it down in three or four straightforward sentences, checking my tone to avoid condescension.
3. I must always be kind, specific, and helpful—à la Ron Berger of EL Education (n.d.).

As a result, I am better equipped to apply emotional intelligence skills and strategies when I respond to my students and others. But like anyone else, I have my bad days and am still working on improving my emotional intelligence.

In my personal emotion management work, I have significantly benefited from the work of James J. Gross, professor and emotions researcher at Stanford University. His research concludes that we humans can learn to modulate and alter the emotions we experience, and it shows that the result of modulation determines our last emotional response (Gross, 2015). Learning that our lived experiences shape how we feel our emotions, I found Gross's process model of emotion regulation helpful for changing how I experience my most difficult emotions. Rather than allowing them to control me, I have developed a healthier mindset for the difficult moments. Due to widespread acceptance that emotional regulation is closely associated with psychological and physical health, Gross has extended the model he first introduced in 1998 (Gross, 1998), detailing five strategies to focus on during emotion regulation (Gross, 2015).

1. **Situation selection** is how you deliberately choose the situation you'll be in to influence the emotional experience you're going to have. For example, you lost your job. Instead of staying home alone to experience negative emotions, you choose to be in the company of caring friends for emotional comfort.
2. **Situation modification** is how you change what's happening in a situation for emotional flow. For example, your friends ask you why you lost your job. You can choose not to talk about it and ignore your emotions, or to process what happened to you with people you trust.
3. **Attention deployment** refers to determining where you will direct your attention and focus, and how much of your attention you will give to a certain situation. This strategy is critical in the emotional regulation process. For example, while in the company of friends, are you going to be present with them in the moment, or will you constantly check your phone for potential job prospects?
4. **Cognitive change** is an intentional change of how you think about a situation to alter what it's making you feel. For example, after seeing your friends, you are able to reflect on losing your job by objectively looking at your role in what happened. Perhaps you had some fault in losing your job and need to improve your job performance, or maybe you had no fault. Developing the capacity for cognitive change is vital for making peace with what happens to us that we deem unfavorable.
5. **Response modification** refers to suppressing or modifying an emotion after it has been fully generated. This strategy can be ineffective because suppressing an emotion can cause us to produce more of that same emotion (Gross, 2015). For example, choosing to suppress your negative emotion while in the company of friends doesn't mean the emotion will disappear. Instead, it can keep coming up until you learn to process it effectively.

Figure 1.1 illustrates the progression of emotions.

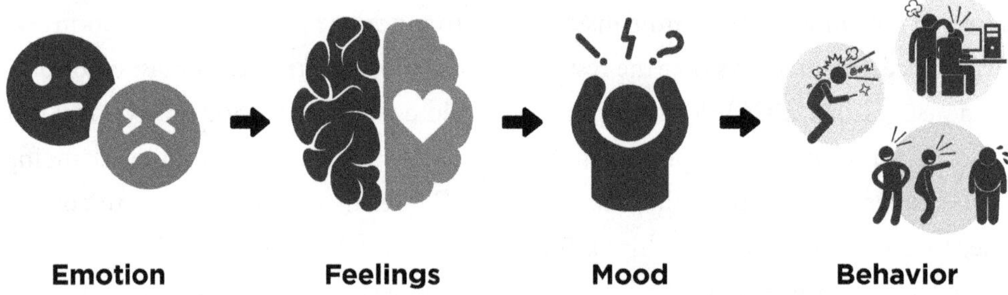

FIGURE 1.1: Progression of emotions.

To begin addressing my own emotional regulation, I developed a handy three-step emotions planner using my insights from the process model of emotion regulation along with the recommendations I received from the emotional intelligence appraisal (Bradberry & Greaves, 2009). The new tool provided me with a much more streamlined and simple process to implement daily or as needed. I found that by paying closer attention to situations and triggers, over time, I began changing how I would experience certain difficult emotions (mainly annoyance and grief). I eventually learned to conquer some of them as I experienced small successes in showing up emotionally and better responding to situations. I even learned that in certain situations (mainly where people lack integrity), I had to remove myself because I couldn't change my emotional responses or make the situations better through dialogue. I've tailored this emotional intelligence appraisal tool (figure 1.2, page 27) for all educators to use.

Working through the emotions planner helped me understand and establish healthy boundaries in my relationships. Additionally, I have learned to free myself of how I used to experience and deal with many negative emotions that have plagued me throughout most of my life. I have come to understand that I no longer have to be a victim of the conditioning of my past circumstances; this realization was very freeing and improved many aspects of my life and relationships. I hope that sharing my story shows that emotional transcendence is possible even for those of us who have struggled for years. Here are some tips for getting the most out of working with the emotions planner.

- Objectively state the situation in column 1 by sticking to the facts.
- Label your primary and secondary emotions in column 2 without passing negative judgment on yourself or others. Simply state what you are experiencing and feeling.

- Don't make the emotional regulation strategies you identify in column 3 about changing the behavior of others. Instead focus on improving your responses to the situation.

Name: Jorge Valenzuela		
Situation	**Emotion**	**SEL Strategy**
A close friend continues to lie to me—at times about trivial items but recently about more serious items, like his whereabouts and ability to cover his portion of our dinner tab.	Eight primary emotions: ☑ Anger ☐ Anticipation ☐ Joy ☐ Trust ☐ Fear ☐ Surprise ☐ Sadness ☑ Disgust Use the space provided to elaborate on other emotions you may be experiencing in tandem with a primary one. Use Plutchik's (2001) wheel of emotions as a reference. *Annoyance* *Loathing*	☐ Self-management ☑ Social awareness ☑ Relationship skills ☑ Self-awareness ☐ Responsible decision making Use the space provided to elaborate on how you will use the SEL skills to regulate your emotions. *Self-awareness: I labeled the emotions I experienced.* *Social awareness: To empathize with my friend, I speak with him to learn what causes him to lie and break trust in our relationship.* *Relationship skills: I will need to set my boundaries firmly and respectfully.*

FIGURE 1.2: Example emotions planner for educators.

Now that you're developing a better understanding of emotions and you have a tool for labeling and recognizing them, you can begin gauging where your emotions reside and identifying effective regulation strategies by regularly using the emotions planner. For example, use this simple check-in in response to feeling off or having trouble restoring your inner peace after a difficult social interaction. Figure 1.3 (page 28) offers additional examples of using the tool.

Please try out the emotions planner for educators for yourself using the blank reproducible version of this form at the end of the chapter (page 31). First, identify a situation at school where you struggled. Next, work to identify appropriate SEL strategies to effectively regulate your emotions.

Situation	Emotion	SEL Strategy
Major Loss: Divorce Breakup Death of loved one Unemployment	Eight primary emotions: ☑ Anger ☐ Anticipation ☐ Joy ☐ Trust ☑ Fear ☐ Surprise ☑ Sadness ☐ Disgust Use the space provided to elaborate on other emotions you may be experiencing in tandem with a primary one. Use Plutchik's (2001) wheel of emotions as a reference. Rage Grief	☑ Self-management ☐ Social awareness ☐ Relationship skills ☑ Self-awareness ☑ Responsible decision making Use the space provided to elaborate on how you will use the SEL skills to regulate your emotions. I won't be afraid to ask for help from family, friends, or a therapist. I will take time to feel and heal and do things I enjoy. I will take care of my physical health, preserve memories, and join a support group.
Argument: Partner Friend	Eight primary emotions: ☑ Anger ☐ Anticipation ☐ Joy ☐ Trust ☐ Fear ☐ Surprise ☐ Sadness ☐ Disgust Use the space provided to elaborate on other emotions you may be experiencing in tandem with a primary one. Use Plutchik's (2001) wheel of emotions as a reference. Annoyance	☐ Self-management ☐ Social awareness ☐ Relationship skills ☐ Self-awareness ☐ Responsible decision making Use the space provided to elaborate on how you will use the SEL skills to regulate your emotions. I will gain the other's perspective, identify win-win solutions, apologize, and revisit shared agreements for relationship management and disagreements.

FIGURE 1.3: Example emotions planner for educators (experiencing a major loss and a disagreement).

As you can see, you can leverage the simple emotions planner tool to emotionally check in with yourself as needed. It makes emotional regulation simpler to manage, and with a little practice, you can begin to see success that you can pass on to others (like students, family, and friends).

Journal to Boost Emotional Intelligence Over Time

Thus far, this chapter has provided you with two reliable methods for identifying emotions in an incident-based situation. Journaling can be another powerful life management tool you incorporate into a self-care regimen to practice regular emotional awareness and boost emotional intelligence over time. You don't have to be in crisis mode for it to aid in managing thoughts and feelings throughout your day. Not a new practice, journaling can help give you clarity while deconstructing difficult and stressful problems. For example, expressive writing is a type of journaling that can transform one's life by creating a cohesive personal narrative that links emotions to specific events. This type of journaling strengthens immune cells and is associated with lowering depression and anxiety and improving moods and social relationships (Pennebaker, 1997).

Journaling is an amalgam of one's take on what happens in their life and one's inner feelings, which is critical for reflecting on and processing lived experiences. With dedication to the practice of expressive writing, we eventually don't have to always write to process thoughts—we begin to think them through (Grothaus, 2015). For me, journaling serves as helpful in unpacking my thoughts and feelings about positive events, like trips or nature outings. Taking time to reflect and journal independently on my first hiking trip with family friends led to establishing family hikes as a twice-yearly tradition. Here are a few ways to begin or improve your journaling (Baikie & Wilhelm, 2005; Bastos, 2022).

- **Personalize your writing and make it private:** Making your writing private means you don't have to share it with others. This creates an emotionally safe and honest space.
- **Write frequently:** Start small with twenty to thirty minutes three to four times a week. I started small and now easily dedicate ninety minutes a day to my various writings.
- **Reflect for metacognition:** When writing about events in your life, consider alternate perspectives about your moods and decisions related to specific emotions.
- **Structure your writing:** Use a framework or methodology that works for you. At times, I journal in gratitude or prayer, addressing God. Other times, I simply list my lived events and the range of emotions concerning them beside bullet points.

Don't overthink journaling—with practice, your flow will eventually come. The point here is to journal in a manner that helps you develop good emotional regulation and healthy thinking dispositions. Do what will make the practice beneficial for you.

Summary

Understanding the CASEL 5 and emotional intelligence basics is the required foundational knowledge to begin using the Equity and SEL Integration Framework in your classroom. The excellent research-based resources in this chapter help educators consider how they can implement SEL competencies to best serve their unique community of learners. Additionally, taking the time to unpack and regulate their own emotions through an emotions framework and planner seeds the emotional intelligence growth required so that educators can help students do the same. (This will be expanded on in steps 4 and 5 of the Equity and SEL Integration Framework.)

Emotions Planner for Educators

Situation	Emotion	SEL Strategy
	Eight primary emotions: ☐ Anger ☐ Anticipation ☐ Joy ☐ Trust ☐ Fear ☐ Surprise ☐ Sadness ☐ Disgust Use the space provided to elaborate on other emotions you may be experiencing in tandem with a primary one. Use Plutchik's (2001) wheel of emotions as a reference.	☐ Self-management ☐ Social awareness ☐ Relationship skills ☐ Self-awareness ☐ Responsible decision making Use the space provided to elaborate on how you will use the SEL skills to regulate your emotions.

CHAPTER 2

Assess Your Unconscious Biases and Beliefs About Students

KEY CHAPTER TASKS

- Raise equity for students by learning the effects of implicit and explicit biases on the student population.
- Define and see examples of microaggressions.
- Learn the ways unconscious bias can influence a school environment.
- Lay the groundwork for developing culturally inclusive classrooms.
- Start difficult conversations about bias and equity with your peers.

The previous chapter reviewed research and many SEL possibilities you can use to support students in developing emotional intelligence skills with the CASEL 5 competencies. Make sure you have begun the self-work for developing your emotional intelligence skills before embarking on step 2. Understanding, labeling, and regulating emotions is only the first step in our self-work, which will continue as we begin to assess our own biases.

Whether or not we're aware of them, we all have biases (Steinhauser, 2020). Having biases doesn't make us terrible people, but we must recognize and change the ones that lead to unintended and destructive student outcomes. First, we must understand that some of our biases are *explicit* (meaning we know we have them) and others are *implicit* (meaning we may not be fully aware of them). According to Tammy Xu (2022), a *Built In* staff writer, "Unconscious biases, or implicit biases, are attitudes that are held subconsciously and affect the way individuals feel and think about others around them. Subconscious attitudes aren't necessarily as well-formed as coherent thoughts, but they can be very ingrained."

As teachers, we have problematic implicit biases when we don't do the inward-out work to recognize how they cause students harm. Ignorance is not bliss when your actions have negative effects for vulnerable people around you. Remember, sometimes our intent doesn't match our impact.

To raise equity in schools, ways must exist for us educators to safely work on recognizing and understanding our biases and patterns that harm students. Still, I observe that school culture can make it difficult for educators to express their biases to others without being shamed—even when they do not mean to harm. Professor Heather Thompson Day (2020) tweets, "There is a difference between a person who hurts you by making a mistake, and a person who hurts you by continuing a pattern. Mistakes can be forgiven. Patterns should be broken." Day's quote is powerful because it doesn't make excuses for those who harm others unconsciously. Instead, it opens a way to redemption by doing the work of unlearning harmful patterns. It also calls for healing for those harmed when they forgive a transgression but the destructive patterns continue.

According to Cheryl Staats (2014), a research associate at The Ohio State University's Kirwan Institute for the Study of Race and Ethnicity, people's implicit biases often contradict the beliefs they profess. My coaching work has led me to consistently interact with many educators since 2012; although numbers vary, working with fifty to three hundred people a week is my standard. And I have never met a teacher who expressed they do not care about the students they serve. Instead, they profess to love their students and display compassion and sympathy for the difficult circumstances they endure. I do believe them. For many of us, however, implicit biases cause a lack of empathy for students we don't culturally identify with. This lack of empathy often shows in how teachers discipline and penalize students for infractions—particularly Black and Brown students.

Data from the U.S. Department of Education tell us that in the 2017–2018 school year, schoolteachers were (USA Facts, 2021):

- Seventy-nine percent White and non-Hispanic
- Nine percent Hispanic (of any race)
- Seven percent Black and non-Hispanic
- Five percent identify as "other"

Data from the 2017–2018 school year also reveal racial disparities in how schools disciplined Black students compared to their White peers across all ages and grade levels (National Center for Education Statistics, 2020). Here are some of the most troubling numbers uncovered by the National Center for Education Statistics (2020).

- Black preschoolers are 18 percent of the enrolled preschool population but receive 43 percent of out-of-school suspensions.
- Fifteen percent of K–12 public school students are Black, but they make up more than 30 percent of students who are suspended, expelled, or arrested.

Therefore, assessing and knowing what we believe about students and expect for their academic success is critical to more equitably engaging them in SEL and education in general.

In this chapter, we will examine in more detail the adverse effects of implicit biases and microaggressions on students. I will then provide examples of implicit biases and microaggressions that frequently occur in schools, and include a series of useful strategies for recognizing and confronting biases in ourselves.

Effects of Implicit Bias and How to Begin the Work

For educators, a dangerous side effect of implicit bias is how it influences behavior that lowers equity for students. Implicit bias makes us categorize students according to identity labels and cultural stereotypes without giving these labels much thought and, worse, without knowing the harm they cause (Cherry, 2020a). According to Packback content coordinator Ariam Tesfaye (2022), unconscious beliefs and attitudes can lead to erroneous expectations about the overall potential of Black, Indigenous, and people of color (BIPOC) students and prevent these students from receiving academic opportunities. Table 2.1 (page 36) exemplifies the effects of such stereotypes.

Studies show the disastrous consequences for students of color when their teachers and schools don't fully comprehend how limiting beliefs and lowered expectations impact their academic and personal success. According to researchers Travis Riddle and Stacey Sinclair (2019), implicit bias impacts racial disparities in school-based discipline in the United States, with Black students liable to face disciplinary action at disproportionately higher rates than White students. This puts them at higher risk for negative life outcomes, including lack of employment and incarceration. Riddle and Sinclair (2019) use federal data spanning over thirty-two million students at approximately ninety-six thousand schools to show the association between county-level racial bias rates and the disciplinary gap between Black and White students across five types of corrective actions (in-school suspensions, out-of-school suspensions, law enforcement referrals, school-related arrests, and expulsions).

In addition, researcher Hua-Yu Sebastian Cherng (2017) examines the negative impact that teacher perceptions and beliefs of student ability have on both African American and Latinx learners' academic achievement. Cherng's (2017) study reveals

TABLE 2.1: Implicit Stereotypes With Their Systemic Enforcements and Associated Traumas to Students

Example of a Societal Issue Affecting Students	Systemic Conditions	Associated Traumas
Implicit stereotypes involve the prereflective attribution of particular negative qualities to members of a socially repressed group (Greenwald & Banaji, 1995). For example, a teacher might believe that students from a particular background will not prioritize their academic achievement, which puts those students at a disadvantage before they enter their school or meet the specific teachers. This disadvantage is significantly amplified for students who don't have advocates. Teachers can become advocates for these isolated students by prioritizing learning about the students' academic goals and encouraging the students toward opportunities that can help them achieve the goals.	Implicit stereotypes create unconsciously endorsed, unintentional, and sometimes uncontrollable thoughts and beliefs that hold particular members of a group back in a school or society. For example, the teacher who stereotypes students from a particular background as not prioritizing their academic achievement will exclude those students from critical scholastic opportunities (like the SAT, college prep courses, and other programs). The teacher thus harms the students by causing them to miss out.	The effects of implicit stereotypes are devastating to students and can lead to discrimination based on their race, gender, social class, or religious group. Associated traumas for victims include symptoms of disorganization, lack of confidence, emotional distress, racial trauma, and devalued social identity.

instances where mathematics and English language arts teachers lowered expectations because they perceived the content to be too difficult for their students of color. Biases therefore decreased students' schooling by almost a third of a year in English and 0.2 of a grade point in mathematics (Cherng, 2017).

Implicit bias or unconscious bias is also referred to as *implicit social cognition*, or deep-seated prejudice situated below the conscious level within the brain. In schools, implicit social cognition plays out when educators unconsciously hold attitudes toward students of color and associate stereotypes with them. Although teachers do not want to believe they stereotype students or allow their conscious or unconscious biases to impair their treatment of them, these harmful beliefs and actions negatively affect students in the long term if not appropriately examined. For example, a student traumatized by implicit prejudice, bias, or stereotypes, as depicted in table 2.1, may have difficulties relating to others and developing self-esteem (Willen & Allan, 2021).

Microaggressions

All of us, as people, possess unconscious biases that cause us to instantly judge others on how they look and how well they communicate, thus categorizing them according to cultural stereotypes with prejudice. We may even hold an implicit bias against the groups we belong to. In society, implicit bias becomes apparent through daily and commonplace *microaggressions*, which are an outgrowth of implicit bias. Psychiatrist Chester M. Pierce coined this term in the 1970s to refer to intentional or unintentional verbal, behavioral, and environmental offenses committed against people of color (Treadwell, 2013). Using microaggressions to demean others also extends beyond race to include LGBTQ people, people with disabilities, women, and other marginalized groups. Table 2.2 (page 38) features various examples of microaggressions and the messages they send.

As we see in table 2.2, microaggressions are harmful because they are used to communicate hostile, derogatory, and racially motivated slights and insults. Even someone's belief that they can't have racial biases because they have friends who are people of color could potentially hurt their friends when openly communicated. That is because this person is using their friends' racial identity for their own social currency, which reduces those friends to representative tokens of their race as opposed to complex individuals. The good news is we can transcend our implicit biases and destructive behavior over time by purposefully doing the work prescribed in the upcoming strategies section (page 41), either individually or within our schools.

Examples of Unconscious Biases in Schools

Implicit bias and microaggressions take on many forms in classrooms. Assessing these forms is critical because whether a teacher believes students can succeed academically and expects them to do so has been shown to affect how well the students do (Gershenson, Holt, & Papageorge, 2015). Teachers need to be aware of how their implicit biases influence those expectations.

It is impossible to examine implicit bias without tying it to structural racism and how it manifests for students of color and students of stigmatized and culturally marginalized groups. Here are a few example manifestations for teachers to consider.

- Teachers unconsciously categorize students according to racial and cultural stereotypes.
- Teachers may presume that students who belong to other cultures and speak with different accents are poor writers and communicators of the English language.

TABLE 2.2: Microaggressions and the Messages They Send

Theme	Microaggressions	Messages
Alien in own land: When someone assumes Asian Americans and Latinx Americans are foreign born	"Where are you from?" "Where were you born?" "You speak good English." A person asks an Asian American to teach them words in their home language.	"You are not American." "You are a foreigner."
Ascription of intelligence: When someone assigns intelligence to a person of color based on their race	"You are a credit to your race." "You are so articulate." A person asks someone of Asian descent to help with a mathematics or science problem.	"People of color are generally not as intelligent as White people." "It is unusual for someone of your race to be intelligent." "All Asian people are intelligent and good in mathematics or science."
Color blindness: When a White person makes statements that indicate they do not want to acknowledge race	"When I look at you, I don't see color." "America is a melting pot." "There is only one race: the human race."	"Your racial or ethnic experiences are invalid." "You must assimilate or acculturate to the dominant culture." "Your experiences as an individual racial or cultural being are invalid."
Assumption of criminality or criminal status: When someone presumes a person of color to be dangerous, criminal, or deviant based on their race	A White person clutches their purse or checks their wallet as a Black or Latinx person approaches or passes. A store owner follows a customer of color around the store. A White person waits to ride the next elevator when a person of color is on the current one.	"You are a criminal." "You are going to steal." "You are poor." "You do not belong." "You are dangerous."
Denial of individual racism: When a White person makes a statement that denies their racial biases	"I'm not racist. I have several Black friends." "As a woman, I know what you go through as a racial minority."	"I am immune to racism because I have friends of color." "Your racial oppression is no different from my gender oppression. I can't be a racist. I'm like you."
Myth of meritocracy: When someone makes statements that assert race does not play a role in life successes	"I believe the most qualified person should get the job." "Everyone can succeed in this society if they work hard enough."	"People of color are given unfair extra benefits because of their race." "People of color are lazy and incompetent, and they need to work harder."

Theme	Microaggressions	Messages
Pathologization of cultural values or communication styles: When someone expresses the notion that the values and communication styles of the dominant White culture are ideal	"Why do you have to be so loud and animated? Just calm down." (Spoken to a Black person) "Why are you so quiet? We want to know what you think. Be more verbal. Speak up more." (Spoken to an Asian or Latinx person) A person dismisses an individual who brings up race and culture in a work or school setting.	"You should assimilate to the dominant culture." "You should leave your cultural baggage outside."
Second-class citizen: When a White person receives preferential treatment as a consumer over a person of color	Someone mistakes a person of color for a service worker. A taxi driver passes a person of color and picks up a White passenger. A person of color is ignored at a store counter as attention is given to a White customer farther back in line. Someone says phrases such as, "You people . . ."	"People of color are servants to Whites. They couldn't possibly occupy high-status positions." "You are likely to cause trouble or travel to a dangerous neighborhood." "Whites are more valued customers than people of color." "You don't belong. You are a lesser being."
Environmental microaggressions: When microaggressions are exhibited at systemic and environmental levels	A college or university has buildings that are all named after White heterosexual upper-class males—often with blatantly oppressive legacies and backgrounds. Television shows and movies feature predominantly White programs without representation of people of color. Public schools in communities of color have overcrowding. An overabundance of liquor stores are in communities of color.	"You don't belong." "You won't succeed here." "There is only so far you can go." "You are an outsider." "You don't exist." "People of color don't or shouldn't value education." "People of color are deviant."

Source: Adapted from Sue, 2020.

- Teachers may assume that certain students know how to seek assistance when struggling academically. Unfortunately, many learners with academic challenges hesitate to ask for help because of how others may perceive their intelligence (Good & Shaw, 2022).
- Mathematics teachers may perceive their class's rigor to be too challenging for both Black and Latinx students.
- Teachers may assume that their students who belong to certain social groups have limited intellectual abilities, which lowers their academic achievement expectations.
- Science teachers may perceive their class to be too difficult for all non-Asian and non-White students.

IMPORTANT NOTE FOR TEACHERS

In some cases, students who are privileged or who are labeled academically and intellectually gifted are also victimized with limiting and false beliefs, which result in neglect of their social-emotional well-being. This is why I added "beliefs about students" to this step in the Equity and SEL Integration Framework; equity is for *all* students. Myths and misconceptions about academically and intellectually gifted students that teachers should rectify include the following.

- They will succeed in life no matter what.
- They love school, and that's why they get high grades.
- They are good at everything they do.
- They tend to be more mature than other students their age.
- Their innate curiosity causes them to be self-directed.
- They don't need help; they'll do fine on their own.
- Teachers in our school challenge all the students, so they will be fine in the regular classroom.
- If we're challenging their brains, we're servicing their needs.
- They know how to speak up for themselves.
- They don't need scaffolding.
- All their parents are heavily involved in their education and general well-being.

Scholastically, implicit bias can lead students to not try out for the mathematics or soccer team or not enroll in a computer science course for fear of failure. Socially, implicit bias can result in students' self-induced isolation because they feel unwanted or unseen by others. Psychologist Melanie Greenberg (2017) points out that negative thoughts about oneself can lead to depression and require targeted self-work to change. Therefore, it is incumbent on teachers who want to be equitable and just in their practices to learn about their students, their needs, and their challenges, even when that conflicts with what these teachers have been taught or currently believe. Teachers who want to address their biases need to begin with themselves and consider various strategies for revealing and remedying biases in their classrooms. It is trendy for many schools and organizations to tackle this collectively through DEI programs. The strategies that follow include some recommendations for starting this work on your own or with colleagues.

IMPORTANT NOTE FOR TEACHERS

To make DEI practices systemic and effective in schools, school leaders must have teachers work in collaborative teams to tackle the items outlined in this chapter regarding biases. Start small. Systemic change takes time. It's impossible to completely eradicate implicit bias, hate, misconceptions, or false beliefs in our school buildings. Therefore, set realistic goals, focusing on small, high-leverage steps to yield tangible shifts in colleagues' interpersonal dynamics.

The primary goal should be making faculty meetings intellectually safe spaces where teachers and staff feel comfortable either voicing their views or getting the necessary feedback when their perspectives need further development. Educators *collectively* need to create positive change in the schoolwide climate, culture, policy, routines, and rituals before it can occur with students.

Strategies for Assessing Unconscious Biases

In this section, we will explore three practical strategies for assessing implicit biases in yourself and in other school staff: (1) starting and sustaining difficult conversations as a faculty, (2) curating digital resources for combating implicit bias and microaggressions, and (3) developing culturally inclusive classrooms by establishing learning partnerships and ground rules. While these strategies primarily address biases that are present and influential in the classroom, there are elements of these strategies that apply to personal biases outside of education. You may consider how these methods can apply to your personal relationships.

Start and Sustain Difficult Conversations as a Faculty

Difficult conversations will be much more successful if you proactively set parameters for what they entail and how team members conduct them. Therefore, school leaders can use circle practice (see chapter 8, page 137) to provide structure to difficult conversations between educators (Davenport, 2018). Other discussion protocols, like In2Out, can also help school teams establish equity of voice, set norms and a structure for continued learning and discussions, and define microaggressions to develop a schoolwide culture of inclusivity where everyone is proactively protected from harm (Harvard Graduate School of Education, 2017; Valenzuela, 2022c). The three steps to implementing the In2Out protocol are as follows:

1. **(In) Written Reflection.** This step is essential for priming colleagues for discussion by having them write their thoughts—beginning with their own experiences. A powerful norm to lift up here is that they don't share what they write with others. Instead, this is an opportunity to formulate their thoughts about the topic in a safe space.
2. **(2) Pair Share.** This step requires the facilitator to share a prompt to help colleagues make meaning and begin conversations with a peer. The protocol norm is to do this in pairs, but if your class doesn't have even numbers, triads work too.
3. **(Out) Table Talk With Peers or Entire-Class Discussion.** The final step is for broader discussion and reaching consensus about how to collaboratively commence with learning. Facilitators introduce another prompt and can choose to make it a table talk with more than two peers or a whole-group discussion. (Valenzuela, 2022c)

Additionally, creating transformational norms and shared agreements to model and implement with staff during circles can create a safe and inclusive environment. Here are some good ones to consider.

- **Everyone participates:** Students need their teachers to be on the same page about DEI issues for raising equity throughout a school. Many educators are unsure of how they can add to difficult discussions when they are nervous or feel ignorant about DEI topics. Participation does not mean that everyone will speak, especially if people are uncomfortable sharing, but it does mean that everyone will look and pay attention to whoever is speaking.

- **Create a safe space that doesn't shame colleagues:** Do not pressure people of color to lead the work or discuss any traumatic experiences in a group setting. Everyone, including people of color, can contribute depending on their level of comfort. Consider inviting DEI experts who are knowledgeable about biases, facilitation, research, and methodology. The goal is to create safe spaces that don't shame or isolate colleagues. Unfortunately, when these conversations are held without shared agreements or input from all colleagues, some feel called out, isolated, and blamed for today's conditions. This is not productive and does not get us closer to raising equity for students.
- **Speak from the heart and with respect, and be open to feedback from colleagues:** Everyone must be comfortable expressing themselves and open to receiving feedback when their perspective needs to change because it harms others. Facilitators should take practical measures to create an atmosphere of comfort for people to share. For example, they can open a discussion circle with conversations unrelated to implicit bias, making participants feel more comfortable sharing with colleagues before the "uncomfortable topics" begin. A helpful strategy for building camaraderie in the room is to suggest that smaller groups practice vulnerability first—thus giving them the tools and trust to tackle harder conversations together.
- **Listen from the heart:** Colleagues must listen to one another without judgment, even when they disagree on an issue. However, this may be difficult or impossible when emotions run high. Facilitators need to know participants' breaking points and when to table a highly explosive hot topic—especially if it's a trauma trigger for them. Instead of asking participants to express their views, facilitators can ask vulnerable staff to describe how the occurrence triggers them and makes them or students feel. In contrast, other staff focus solely on empathizing with the vulnerable staff, writing down some of their exact statements without revising them. The hope here is for constructive dialogue to occur over time, thus causing *some* colleagues to eventually change their limiting beliefs about students.
- **Whatever is said in the circle remains in the circle:** This agreement allows everyone to speak freely without fear of having anything they say held against them. When this norm is understood, trust will develop.

Curate Digital Resources for Combating Implicit Bias and Microaggressions

Gather research-based, universally accessible resources on complicated topics to help your peers understand the topics on their own time. To gauge the quality of selected resources, I recommend auditing them to ensure they include authentic narratives of those most impacted and marginalized by bias and microaggressions. So often, historical accounts of prejudice and oppression minimize the truth, making it appear more palatable for audiences—thus misrepresenting BIPOC (Erdman, 2021). These resources should include videos, how-to blogs, published research, and replicable activities for the classroom and teacher professional learning. Please find a sample vetted list of resources in appendix A (page 193).

While people are learning about an oppressed group, mindsets to encourage include but are not limited to being open, being empathetic, not making it about you, and moving from cultural competence to cultural proficiency (Childs, 2020; Sieck, 2021).

Develop Culturally Inclusive Classrooms by Establishing Learning Partnerships and Ground Rules

Culturally responsive teachers understand the cultural nuances required for connecting with students (Rucker, 2019). The seven principles of culturally responsive teaching by equity expert Gary R. Howard (1999) can provide excellent guidelines for helping teachers and students create learning partnerships in classrooms. The seven principles for culturally responsive teaching are

1. Students are affirmed in their cultural connections.
2. Teachers are personally inviting.
3. Learning environments are physically and culturally inviting.
4. Students are reinforced for academic development.
5. Instructional changes are made to accommodate differences in learners.
6. The classroom is managed with firm, consistent, loving control.
7. Interactions stress collectivity as well as individuality.

To re-engage struggling students who are often labeled as underprepared, collaborative teacher teams can collectively answer the following questions and see what they can do differently for their learners.

- "Which students in our school tend to get the most office referrals?"
- "Which students do we tend to struggle with behaviorally or academically? Are there any trends?"

- "Do we have any unconscious biases related to our students who struggle?"
- "How can we establish learning partnerships with our students who struggle?"

More information about culturally responsive teaching and engaging students appears in chapter 7 (page 121).

Summary

Examining and changing our beliefs is not easy and will take time, but our students are worth it. Some of them may lack confidence, struggle with identity, lack a sense of belonging, experience hardships or bullying, have learning disabilities, lack social skills, or have knowledge gaps. Additionally, many students face challenges in both their homes and communities. Discussions about systemic racism in the United States will allow schools and educators to see the tangible effects of both societal and educational divides and how students of color are the most impacted and vulnerable to inaction (Gonser, 2020). The key takeaway from this chapter is we must do critical self-work to prepare to remove the isolation that often impedes students' social and academic success. We must work with like-minded colleagues to strategically use vetted strategies and protocols. Doing so will assist us as we move to the third step of the Equity and SEL Integration Framework: improve knowledge of students.

CHAPTER 3

Improve Your Knowledge of Your Students

KEY CHAPTER TASKS

- Raise equity by getting to know your students better.
- Create a culturally responsive teaching plan.
- Connect with students using an empathy map.
- Model empathy for students.

In step 2, we focused inward to learn more about ourselves. In step 3, we focus on learning about students. Along with step 1 (learn the basics of the CASEL 5 and emotional intelligence), these are steps you can sequentially implement for individual teachers to make an impact with SEL and for collaborative teams to make an impact through DEI efforts. The endgame of taking these prescribed steps is to raise equity for students, appropriately engage students in SEL, create intellectually and physically safe spaces for all, and help students become better learners.

The Instructional Benefits of Knowing Your Students' Skills and Interests

In the context of this chapter, increasing our knowledge of students has two critical dimensions for us as teachers to consider: (1) to know them as individuals and (2) to know them as learners. We want to focus on their interests, assets, and cultural identities as individuals, as this helps us better understand their needs, motivations, and overall personalities. Understanding students as individuals also requires building rapport and forming relationships to better connect with them. Our knowledge of them as learners meshes with what we know about them as individuals. There are two primary benefits to knowing students as learners after knowing their individual qualities.

1. What we know about students as individuals lets us make academic and SEL content as personalized as possible. This means framing the context of lessons and projects in ways that compel and engage students emotionally.
2. Knowing students' academic and SEL needs helps us make better instructional decisions. When considering SEL teaching strategies, for example, we can use visible learning and teaching approaches to sharpen how we see learning; we can see learning through students' eyes and thus evaluate teaching from their perspectives (Hattie & Yates, 2014).

Moreover, knowing students enables us to make data-informed instructional pivots as needed throughout the curriculum. According to John Hattie and Klaus Zierer (2017):

> The key to successful teaching and learning processes lies in measuring student achievements and applying the results in the further course of a lesson—especially by the teacher. These teachers can make learning visible and draw the right conclusions for their teaching, and then the greater their students' learning progress can be. (p. 16)

In the subsequent sections of this chapter, I will unpack how becoming culturally and socially competent can help us raise equity by improving our knowledge of students. First, I want to briefly lay out how knowing our students as individuals and learners will improve our instructional decisions.

Research conducted by Benjamin N. York (2014) reveals that teachers' knowledge of individual students' skills can effectively increase achievement for diverse learners. Knowing the unique skills of individual students for making better instructional decisions has strong empirical support in previous literature (Connor et al., 2011; Connor, Morrison, Fishman, Schatschneider, & Underwood, 2007). Therefore, knowing our students as individuals can make us more impactful and effective teachers (ReachOut Schools, 2022).

Teachers who do not know their students well cannot design truly personalized student-centered learning and motivational experiences that help them thrive socially and academically (Barkley, 2019). On the other hand, teachers who know their students as both people and learners are familiar with their strengths, interests, and SEL needs and can thus help them thrive (Schultz, 2015). Therefore, as educators, we must take on the task of knowing our students as individuals in order to discern the best way to teach them academic content.

Cultural Competence and Knowledge of Students

Educators need to become more culturally and socially competent by continually improving their knowledge of students so they can deliver more relevant lessons. Getting to know students deeply for becoming more culturally responsive is not a new concept in education (Safir, 2017). Getting to know students has logical connections to developing and implementing culturally responsive teaching strategies and lessons for diverse learners. According to coauthors and personalized learning experts William Powell and Ochan Kusuma-Powell (2011), strategies for improving knowledge of students to inform teaching may include the following.

- **Creating a classroom environment that is psychologically safe for all students:** For example, be aware of self and students; support students to do the same for each other. Model what it means to show oneself without fear of negative consequences or harm to one's self-image by admitting mistakes and showcasing your authentic self at all times.

  To involve the entire class, create a set of shared agreements on what the students need to do to show up at their best daily. Get everyone's input on these classroom norms. An excellent norm to uplift students is to critique work and not people. Feedback protocols help keep critique on schoolwork while allowing learners to express themselves. Discussion protocols like In2Out can also help students confidently open up about SEL and academic topics without fear of consequences (Edutopia, 2016; Valenzuela, 2022c).
- **Determining each student's readiness to engage in learning during lessons:** For example, conduct readiness check-ins with students, particularly at the start of a class and before work time, allowing them some wait time for processing and reflection. Also, encourage students to check in with their peers during group and partner work.
- **Identifying multiple entry points to concepts and skills so that the content becomes more engaging to students:** For example, provide several examples of new concepts during lessons using different media, such as video, images, stories, and various informational texts. Also, allow students to demonstrate and transfer skills through apps, tools, or other methods they are familiar with and like. Making the content more engaging in this way leads to students' academic success.

- **Leveling up emotional intelligence skills for use in the classroom:** For example, as often as needed, revisit the section titled Strategies for Understanding Your Emotions (chapter 1, page 15). Mastering emotional intelligence takes time, and you will continue to make mistakes—the key is to catch and improve on them as they arise. It's also important to focus on problem areas (such as anger, grief, and reactions to triggers).

According to educator Zaretta Hammond, culturally responsive teaching is about building the learning capacity of the individual student, and empathizing with students is a critical step in this pedagogical transformation (Gonzalez, 2017). The following section provides an equity-yielding strategy called *empathy mapping*. Teachers can use this strategy as a scaffold for empathizing with students while simultaneously increasing their familiarity with students to inform instruction and other equitable outcomes.

The Empathy Map

An empathy map is a tool that visually captures knowledge about behaviors, attitudes, needs, strengths, struggles, emotional states, and other key attributes of students (Peixoto & Moura, 2020). Conceived by Dave Gray, founder of XPLANE, and originating in user experience design, empathy maps can also help grade-level planning teams purposefully empathize with their students and develop more equitable and personalized lessons (Bland, 2020).

Figure 3.1 (page 51) shows an example of a completed empathy map. A blank reproducible version of the figure is available at the end of this chapter (page 59).

Being mindful and empathic toward students, or being able to share in their feelings, is an essential SEL skill for educators to possess when planning instruction (Gumper, 2020). Therefore, creating empathy maps can be a great first step when designing equitable lessons and other school outcomes for students. Empathy mapping is a strategic and straightforward equity-based activity that teachers can collaboratively do with school stakeholders like administrators, school counselors, instructional assistants, and teacher planning teams to build empathy for students.

The premise for using empathy maps as part of the lesson-ideation process is that developing relevant lessons requires understanding our students' true needs. Designing maps helps teachers consider the students' perspectives and spotlight their goals, interests, and challenges. This practice is powerful because oftentimes, the teachers realize the social and cultural competence they must acquire to better serve their students while they are creating an empathy map. Advocating for students doesn't have to be a matter of convincing because empathy mapping puts the adults

Interests and Goals

- To improve English speaking and writing skills
- To become a lawyer
- Loves to play fútbol (soccer) and Latin dance

Areas of Strength

- Fluent in Spanish
- Empathetic toward others
- Good listener

- Systems thinker
- Mastered multiple Latin dances

Academic Needs

- To improve decoding skills in reading
- To gain exposure to academic language
- To learn more about how the U.S. judicial system works

SEL Needs

- Labeling emotions
- Managing stress
- Asking for help

Career Needs

- Initiative
- Leadership skills
- Punctuality
- Flexibility and adaptability

FIGURE 3.1: Example completed empathy map for an English learner.

on the same page about the students' needs. When used in the classroom, empathy maps provide the following benefits for teachers and students.

- Increased empathy for students
- A tool for making instructional decisions
- An equity-based tool for teachers
- Better insight into the lives and academic struggles of students
- Insights gleaned from research and data collections
- A tool for reflection on educators' own practice
- Common understanding among adults in a school

It is also possible to leverage the empathy map to synthesize research observations and reveal more in-depth insights about a student's or students' needs. The recommendation here, however, is to include mapping in early instructional design stages or to determine what DEI outcomes would be equitable for students.

The exercise of empathy mapping helps teachers approach interactions and instruction from learners' point of view before creating their lessons. Teachers can use it to consider ideas for SEL content (like empathy for others), specific reading and writing skills (such as grammar and punctuation), discussions on issues pertaining to race, or the use of a specific teaching strategy (among other instructional considerations). Additionally, teachers can update empathy maps with student benchmark and biweekly assessment data and what they learn from interacting with and knowing their students. Updating the maps as needed (such as once a semester) can also help foster positive social interactions and academic improvement in both schools and individual classrooms. The following sections explain how to effectively create, label, and use empathy maps to improve your knowledge of students.

Create an Empathy Map

To begin your empathy map, gather relevant data and information about your students. These items may include assessment data; the students' goals, hobbies, and interests; and their areas of academic, career, and social needs. Traditionally, teachers collect student information through polls, surveys, and observations of their students' work (such as reflection journals, essays, digital portfolios, and project-based learning passion projects). However, you can also glean knowledge about students through classroom discussions. During these discussions, check in on learning; build a rapport; pay attention to issues they care about; and recognize what gifts and abilities they have, how they transfer learning, and what they voluntarily talk about.

Label Your Empathy Map Sections

Companies have popularly used empathy maps in product development to better understand their customers' needs by gaining insight into their experiences with particular products (Gray, Brown, & Macanufo, 2010). Labels businesses commonly use in their empathy maps include *thoughts* and *feelings*, and *think and feel* and *say and do as a result of trying a product*. However, we teachers can easily adapt empathy maps in our instructional design process by making a few tweaks to their labels. For academic classrooms, I suggest using the following labels to help us better understand the learners we serve.

- **Interests and goals:** All students have their own interests, goals, and hobbies. These are things that motivate and inspire them and that should be considered when we are planning our lessons.
- **Areas of strength:** All students have areas where they excel. Use this knowledge to help them grow in other areas.
- **Academic needs:** Here, teachers should focus on fundamental academic concepts and skills related to the specific subject they teach (like reading and writing, proportional reasoning, integer operations, and others).

Important concepts that connect learning across various classes should also be addressed in this section; these include key knowledge, understandings, and skills students will need for making cross-curricular connections.

- **SEL needs:** All students have some areas of weakness in the five SEL core competencies and their associated skills. SEL skills are scientifically proven to help in building a less stressful and more positive school climate (Darling-Hammond & Cook-Harvey, 2018). Here, teachers should initially focus on students' having and enacting good self-management strategies for self- and social awareness. Self-management is vital for helping them understand their environment, themselves, and others. Furthermore, self-management strategies are imperative for having good social interactions and developing responsible decision-making skills. Tips for doing this effectively appear in subsequent sections of this chapter (and see chapter 4's The Importance of Understanding and Labeling Emotions section, page 62).
- **Career needs:** This is an optional label, as not all teachers focus instruction on career skills and pathways. However, career and technical education teachers can provide direction to colleagues who are mapping to set critical career development milestones for students. Students considering postsecondary ambitions like college or technical school can also go into this field.

Use the Empathy Map

The empathy maps we design are helpful only if we *use* them. I like to use mine to guide instructional decisions that best support my learners (such as instructional scaffolds and personalized learning) and avoid cognitive overload by only incorporating activities that promote a productive learning struggle. *Productive struggle* in learning includes processes that support students' knowledge construction and problem-solving skills, and it is especially critical when students face new problems. If their struggle is not productive, they can become frustrated and give up (Blackburn, 2018; Grafwallner, 2021; Vygotsky, 1978).

For example, a student who needs to improve her English speaking and writing skills and who aspires to become a lawyer can engage in a project designed to have her learn about the judicial system in tandem with practicing her decoding skills for reading familiar words but in the context of the law. Knowing that she belongs to the Latinx community empowers me to create opportunities for her to see herself represented in various informational texts. Empathizing with her appreciation for soccer and Latin dances allows me to seek colleagues' recommendations for finding or creating extracurricular activities that support those passions.

Similarly, when we know that some of our students are interested in pressing social justice issues (like fighting the oppression of Asian Americans and Pacific Islanders [AAPI], LGBTQ people, and BIPOC), codesigning learning experiences, school activities, and schoolwide themes around what matters to them becomes a simpler endeavor. For example, we could design projects that tackle various environmental issues (such as transportation, carbon footprint reduction, and energy) for students who love both the environment and advocacy. These can be powerful civic learning experiences.

A Plan to Increase Social and Cultural Competence

In this section, you will learn how to create a relevant equity and SEL plan. These plans shouldn't entail simply following scripted resources or how-to blogs. Instead, we will consider relevant pedagogies (like restorative justice), learn through firsthand accounts, consider the needs of others from diverse backgrounds, and apply sound classroom practices to help students become better people and learners. To be truly impactful, we need to truly know our learners. We need to know and better understand what they may be experiencing internally or what may be plaguing them socially. The following is a short list of reasons why some students bear tremendous emotional tolls, feel isolated from others, or feel marginalized in school.

- **Sexual orientation and gender identity:** LGBTQ youth who do not have trusted people to discuss sexuality with may suffer isolation and lack social support. Often, they have minimal contact with others in the LGBTQ community and experience social withdrawal and victimization (The Proud Diplomat, 2018).
- **Poverty:** One in six students in the United States lives in poverty (Children's Defense Fund, 2020). Research also shows that compared to more affluent classmates, students who grow up in poverty tend to struggle academically and have difficulty performing on grade level (Walker, 2016).
- **Racial bias:** Education researchers have hypothesized that implicit bias can impact racial disparities in education—including differences in academic achievement and disciplinary actions between Black and White students (Dhaliwal, Chin, Lovison, & Quinn, 2020). Additionally, Black students exposed to chronic racism have experienced increased anxiety and poor mental health conditions (Anderson, 2020).
- **Religious persecution:** Students across the United States who belong to minority religious groups report having experienced bullying, which vastly affects their social and emotional well-being (Johnson, 2018). Muslim,

Jewish, and Sikh students have expressed concern about being perceived to be connected to terrorism because of their religious attire and heritage (Guo, 2012; Johnson, 2018; Rogers et al., 2017). Studies show that Muslim students are more likely to experience bullying at school than peers of other faiths; one in four incidents involve adults (Mogahed & Chouhoud, 2017).

- **Subjection to violence:** Violence in schools involving students can occur on the way to or from school property or a school-sponsored event. Violent acts, including bullying, pushing, and shoving, can lead to emotional harm alongside physical harm. Physical assault with or without weapons and gang violence can lead to severe injury or death (Centers for Disease Control and Prevention, 2016).

If we don't understand what's happening with our students, we won't have the right words to talk to them. If we don't have the right language or know the data on the preceding issues, we may cause our students to feel more isolated or triggered when we try to engage in delicate conversations. To better understand equity issues, we must know the conditions that led to the inequities and the subsequent disadvantages and trauma caused to our most marginalized and vulnerable students. We can help these students in our classrooms if we learn to apply appropriate strategies from the teaching approaches that are designed to help us improve our SEL plans. Those approaches include the following.

- **Culturally responsive teaching:** This pedagogy is grounded in teachers' possessing the cultural competence and know-how for teaching in cross-cultural or multicultural settings. This approach is also referred to as *culturally relevant teaching*.
- **Trauma-informed teaching:** This pedagogy has teachers consider trauma and its impacts on learners when designing and implementing teaching strategies. Being trauma informed is a mindset and a lens through which educators can choose to view their students to build a better rapport and better relationships, create classroom environments that resolve conflict, encourage discourse, and improve teaching.
- **Restorative justice:** In schools, restorative justice helps students take better ownership of actions and behaviors and provides steps to make things right for those they hurt or negatively impacted. Through restorative practices, restorative justice takes a communal approach in classrooms to assist both victims and offenders in healing and understanding.

See chapters 6, 7, and 8 (pages 107, 121, and 137, respectively) for more on updating your SEL plan with culturally responsive teaching, trauma-informed teaching, and restorative justice.

Strategies for Updating Your SEL Plan With Practices From Corresponding Pedagogies

Seeing how we can update our SEL plan with a corresponding pedagogy can be confusing, especially with so much information at our disposal (such as in literature, podcasts, social media, and others). I think the most important things for us teachers to consider are our students' actual needs. For example, if I teach students from different cultures and backgrounds, I will need to be more culturally responsive to connect with them. Or, if tensions rise among my students because they are arguing and one feels wronged by another, I will need to momentarily pivot from teaching to restore justice before the issue escalates further. The following strategies will help educators align the needs of students with best pedagogical practices.

Create Your Culturally Responsive Teaching Plan

I recommend using a simple graphic organizer to include some best practices for future lessons and start improving your SEL plan with foundational culturally responsive teaching practices. Figure 3.2 (page 57) is an example plan I developed for how I would start being more culturally responsive in my teaching while maintaining the proper rigor to help my students become better learners. A blank reproducible version of the figure is available at the end of this chapter (page 60).

Create a Restorative Justice Teaching Plan

As hard as we try to make every student feel seen and celebrated for who they are, there will still be times when a student feels isolated or wronged. There will be times when our classroom climate feels tense because a conflict between students is causing some not to feel as close or connected to the whole, and we need to get everyone back on the same page. It's up to us to restore a shared sense of equity, inclusivity, and synergy in our classrooms in those moments. When I was ready to introduce a restorative justice process to my students, I used the same simple graphic organizer pictured in figure 3.2 to keep focused on three things: (1) the needs of students, (2) best practices, and (3) how I would follow up to improve my own understanding. You can see the result of this effort in figure 3.3 (page 57).

Needs of Students	Best Practices	Follow-Up
Make learning more relevant to my students. Help my students improve their confidence by becoming better learners. Help students use systematic approaches to deconstructing and solving academic and real-life problems.	Design lessons that accurately represent my actual students (through their cultures, lives, and interests, for example). Form genuine relationships with my students and earn their trust. Use frameworks for teaching students to think critically and use visible-thinking routines during the learning process.	Read *Culturally Responsive Teaching and the Brain* by Zaretta Hammond (2014) to learn the research of how culturally responsive teaching connects to neuroscience. Attend a district-held training on culturally responsive teaching. Create empathy maps for my students. Design learning experiences that promote intellectual challenge and accomplishment for all students by having them problem solve, learn deeply, and produce their best work.

FIGURE 3.2: My culturally responsive teaching plan.

Needs of Students	Best Practices	Follow-Up
Make wrongs right between students. Address grievances in the classroom. Get my class back to a sense of community after a disruption to learning occurs.	Conduct restorative circles with students. Facilitate one-on-one and whole-class conversations. Model use of empathy for perspective taking.	Read a blog on holding restorative circles, and practice with my grade-level collaborative team prior to implementing with students. Design prompts for starting conversations in the classroom. Create a lesson on empathy mapping for students.

FIGURE 3.3: My restorative justice teaching plan.

Model Empathy for Students

This chapter has focused on increasing our knowledge of students for empathizing with them and for raising equity. Here, we've learned to empathize with them by using concrete strategies like empathy mapping, improving our social and cultural competence with culturally responsive teaching, and using other trauma-informed practices and restorative justice to assist students when they experience emotional difficulties.

However, as teachers, we can model empathy for them in our everyday interactions by simply listening to and honoring their words and making eye contact. I learned that from my daughter, who told me she felt disconnected when we chatted because I either was on my phone or cut her off by switching topics and I couldn't recall what she said. She taught me that the best way to model empathy is to hear what she says and honor that without adding to or taking away from her words—sometimes, I even write them down so that I don't forget. As a result, I've been able to bring that level of empathy into my classrooms with students and into my interactions with colleagues. At times, I do come up short, but it's my experience that students just want us to try our best.

Summary

By now, we should know the value of finding useful ways to understand students culturally, socially, and academically before attempting to teach them emotional intelligence skills. We assessed our own biases in chapter 2 and have now improved our knowledge of students in this chapter through engaging in empathy mapping and taking the time to become better informed. Next, we may discover essential items to consider for helping students learn and apply emotional intelligence skills in chapters 4 and 5.

Empathy Map Template

Interests and Goals	Areas of Strength	Academic Needs
SEL Needs		Career Needs

Template for Updating Your SEL Teaching Plan

Needs of Students	Best Practices	Follow-Up

CHAPTER 4

Help Students Develop Emotional Intelligence Skills

KEY CHAPTER TASKS

- Identify the different kinds of emotional intelligence skills.
- Help students label and understand their emotions.
- Help students find appropriate emotional regulation strategies.
- Teach responsible decision-making skills to students.
- Help students understand other people's emotions.

Steps 1–3 of the Equity and SEL Integration Framework are designed to give educators the needed insight, knowledge, and perspective to effectively activate SEL in themselves and in their lessons. Although I consider step 1 universal for all (we all need emotional intelligence), steps 2 and 3 are designed to help *you* assess your beliefs and improve your knowledge of students based on your teaching context. Step 4 enables us to use what we know about students to help *them* develop or enhance their emotional intelligence skills.

Emotional intelligence is the ability to be aware of, control, and express one's emotions while also being able to handle others' emotions judiciously and empathetically. Teachers can help students improve their emotional intelligence by having them do some of the same self-work available to educators in chapter 1 (page 15). To recap, emotional intelligence develops when we understand emotions and learn to label and regulate them—which is what we are trying to teach students through the CASEL 5 competencies for improving their personal and social competence. Remember, these are the basics and the critical first steps for learners to become self-aware, manage their emotional state, prepare for learning, and equip themselves for other life events.

Also remember, SEL is not meant to replace professional trauma-informed therapy, nor should SEL skills be taught or utilized independent of curriculum (Cohen,

Opatosky, Savage, Stevens, & Darrah, 2021). Giving students an awareness of and the tools to manage their emotions will help them better accept themselves, understand their situations, and be less self-judgmental when experiencing unpleasant feelings like envy, anger, and annoyance. We can help students learn to notice how they feel instead of penalizing themselves for not feeling or acting better, which will serve them well beyond the kindergarten through twelfth-grade experience. In doing so, and with practice, students will understand themselves and others better, which will result in their making better decisions in and out of the classroom.

This chapter focuses on three emotional intelligence competencies that make up the CASEL 5: (1) self-awareness, (2) social awareness, and (3) responsible decision making. It will first deepen your understanding of these concepts as well as offer strategies for helping students label emotions, including giving students the emotions planner from chapter 1 (page 31) as part of an emotions check-in as needed. I haven't revised the emotions planner for students because I continually see in my coaching work that teachers have more success modeling tools they've already used. We will then focus on the connection between emotional intelligence and responsible decision making and study strategies for enhancing this skill.

IMPORTANT NOTE FOR TEACHERS

Remember, SEL is also an academic intervention for developing better learners. Consider the emotions planner activity as a cognitive process students can use throughout their lives for labeling and regulating emotions; restoring their inner peace; and preparing for learning, work, or play. I tell students that the planner can help them organize their thoughts, new learning, reflections, and next steps regarding their complex emotions. I also always show them a planner I completed myself (see figure 1.2, page 27). I do this because I want them to know that even adults face difficult emotions and need assistance for managing them. I also get better responses from students when they know I'm asking them to do something I am implementing for myself.

The Importance of Understanding and Labeling Emotions

Students need to understand that emotions are part of human nature. Emotions give them information about their internal experiences and help them know how to best respond in all situations. Babies, infants, and young children before preschool age (three to five years old) all sense emotions and react to behaviors like laughing, touching, making facial expressions, or crying (Mcilroy, 2022). Although they feel and display emotions, young children from infancy and before school age can't always name them yet, explain what they experience internally, or describe why they feel the way they do in a given situation. Instead, they often react to their emotions. Reacting to emotions in early development is primal, and it's a good thing because it informs caregivers of how to best serve their needs (Mcilroy, 2022).

Unfortunately, as students move through the stages of adolescence, many don't have adults in their lives to coach them through their complex emotions. As a result, they don't fully comprehend emotions and often continue to react to them, which can be problematic in the classroom. The good news is children can become more skilled in understanding their emotions if they encounter SEL in school starting at ages three to five (Mcilroy, 2022). The following two sections detail how understanding emotions and knowing how to label them will help students become more self-aware and socially aware.

Self-Awareness

Instead of reacting to emotions as they did when they were younger, students in any grade can learn to identify their emotions and describe them using words (Cohen et al., 2021). With time and practice, they can get better at knowing what they experience and why, as well as the triggers that bring up these emotions. This range of skills is called *self-awareness* and is critical for emotional well-being and self-management.

To help learners get started, the first thing we need to do is help them name the emotions they experience. As previously covered in chapter 1 (page 15), psychologists call this *labeling* (David & Congleton, 2013). Once students can accurately label their emotions, we can then help them identify and implement an appropriate SEL strategy for getting themselves back in a peaceful state. We will learn to use daily emotions check-ins for this purpose and tie them to either impactful current events, happenings in the classroom, or the concepts and student work in the day's lesson.

You can begin the labeling process early in the school year by engaging your students with Plutchik's (2001) wheel of emotions and using the following simple steps for improving their understanding of emotions.

1. Introduce students to Plutchik's (2001) wheel of emotions as a tool to simplify their emotions. If possible, print them a copy, or keep a poster-size version somewhere visible in the classroom. See chapter 1, page 21, to revisit Plutchik's wheel of emotions.
2. Have students identify and discuss the eight primary emotions on the wheel: (1) anger, (2) anticipation, (3) joy, (4) trust, (5) fear, (6) surprise,

(7) sadness, and (8) disgust. Structures for discussion may include In2Out and circle practice (Davenport, 2018; Valenzuela, 2022c). Good question prompts to guide discussions in either structure may include the following.

- Describe a time when you saw someone on TV or a character in a story experience one of the eight primary emotions. What secondary emotions do you think they also experienced, and how did those visibly affect their mood?
- Think of a time when a caregiver or teacher introduced a new strategy for overcoming a difficult emotion. How did the adult explain and model the process in ways that allowed you and other students to understand how to overcome the emotion?
- How do we know when emotional intelligence is part of our classroom culture, and how can each of us do our part?

3. Have students identify other emotions on the wheel, and help students connect them to the eight primary emotions. Be very careful not to trigger them. Have the students pick an emotion and identify feelings along with some preferred regulation strategies.
4. If possible, role-play different scenarios where students pretend to experience one of the basic emotions and ask students about possible self-management strategies they can implement for managing the difficult ones (like anger, sadness, and disgust). I like to give students the opportunity to contribute to lessons, but if they are unsure, this is where you can step in and suggest and model some good strategies. Discovering possible self-management strategies is a very powerful realization for students, as it serves to help them identify emotional triggers and begin planning how to respond.

The following vignette describes how a teacher might use Plutchik's (2001) wheel of emotions during a lesson to help her students recognize and label their emotions using technology.

During initial emotions check-ins with her students, Kelly noticed that some students were having difficulty identifying the names of the emotions they were experiencing and kept referring to low-level terms like happy, angry, *and* sad *instead. She wanted them to understand that emotions are complex and can influence their decisions, change their view of the world, and cause them to evaluate situations they encounter in different ways depending on which emotions they are feeling. Therefore, Kelly displayed a graphic of Plutchik's (2001) wheel of emotions and talked her students through the eight primary emotions. Together, they categorized the eight emotions and how they tie to other emotions they may experience. She also provided a shared online copy of the emotions wheel graphic, which students could access daily as a scaffold for pinpointing their emotions during emotions check-ins.*

IMPORTANT NOTE FOR TEACHERS

K–3 students may find the wheel too complex and overwhelming for labeling their emotions. Try using emojis or other visuals that will accomplish the same goal. You can introduce students to the wheel of emotions or emojis either in person or virtually using a simple graphic. Keep the graphic displayed by sharing your screen and having the graphic accessible in your learning management system so students can reference it for quickly assessing and labeling their emotions.

Social Awareness

Unlike self-awareness (focusing on self), *social awareness* involves considering the perspectives of others, including diverse groups and communities, and subsequently applying that understanding to interactions with those people. Moreover, social awareness is a learned skill that requires individuals to label their emotions and then find and apply appropriate strategies for relationship building and conflict resolution.

Social awareness of others typically develops throughout childhood, even before schooling, as children establish friendships and begin empathizing with others (Mcilroy, 2022). This awareness increases significantly throughout adult life as people increasingly need to understand others' views and perspectives in their personal and professional spaces. Additionally, both students and adults need to collaborate with others, whether at home or in school, and establishing good interpersonal relationships and interactions requires everyone to learn the basics about building a rapport.

Building a keen social awareness of others in elementary school is easier if information about social awareness is readily available and if the adults in students' lives model it appropriately. Unfortunately, scrolling through a student's social media feed or scanning the local news, one can see that social awareness is lacking throughout politics and society. Beyond the outright trolling and bullying among young people on apps, political discord can get highly inflamed, as commentators don't always express respect and regard for others who don't share their views. Data suggest that 85 percent of U.S. adults say political debate has become more hostile and less socially respectful (Drake & Kiley, 2019). Additionally, most people in the United States agree that elected officials should avoid inflammatory language because it could promote violence (Pew Research Center, 2019).

Although world and school conditions may discourage us, we can use SEL to help our students improve their perspectives for becoming kinder and more empathic toward others. The following key, calculated steps can help students navigate the basics of labeling their emotions for social awareness.

1. Students must recognize, or label, how they are showing up emotionally in their social interactions. They should begin labeling their emotions using either Plutchik's (2001) wheel of emotions or emojis for younger students. Figure 4.1 features an emoji chart for basic emotions.
2. Students must become keenly aware of how others are reacting or responding to them emotionally. This can be as simple as checking for body language, eye contact, voice tone, and tolerance to interact. According to the Watson Institute (2022), students have four critical components to consider when interpreting body language during social interactions.
    a. **Facial expressions:** Subtle cues can indicate whether someone's response is good, standoffish, or neutral.
    b. **Posture:** Body positioning—mainly of the head, back, and shoulders—can be informative.
    c. **Gestures:** What others do with their hands can indicate aggressiveness or peaceful emotions.
    d. **Stance:** This includes how someone stands and uses their arms (such as folding them across the chest).

Without these insights, students will find it difficult to learn and apply the appropriate relationship skills in different social situations. Plutchik's wheel or emojis can also be a suitable scaffold for helping learners assess where they think a peer's emotions reside.

Types of Basic Emotions

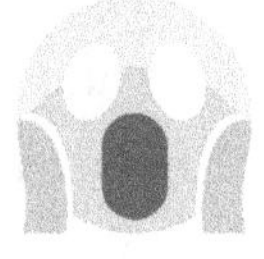
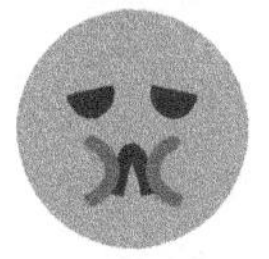

1. Happiness 2. Sadness 3. Fear 4. Disgust 5. Anger 6. Surprise

FIGURE 4.1: Emoji chart for basic emotions.

In figure 4.2, let's examine a planner that covers a few different social interactions to see how students can begin to put these two key points into action. A blank reproducible version of this figure is available at the end of the chapter (page 85).

Difficult Social Interaction	**How the Student Is Showing Up Emotionally**	**How Others Are Reacting or Responding to the Student Emotionally** *(Check for body language, eye contact, voice tone, and tolerance to interact.)*
Experiencing a first day at a new school	Eight primary emotions: ☐ Anger ☑ Anticipation ☐ Joy ☐ Trust ☑ Fear ☐ Surprise ☐ Sadness ☐ Disgust ☑ Other emotions: Nervousness	Some students are avoiding interacting with me and turning their bodies away from me. Some even avoid eye contact.
Winning an essay contest	Eight primary emotions: ☐ Anger ☐ Anticipation ☑ Joy ☐ Trust ☐ Fear ☐ Surprise ☐ Sadness ☐ Disgust ☑ Other emotions: Pride	Not all my classmates are sharing in my enthusiasm, and it's evident from their body language, lack of eye contact, and voice tone.
Arriving at school with a new haircut (one the student doesn't like)	Eight primary emotions: ☐ Anger ☐ Anticipation ☐ Joy ☐ Trust ☐ Fear ☐ Surprise ☑ Sadness ☐ Disgust ☑ Other emotions: Embarrassment	Some of my classmates are snickering and pointing at me.

FIGURE 4.2: Emotions planner for students (featuring examples for learning to recognize how others are showing up in social interactions).

Strategies for Understanding and Labeling Emotions

So far, we have helped students realize how they emotionally respond to situations. We've taught them how to label their emotions when they feel them and to trace them back to one of eight base emotions for better understanding. Now, we can help students choose and implement SEL strategies that will allow them to restore inner peace to prepare them for learning. *Inner peace* refers to being in a state of tranquil emotional and mental stability while exercising control over negative thoughts, moods, and impulsive reactions (Shea, 2017). An important item for teachers to consider is that although modeling and discussing SEL strategies with students as needed is impactful to learning, interventions are most effective when applied in forty lessons or more (Hattie, 2009). Researcher Catherine Cook-Cottone's (2013) work on *dosage* also supports that the best results occur when strategies are measured, predictable, and consistent in delivery.

Self-Manage With the Emotions Planner

Try doing an emotions check-in using the emotions planner for students. Figure 4.3 (page 69) features examples in each of the core content areas. A blank reproducible version of this figure is available at the end of the chapter (page 84). Initially, you may need to help students find and implement new emotional regulation strategies. Eventually, both the teacher and the student can work to identify SEL strategies to effectively regulate any of the student's emotions.

Educators can leverage the emotions planner during a minilesson to have students conduct an emotions check-in before individual or cooperative work time. It's important to help students resolve negative emotions before they solve problems independently. The following vignette describes an example of this strategy in action.

> *Michael, an elementary school teacher, had assigned his third graders journal entries as a final product for an English language arts project. He noticed that some of his learners were resistant to writing reflectively for their journals. After conducting an emotions check-in using Nearpod, he learned that many students felt anxious about the required learning for the new task. So Michael dived into a trusted bank of SEL strategies for combating anxiety and decided to adopt breathing techniques to help anxious students overcome their negative feelings and restore their internal peace. First, Michael practiced on his own, and then, he used his videoconferencing tool's breakout room feature to model the breathing techniques for small groups of students. He found these tactics to be helpful and less invasive for the struggling students.*

Subject	Emotion	SEL Strategy
English language arts: Complete journal entry	Eight primary emotions: ☐ Anger ☐ Anticipation ☐ Joy ☐ Trust ☐ Fear ☐ Surprise ☐ Sadness ☑ Disgust ☑ Other emotions: Boredom Loathing	☐ Self-management ☐ Social awareness ☐ Relationship skills ☑ Self-awareness ☑ Responsible decision making Use the space provided to elaborate on how you and your teacher will use the SEL skills to regulate your emotions. *Teacher will provide duties, model, and make learning relevant.* Student will recenter and focus on being present.
Mathematics: Fractions quiz	Eight primary emotions: ☐ Anger ☐ Anticipation ☐ Joy ☐ Trust ☐ Fear ☐ Surprise ☐ Sadness ☐ Disgust ☑ Other emotions: Apprehension	☐ Self-management ☐ Social awareness ☐ Relationship skills ☑ Self-awareness ☑ Responsible decision making Use the space provided to elaborate on how you and your teacher will use the SEL skills to regulate your emotions. *Teacher will provide scaffolds to support learning.* Student will provide positive self-talk and positive visualization.

FIGURE 4.3: Emotions planner for students (featuring examples from each of the core content areas).

continued →

Subject	Emotion	SEL Strategy
Science: Use of simulations	Eight primary emotions: ☐ Anger ☐ Anticipation ☐ Joy ☐ Trust ☐ Fear ☑ Surprise ☐ Sadness ☐ Disgust ☐ Other emotions: ____________	☑ Self-management ☐ Social awareness ☐ Relationship skills ☑ Self-awareness ☐ Responsible decision making Use the space provided to elaborate on how you and your teacher will use the SEL skills to regulate your emotions. *Teacher will restate instructions, encourage student to ask for help, and teach breathing techniques.* Student will practice breathing techniques.
Social studies: Study on civil rights	Eight primary emotions: ☑ Anger ☐ Anticipation ☐ Joy ☐ Trust ☐ Fear ☐ Surprise ☐ Sadness ☐ Disgust ☐ Other emotions: ____________	☐ Self-management ☐ Social awareness ☐ Relationship skills ☑ Self-awareness ☐ Responsible decision making Use the space provided to elaborate on how you and your teacher will use the SEL skills to regulate your emotions. *Teacher will model breathing techniques.* Student will focus on breathing, take a walk or step away, and count up to or down from ten.

IMPORTANT NOTE FOR TEACHERS

Typically, I conduct the check-ins with students on my classroom whiteboard or in Nearpod (https://nearpod.com). However, you can conduct check-ins verbally, in student journals, via your learning management system, through student engagement apps like Pear Deck (https://www.peardeck.com) or Seesaw (https://web.seesaw.me), or in a shared document like a Google Doc (https://docs.google.com).

Another essential item to consider when conducting check-ins is that learning to intentionally manage emotions in positive and healthy ways is only possible when people understand emotions. Managing and expressing emotions is therefore a separate skill from labeling them. Be sure to impart that tidbit to your students as their emotional intelligence capacity increases.

The following vignette describes a teacher using emotions check-ins to support her students' SEL.

Janet, a middle school teacher, used emotions check-ins to support her students' social-emotional needs whenever the students learned a new concept in lessons or traumatic situations arose. For example, when her school began hybrid teaching in March 2020 due to the COVID-19 pandemic, she noticed many students displayed anxiety or apathy toward some of her initial lessons and projects. She created a simple emotions check-in via a shared online planner so students could begin labeling and discussing the difficult emotions many of them were experiencing. Janet encouraged her students to digitally share their planners with her; this allowed her to curate strategies she could model for her students to help them be more peaceful in her SEL-infused remote lessons.

Identify Other People's Emotions

Check-ins on students' social awareness of relationship skills must be in response to social interactions. Figure 4.4 (page 72) features two examples of difficult social interactions. In the third column, the teacher and student work together to identify SEL strategies to effectively regulate any of the student's emotions. A blank reproducible version of this figure is available at the end of the chapter (page 85).

Difficult Social Interaction	Emotion	SEL Strategy
Argument: Sibling or friend disagreement	Eight primary emotions: ☑ Anger ☐ Anticipation ☐ Joy ☐ Trust ☐ Fear ☐ Surprise ☐ Sadness ☐ Disgust ☑ Other emotions: Annoyance	☐ Self-management ☑ Social awareness ☐ Relationship skills ☐ Self-awareness ☑ Responsible decision making Use the space provided to elaborate on how you and your teacher will use the SEL skills to regulate your emotions. The teacher will help identify win-win solutions and hold space with a restorative circle. I will gain the other's perspective and apologize.
New setting: School or class transfer	Eight primary emotions: ☐ Anger ☑ Anticipation ☐ Joy ☐ Trust ☐ Fear ☐ Surprise ☐ Sadness ☐ Disgust ☑ Other emotions: Apprehension	☐ Self-management ☑ Social awareness ☐ Relationship skills ☑ Self-awareness ☑ Responsible decision making Use the space provided to elaborate on how you and your teacher will use the SEL skills to regulate your emotions. I will think positively, remember that apprehension starts in the mind before it manifests physically, clearly organize my ideas about the new setting, and practice social skills in an environment similar to the new school or class.

FIGURE 4.4: Emotions planner for students (featuring examples of difficult social interactions).

The following vignette describes an example of this strategy in action.

Courtney, a middle school history teacher, assigned her class a collaborative activity during a project on the U.S. Civil War. The students would work in pairs or triads to create their final products. Midway through the designated chunk of work time, two students began quarreling loud enough that everyone in the class heard it. All the students shifted their attention to Courtney to see what she would do to defuse the situation and assist the two in restoring peace. Using one-to-one conversation as a de-escalation practice with both students, she was able to get them to reflect on better ways to deal with conflict in the future. Luckily, conducting emotions check-ins using the planner was an established practice among Courtney's students, as she consistently and intentionally modeled using the tool to improve emotional intelligence skills.

After the two students labeled their emotions about their heated debate, one determined that an apology was due to their classmate. Since the incident disrupted the entire class, Courtney engaged the entire class in a restorative circle to coach students in restoring justice through heartfelt apologies. Therein, Courtney explained to students they could always take a moment to apologize to others if they ever needed to. She said, "We won't always get things right. Mistakes are inevitable, and sometimes, we will need to apologize to someone. At times, a simple apology suffices, and other times, we will need to make things right by restoring justice. Here are three parts to an effective apology: (1) 'I'm sorry,' (2) 'It's my fault,' and (3) 'How can I make things right?'"

The students in question apologized to each other and their classmates for the disruption. At the closing of the restorative circle, all the students recorded the three parts to an effective apology in their bank of SEL strategies for future use.

IMPORTANT NOTE FOR TEACHERS

You will not always have to dedicate a significant amount of time or involve your entire class to improve social interactions. Use your discretion to determine what's best for everyone (including victims and offenders). Suppose a social interaction affects the entire class (as in the preceding vignette). In that case, a restorative circle and whole-class discussion may allow aggressors, victims, and bystanders the opportunity to heal and a platform to speak about how the occurrence impacted them (Heiskala, 2018; Miner, 2010). It also provides the space for getting the class back on the task of learning. But if social interactions are not disruptive to the entire class and involve only two or a few individuals, then don't involve others unnecessarily.

Hold Tiered Conversations

While addressing grievances between students through restorative justice, we must know when it's best to hold space for either one-to-one conversations or whole-class conversations with the students. For example, when I wasn't trauma informed and had no idea how to implement restorative practices, I made the mistake of triggering an already-angry student in front of his classmates (following a heated verbal exchange with his peer). I asked why he felt the need to make threats of violence every time he got upset. I thought I was reasoning with him; instead, I upset him more. Another time early in my teaching career, I took away a week of recess from an angry student while he was threatening to fight another student. Again, I made the mistake of giving him the consequence in front of his peers before defusing the conflict—thus making the situation worse.

Luckily, an assistant principal taught me that when students are upset, it's best to defuse the situation by helping them de-escalate instead of questioning them or disciplining them while they are still highly emotional. Structured one-to-one conversations aimed at assisting the students in regulating their difficult emotions will probably be better received. Challenging or penalizing angry students might trigger previous trauma, making them feel like their back is against a wall and they have nowhere to turn and nothing to lose. It also might make some feel like you don't care about them, which will trigger previous feelings of abandonment. I took my assistant principal's advice very seriously and learned better strategies for helping angry students with one-to-one conversations. The following are de-escalation and conversation strategies that have served me well.

- Remain calm yourself, and don't overreact by raising your voice or posturing if a student is expressing anger or appears out of control. I have seen this trigger amplify angry moods and behaviors. When speaking to the student, validate their emotional state and speak in calm, soothing tones. This works well when the adult has already built a positive rapport with the student. If this is not yet the case for you, try to get assistance from another adult who has built trust with the student.
- Know the signs that a young person is highly stressed, including raising one's voice, lashing out, and making inappropriate and threatening remarks to oneself and others. Anxiety-fueled movements such as shaking and fist clenching also indicate that this student is in crisis mode and needs de-escalation (Vollrath, 2020).

- Calmly and respectfully address the student, and acknowledge that you are aware they are upset. Let them know that you are there to help them through the difficult emotions they are currently experiencing. Gently redirect them to a designated area for de-escalation and reflection—it's crucial to have a private space for one-to-one conversation (Edutopia, 2018a).

Once you have the student in a private space, allow them time to calm down by helping them redirect their thoughts, breathing, and feelings (Vollrath, 2020). This sort of redirection helps separate the individual from their internal experience. I have found that we teachers can help raise students' awareness that they are temporarily experiencing negative thoughts, feelings, and emotions. I have also seen that teachers can eventually reduce de-escalation time by consistently practicing these techniques. For example, I've seen a trauma-informed teacher successfully get her student to de-escalate when lashing out by beginning with fifteen minutes of de-escalation time and getting it down to five minutes throughout a semester. Powerful techniques may also include using a timer and having the student journal, draw, and process what they experience in a volatile or highly emotional state (Edutopia, 2018a).

Whole-class discussions have many benefits for academic and social-emotional learning; they help students understand content, improve empathy for perspective taking, boost higher-order thinking skills, and practice speaking and listening skills (Common Core State Standards Initiative, 2022; Finley, 2013). Educators can effectively hold space for practical and effective classroom discussions using a circle practice structure (Davenport, 2018) and some of the norms and shared agreements discussed in chapter 8's Use Circle Practice section (page 146).

Emotional Intelligence and Responsible Decision Making

It is tough for students to make good and responsible decisions if they don't understand how to apply emotional intelligence skills. Because SEL focuses on self- and social awareness, we can assist students in exploring how their choices impact themselves and others.

Students have a long time to be adults but a short time to be young. Therefore, it benefits the students when we prepare them for the future by teaching them to apply their emotional intelligence skills as they make emotionally charged decisions. As students navigate the three broad stages of development—(1) early childhood (infancy to age five), (2) middle childhood (ages six to nine), and (3) adolescence (ages ten to nineteen)—they will encounter plenty of challenging choices to make. Although we cannot make their decisions for them, we can help them develop a system for making the best possible ones with emotional intelligence. Enter SEL and the need for decision-making tools and resources. Situations that may put students' emotional intelligence skills to the test and require them to weigh the consequences to themselves and others include the following.

- Peer pressure (regarding drugs, alcohol, sex, gangs, and other pressures)
- Escalation of disagreements with peers
- Dating and social events (the prom, lunchtime socialization, and more)
- Decisions to skip homework for TV or a social event
- Choices to cut school to socialize with peers
- Attempts to discover themselves and find their place (discovering their sexual orientation, for example)
- Plans for after high school (college and career)

Students need to make many other difficult decisions during their time in school. After reviewing this list, you will no doubt realize the enormous amount of stress they face. Whether or not you choose to assist them with making responsible decisions outside your content area or classroom activities, the emotions that their personal lives evoke will enter your classroom with them. And at times, those emotions can impact their learning or the learning of others in their vicinity. That's why SEL works best in schools where it's implemented systemically, and aligned with academic curricula, by *all* adults in the building. I've seen examples of this in schools like Fall-Hamilton Elementary in Nashville, Tennessee, whose staff identify students who need extra support in social, emotional, and academic aspects of life. The students are paired with an adult mentor (staff member) in the building who is not their teacher, and they do check-ins at the start and end of each school day (Edutopia, 2018b). Even designating a place in the school is powerful for fostering the SEL of students who require additional assistance to make decisions and not disrupt instruction.

When discussing the CASEL 5 framework in my professional development workshops, I hear many teachers express that they wish students were less impulsive and would take the time to think through their decisions. As an educator, I've often felt the same. Now that I better understand some of the science behind how decisions are made, I believe teachers must consider the following critical takeaways when they are approaching this component of SEL.

Emotions greatly affect people's choices and behavior, and therefore, many decisions are made unconsciously (Ellis, 2019). Before the age of twenty-five, the human brain is still developing. Mature adults learn to rely on the rational part of the brain, the prefrontal cortex, to make informed and responsible decisions (Campellone & Turley, 2021). Many students across grades K–12 impulsively make decisions using the amygdala, which is the region of the brain that can be hijacked for fight-or-flight responses and trigger emotional responses to immediate outcomes (Raising Children Network, 2021).

This is why students often lead with their emotions when making choices, and it isn't always their fault. In their brains, the link between the prefrontal cortex and the amygdala is still developing; this link is what humans need when considering long-term consequences while weighing decisions. Teachers can assist their learners in strengthening the connection between their prefrontal cortex and their amygdala by coaching them through the decision-making process. Additionally, conducting a minilesson about the amygdala and emotion-based decision-making setbacks will benefit students in learning to combat natural impulses.

Strategies for Fostering Responsible Decision Making

If K–12 students lack a working knowledge of how to apply their emotional intelligence skills, making good, calculated, and responsible decisions can be complicated for them. To clarify, it's not that young people entirely lack appropriate decision-making skills. Rather, the decisions they make in high-stakes situations may be affected by their emotions or a lack of understanding about possible outcomes. For example, a decision made to elevate their social status might come at the expense of another classmate (such as engaging in teasing or bullying). Since SEL focuses on both self- and social awareness, we teachers should help students explore the impact of their decisions on themselves and others.

To simplify the process of strengthening connections within the brain as much as possible, try using a decision-making tool (like the decision matrix or the decision-making checklist) with students. Our aim with decision-making activities is to provide students a systematic approach to responding to their emotions and taking the time to pause, weigh their options, and consider the perspectives of others involved before making decisions. Next are straightforward steps for doing this with your students using both tools.

Use the Decision Matrix

Teachers can help young learners (elementary and middle school students) start thinking about how to frame their decisions by examining their choices, the alternatives, and the natural consequences of whichever path they choose by using a decision matrix. With practice using the tool as a framework, they'll internalize the process and develop a mindset for sound decision making.

The decision matrix method, also known as the *Pugh method* or *Pugh concept selection*, was designed by Stuart Pugh (1981). It is a qualitative method used to sort multidimensional choices. In short, it assists with making tough choices. Business analysts, engineers, educators, and other professionals use the decision matrix as a tool to evaluate and prioritize their lists of options (Peek, 2021; Ramdhani & Jamari, 2018). Typically, teams establish a list of weighted criteria by importance and then evaluate each option against those criteria. Many organizations rely on these types of results for making complex, informed decisions that have a direct impact on their budgets, personnel, restructuring efforts, and partnerships.

The decision matrix is flexible and applicable in a variety of settings, including students' decision making in the classroom. Points are added for positive outcomes and deducted for negative outcomes. After students add up their numbers, they determine the choice with the highest score is the most responsible one. I recommend, at first, assisting elementary school– and early middle school–aged students in comparing multiple decisions to determine the best one.

The responsible decision-making matrix for students (see figure 4.5) helps students process their emotions by reflecting (via independent journaling, conversations with a trusted adult, or goal setting) and focusing on the consequences of the choices. A blank reproducible version of the responsible decision-making matrix for students is available at the end of this chapter (page 86).

Directions: Students can use the responsible decision-making matrix to make healthy decisions between two and three choices. The choice with the highest score can be deemed the most responsible decision.

Possible Decision-Making Choices	**Positive Outcomes** *(Add 1 point for each pro.)*		**Negative Outcomes** *(Subtract 1 point for each con.)*		**Total Scores**
1. Participate in teasing and bullying a peer.	To self	0	To self	–1	–4
	To others	0	To others	–3	
2. Become an ally by showing empathy.	To self	2	To self	0	5
	To others	3	To others	0	

FIGURE 4.5: Responsible decision-making matrix for students—Bullying example.

Include responsible decision-making skill-building strategies in your SEL strategies for students. The following vignette describes an example of using the responsible decision-making matrix for students.

Anisa, a sixth-grade mathematics teacher, noticed that one of her students, John, was snickering at a smaller peer during collaborative work time. Upon further observation of the situation, she learned that John was teasing his classmate. She temporarily removed John from his group and requested he approach her desk. Anisa informed John that teasing is a form of bullying and told him that she would help him make a better decision by weighing his options and evaluating their impact (pros and cons) on himself and others. She then introduced the responsible decision-making matrix for students to him and guided him through completing the activity.

Anisa learned that John and two other classmates had begun to tease their smaller peer at the start of work time. Therefore, Anisa and John determined he had two options to choose from: (1) participate in the bullying with his two friends, or (2) become an ally to the victim. They then labeled the possible choices in column 1 of the matrix.

After Anisa explained the point system for weighing the pros and cons, she and John determined that the first option had no pros (positive outcomes) to either himself or others. Zero was therefore added to both categories (self and others) in row 1 of column 2. For cons, John and Anisa entered –1 for self and –3 for others (the victim and the other two classmates involved in the bullying). They tallied the score in column 4, which totaled –4.

For the second option of becoming an ally to the victim by showing empathy (row 2), John and Anisa applied the same scoring system to the pros and cons. After talking through the pros to self, John determined that choosing this option had two positive outcomes for him: (1) he would be doing the right thing, and (2) he would feel good about himself by choosing to empathize with his classmate and prevent further injustice. The pro for each of his peers was that they would complete their schoolwork with no negative incident. A positive 2 was entered for John and a positive 3 for the others. With no cons to consider for choosing to become an ally, John entered zeros in column 3 for both self and others.

The total in row 2 was 5 points. After tallying the score, Anisa and John discussed what the individual scores meant and agreed that the better decision for John to make was to become his classmate's ally to prevent further injustice and bullying. John agreed to apologize to his peer upon returning to his workstation. After ensuring that her student was safe from further harm, Anisa chose an opportune time to hold space for a restorative circle with all involved.

IMPORTANT NOTE FOR TEACHERS

Keep it simple and include the responsible decision-making matrix in your SEL strategies for students. You can teach students effective use of the tool through the following steps.

1. Introduce the tool as an analytic framework for helping the students make the best possible decisions.
2. Normalize the tool's use for all students in your class by introducing the tool as a universal strategy and not a stigma.
3. Let the students know that the decision matrix is versatile and can be applied to many different types of decisions; encourage them to use it both at home and in the classroom.
4. Model the tool's use in various scenarios the students have encountered or are likely to encounter (such as addressing bullying, de-escalating conflict, and choosing between the fun thing and the right thing). It's crucial to present authentic scenarios here—you may even have students role-play.
5. Take time to explain the point system for weighing the pros and cons (positive numbers for pros and negative ones for cons). Pay close attention to the rules of adding and subtracting positive and negative numbers, especially for younger students (grades 3–6). Using a number line can be particularly helpful with early elementary students; also, model tallying in different scenarios, and have the students practice adding and subtracting with negative numbers.
6. Give students time and space to use the tool and incorporate reflection as part of the decision-making process. Having them list the pros and cons and talk through possible outcomes can be helpful here.
7. Only allow experienced users of the tool to model its use with classmates.

Finally, this is not a tool that students will use forever—it's simply a scaffold for helping them better weigh their decisions. When you see them demonstrating good decision making, you'll know that the responsible decision-making matrix has served its purpose. Hints of growth and maturity may include experiencing fewer weighted consequences of their impulsive behavior and considering the needs of others before making decisions.

Use the Responsible Decision-Making Checklist

High school-aged students may not want to use the responsible decision-making matrix but can still benefit from having a trusted set of steps for responsible decision making. A handy checklist provides a list of items for consideration (Santos, 2019) and another simple and powerful strategy we can put in students' responsible decision-making tool kit. Moreover, a well-designed checklist can help students save time, be specific, reduce human error (Gawande, 2011; Santos, 2019), and tackle decision making as a designer.

When you think about possible steps for a checklist, know that not all checklists are created equal. Atul Gawande (2011), author of *The Checklist Manifesto*, has good suggestions for getting started (Santos, 2019).

- A standard checklist is a good place to start, but allow your students to customize it and make it unique to them.
- Use the checklist to instill discipline in students. Having them work through a process is not the same as checking off boxes.
- Constantly have students review and refine their checklists as they work through the process and their needs change.
- Make checklists practical enough to keep students focused on the most important steps in their decision-making process.

For getting started, here are five steps students can take when making responsible decisions via this problem-solving and decision-making checklist (Positive Action, 2020):

1. Identify the problem.
2. Analyze the situation.
3. Brainstorm solutions and solve the problem.
4. Consider ethical responsibility.
5. Evaluate and reflect.

Using the preceding steps as guidelines, coach your students through several fictitious but complex scenarios to hone their responsible decision-making skills (such as choosing the right career path, addressing insults, and facing peer pressure). Make it a whole-class activity when you introduce the checklist—that way, everyone gets the same message about using the tool. You'll find that discussion about their decisions or decisions by others in the public eye, in tandem with role-playing and decision-making exercises like the responsible decision-making matrix and the responsible decision-making checklist, can assist students in approaching their choices tactfully.

Summary

Helping students with their emotional intelligence skills is challenging, but even more so if we ourselves haven't done the inward work first. Neglecting the previous steps in the Equity and SEL Integration Framework blocks us from having the necessary insight and perspective to be as effective as our classroom requires. This fourth step highlights our role in coaching students to improve their emotional intelligence skills with each of the chapter's presented tools. For SEL, think of these tools as thinking routines that foster critical-thinking and problem-solving skills for learners. Now that we have the emotional intelligence and SEL basics and foundational tools at our disposal, we can activate SEL as needed in daily lessons and across the curriculum, thus keeping SEL as an academic and social-emotional intervention. The following chapter tackles how we can do this seamlessly through our daily instructional design practices and pivoting when we have to keep learning at the forefront.

Emotions Planner for a Social Conflict in the Classroom

Social Conflict	How the Student Is Showing Up Emotionally	How Others Are Reacting or Responding to the Student Emotionally *(Check for body language, eye contact, voice tone, and tolerance to interact.)*
	Eight primary emotions: ☐ Anger ☐ Anticipation ☐ Joy ☐ Trust ☐ Fear ☐ Surprise ☐ Sadness ☐ Disgust ☐ Other emotions:	

Emotions Planner for a Difficult School Subject or Task

Subject	Emotion	SEL Strategy
	Eight primary emotions: ☐ Anger ☐ Anticipation ☐ Joy ☐ Trust ☐ Fear ☐ Surprise ☐ Sadness ☐ Disgust ☐ Other emotions:	☐ Self-management ☐ Social awareness ☐ Relationship skills ☐ Self-awareness ☐ Responsible decision making Use the space provided to elaborate on how you and your teacher will use the SEL skills to regulate your emotions.

Emotions Planner for a Difficult Social Interaction

Difficult Social Interaction	Emotion	SEL Strategy
	Eight primary emotions: ☐ Anger ☐ Anticipation ☐ Joy ☐ Trust ☐ Fear ☐ Surprise ☐ Sadness ☐ Disgust ☐ Other emotions:	☐ Self-management ☐ Social awareness ☐ Relationship skills ☐ Self-awareness ☐ Responsible decision making Use the space provided to elaborate on how you and your teacher will use the SEL skills to regulate your emotions.

Responsible Decision-Making Matrix for Students

Directions: Students can use the responsible decision-making matrix to make healthy decisions between one to three choices. The choice with the highest score can be deemed the most responsible decision.

Possible Decision-Making Choices	**Positive Outcomes** *(Add 1 point for each pro.)*		**Negative Outcomes** *(Subtract 1 point for each con.)*		**Total Scores**
1.	To self		To self		
	To others		To others		
2.	To self		To self		
	To others		To others		
3.	To self		To self		
	To others		To others		
4.	To self		To self		
	To others		To others		
5.	To self		To self		
	To others		To others		

CHAPTER 5

Activate Social-Emotional Learning in Your Lessons

KEY CHAPTER TASKS

- Embed social-emotional learning into your instructional design.
- Use social-emotional learning practices to combat bullying in school.
- Seek instructional feedback from students.
- Help students grapple with difficult or negative emotions.

Now that you've taken the time to work through the concepts and skills in steps 1–4 of the Equity and SEL Integration Framework, you have the right mindset and the needed foundational tools to successfully and equitably activate SEL in your lessons for all students.

Commit to considering the CASEL 5 and its set of skills as integral to student learning as the content standards that you weave into your lesson designs during the ideation process. You must do this if you want SEL to make a lasting impact on students. It won't always be tricky (just as it won't always be easy), but it will always be worth it. Remember, SEL is also an academic intervention because it helps students become better prepared for learning.

There will be times in the classroom when SEL is as simple as conducting an emotions check-in, having students label their emotions, and then having them quickly use a self-management strategy with no significant impact on your content-driven instructional focus. At other times, you will need to halt academic instruction to restore justice and help mend fences between the students experiencing trauma (such as bullying) and those causing the trauma. Doing this seamlessly is critical to raising equity for students who cannot advocate for themselves. Many have experienced a lifetime of harassment and bullying, and they need allies. You won't always do it perfectly, and that's OK; repetition over time and with consistency will make you better.

The better you get at helping students with their SEL using this framework, the better you get at raising equity for your most vulnerable students and making a safe, educational space part of your daily work.

In this chapter, we'll observe the implementation of SEL practices in the classroom. The implementation will occur through preemptive instructional design, backward design methodology, identification of SEL-compatible teacher traits, and the real-world application of SEL to bullying prevention. This chapter also features some introductory material and strategies for student emotional development and steps teachers can take to help that development.

Social-Emotional Learning in Your Instructional Design Practices

When it comes to confidently delivering instruction embedded with SEL, it's always important to pay close attention to sound practices for purposefully planning and teaching lessons. This means intentionally combining education research and personal experiences with actionable instructional strategies to plan lessons. As you learned in chapter 3 (page 47), it's also important to use our knowledge of our students when making instructional decisions. In education, these are often referred to as our *pedagogical strategies* or *instructional design practices* for teaching and learning (Edsys, 2018; Groshell, 2019). Instructional design is necessary for teachers to effectively translate content into learning.

It will take time to learn how to successfully embed equity and SEL into our instructional design practices. But we can continue to make strides over time through committing to consistency, practicing a lot, experiencing failure, and reflecting individually and with colleagues and students. Remember, educators and students cocreate thriving schools with SEL. The key here is for us as educators to never stop learning how to refine our practice.

We must be comfortable acknowledging learning gaps as we become aware of them. When we learn to trust and work well with colleagues and students, their feedback becomes an integral part of our instructional design process. You can seek feedback from students through polls and surveys. Request that colleagues critique your designed lessons, and observe them in action by using simple feedback protocols to structure your conversations. This will be critical for turning deficiencies into assets.

IMPORTANT NOTE FOR TEACHERS

When working to improve our instructional design practices for teaching and learning, we have a lot to contemplate. Mastery takes time, practice, and reflection. The more we try things out, the better we will know how our students respond and ultimately learn. If you need a system for aligning SEL with critical aspects of your instruction, try a simple backward design alignment tool. Use this tool to organize where the emotions check-in strategy from the previous chapter (like the one on page 83 for social conflict in the classroom) can live in your daily lesson plan, and leave a place for SEL activation as needed.

Strategies for Embedding Social-Emotional Learning Into Instructional Design

Teachers who want to make SEL part of their instructional design practices for teaching and learning often ask me the following questions.

- "When would be the best time of year to implement these changes in my instruction?"
- "Should I wait for the start of a new year, or can many of these changes weave into lessons as I go?"
- "Will I often need to stop teaching my academic content to do SEL?"
- "Should my school dedicate a class period or a day a week to address SEL and wellness?"

In the context of this book, embedding SEL into our instructional design means that we understand the value of helping our students with their social-emotional needs as these needs come up in our daily lessons. Although I see the importance of having established wellness days in schools, I prefer to activate most SEL lessons in my teaching as needed and in ways that align with academic content. This prevents SEL from being overdone and possibly viewed negatively by students and parents. For example, a student who needs help with anxiety before a test may benefit from doing quick breathing exercises and learning positive self-talk. A bullied student needs allies and can benefit from a restorative circle format for addressing the bully. The bully will also benefit from learning the impact of their behavior on the victim.

We can also intentionally teach SEL skills along with academic skills. For example, having my STEM students uplift empathy for a consumer in their design thinking is another form of activating SEL in lessons. I've seen students tasked with designing water wells for communities in India where women and children travel long distances with water. The students empathize with these people by carrying filled water jugs around the track that surrounds their football field. This practice gives students some firsthand understanding of the difficulty those Indian communities experience, and it emotionally compels the students to learn about engineering for the greater good.

As you'll see in the following sections, a few simple tweaks to include SEL in our instructional design practices can make our instruction much more equitable for so many students. The previous four steps in the Equity and SEL Integration Framework provide the prerequisite work and tools for effectively activating SEL in our lessons. Undoubtedly, many teachers already have a set of pedagogical strategies at their disposal for planning and facilitating instruction. They can therefore take the knowledge from the previous chapters and begin infusing SEL into what they already do.

But for teachers who are not yet sure where SEL can live in their daily teaching and their overall instructional design, the following sections provide tips for seamlessly implementing it. These sections encourage readers to use a simple alignment tool inspired by Jay McTighe and Grant Wiggins's backward design principles (Bowen, 2017; Wiggins & McTighe, 2005). Readers may be pleased to see that the tool is also helpful for aligning instruction with assessment.

Implement Backward Design Methodology

When I began teaching, colleagues always told me to plan backward—but no one could ever explain it to me in ways that made sense in my young mind. I needed modeling and examples. After I sought professional development and practiced using a powerful alignment tool, backward design methodology became a permanent component of my instructional design process. There isn't only one way to teach. But daily lessons must have flow and alignment. If those are things you need, you can benefit from a quick visual guide, like figure 5.1 (page 91); this can help you ensure that your daily lessons align with learning goals and assessments. A blank reproducible version of this figure is available at the end of the chapter (page 103). You can also use this backward design approach to help you activate SEL as needed throughout your teaching.

Backward design, also referred to as *backward mapping* or *backward planning*, is an instructional design process educators can use to develop logical teaching progressions in lessons, units of study, and courses. The central premise is to begin with the end in mind by stating the desired goals and outcomes for students; then work

Final Product or Performance	Learning Goals and Pacing	Formative Assessments	Lessons, Teaching Strategies, and Scaffolds
Computational artifact	I can investigate and explain each of the four computational thinking elements for computational problem solving. It will take me two days to complete.	1. Student summary of computational thinking elements from the jigsaw activity 2. Computational thinking rubric 3. Emotions check-in if needed 4. Exit ticket following work time	1. Computational thinking minilesson 2. ISTE overview of computational thinking (https://bit.ly/3xw6aOj) 3. Computational thinking elements jigsaw activity 4. SEL strategies if needed
	I can use computational thinking skills to develop visuals of step-by-step algorithms for solving a computational problem with a flowcharting app. It will take me three days to complete.	1. Computational thinking quiz 2. Flowcharting rubric 3. Feedback protocol to assess flowchart design 4. Reflection in design journal entry 5. Emotions check-in if needed	1. Computational thinking elements graphic organizer 2. Teacher modeling of the flowcharting software application 3. SEL strategies if needed
	I can apply computational thinking skills and algorithms in my flowchart to design a computational artifact that others access on the internet. It will take me three days to complete.	1. Computational artifact design rubric 2. Feedback protocol to assess computational artifact design 3. Reflection in design journal entry 4. Emotions check-in if needed	1. Conferencing with teacher during computational artifact design 2. Teacher modeling of various educational technology for computational artifact design 3. SEL strategies if needed

Figure 5.1: Example backward design alignment tool.

backward to identify and develop the appropriate assessments, learning experiences, and instructional strategies and scaffolds to achieve the outcomes (Bowen, 2017). Having a planning tool and framework for mapping instruction backward can help us maintain alignment no matter what we encounter in the instructional day.

PBLWorks (2015) originally created a version of the tool in figure 5.1, inspired by Grant Wiggins and Jay McTighe's (2005) backward design methodology. I used it for its clarity and eventually re-envisioned the design to fit my instructional design and teaching style. The tool does not replace Wiggins and McTighe's *Understanding by Design* resources and professional development through the Association for Supervision and Curriculum Development (ASCD, 2022). Instead, it's a simple four-column design that allows teachers to quickly map their instruction in alignment with summative assessment and daily learning goals. I have found the tool great for helping teachers see where SEL fits and is activated during their instruction.

The first column identifies the final product or performance task students are working on in a particular week. I'm a computer science teacher, so in the example in figure 5.1, my students are working on computational artifacts. A *computational artifact* is anything built by a human with a computer that is accessed on the internet (Valenzuela, 2020c). The second column houses the learning goals in the form of learning targets for each day of instruction. The third column lists formative assessments to check students' understanding of each learning target. And the fourth column lists teaching strategies and scaffolds to support learning for each learning target.

The "emotions check-in if needed" in column 3 can be a formative assessment for checking what emotions students are experiencing regarding the work they must complete that day (including the learning target and final product). Teachers can conduct the emotions check-in for nonacademic issues as well (such as when a student enters the class upset or when a peer conflict arises). In the last column of the emotions planner (see figure 4.3, page 69), teachers and students identify the SEL strategies and lessons teachers can activate, which are also specified in the backward design alignment tool's final column (see figure 5.1, page 91). When teachers take this approach, they can expertly and seamlessly integrate SEL and academic instruction as needed. Many teachers I've coached appreciate this approach because it doesn't overdo SEL—therefore upping its value to them and students.

The following vignette describes an example of this strategy in action.

Dayna, a high school computer science teacher, used the backward design alignment tool for a project where students were creating a computational artifact that end users would access on the web. She began with her intended student outcome by identifying the student product (computational artifact) in the first column. The second column represented the learning goals using three learning targets. The third column listed formative assessments for each learning target to ensure students were capturing and retaining learning. Finally, the fourth column captured the lessons, instructional strategies, and scaffolds Dayna could use to support student learning for each learning target.

Using this template to map and organize her instructional goals, assessments, and student learning experiences provided Dayna the appropriate aerial view for always knowing where she was or needed to be at each step of her pacing. Although her weekly lesson focused on computer science, she could use the emotions planner and teach SEL strategies as needed throughout the instructional day. For example, students who had difficulty with the material may become disengaged and unprepared to participate in learning. Dayna could now use the tools she had learned from step 4 of the Equity and SEL Integration Framework (chapter 4, page 61). Assisting these students with an emotions check-in (see the emotions planner for students in figure 4.3, page 69) followed by a one-to-one conversation and regrounding exercises (like breathing, positive self-talk, and others) may be what they needed to get back on track.

IMPORTANT NOTE FOR TEACHERS

In the preceding vignette, Dayna used the empathy map template (see figure 3.1, page 51) to gather pertinent data on students that would help her make instructional decisions in this class project. Any SEL strategies she used to help students self-manage would come from soliciting feedback from her students who labeled their emotions using the emotions planner (see figure 4.4, page 72). Additionally, educators can solicit students' feedback about their emotions and feelings as they improve in naming emotions through verbally affirming them and reading body language and facial expressions.

Focus on Empathy in Lessons to Prevent Bullying

With the increasing reports of hostile and violent interpersonal interactions due to bias, hate, and bullying among students, I can't stress enough the importance of frequently focusing on empathy and perspective taking in your lessons (Admissionsly, 2020). To scaffold your ability to effectively uplift empathy in teaching, you need to first understand emotional intelligence basics for yourself and your students and know where to activate SEL in your daily lessons using the backward design alignment tool. Also, in preparation for this section, both figure 4.5 (page 78) and the vignette on using the responsible decision-making matrix (see Use the Decision Matrix, page 77) dealt with addressing bullying.

Now that we have this critical understanding and some solid tools at our disposal, let's address essential steps to help improve our learners' social interactions by focusing on empathy for bullying prevention. Bullying removes safety and prevents learning; therefore, bullying is an equity issue. We can address this issue by implementing interventions that will restore justice and hold perpetrators accountable through increased empathy, healing, and restorative practices as part of our SEL plan. Research also supports shifting the national focus from bullying prevention to systemic integration of evidence-based SEL practices into school programs and policies (Divecha & Brackett, 2020).

In chapter 1 (page 15), I described social awareness as the ability to empathize with others, including those belonging to diverse cultures and backgrounds, and take their perspective even when it contradicts one's own. To become empathic toward their peers, students need to know the facts and consequences of hate-motivated bullying for all parties involved, and they need to have access to prevention methods. The following text contains valuable information, general statistics, and curriculum resources for understanding and addressing bullying through an SEL lens and for beginning conversations in your lessons.

There are three types of bullying: (1) verbal, (2) social, and (3) physical. According to StopBullying.gov (2021b), "Bullying includes actions such as making threats, spreading rumors, attacking someone physically or verbally, and excluding someone from a group on purpose." It can affect one student at a time or many, and multiple people can facilitate a single act of bullying at the same time. Bullying has three essential elements: (1) it's unwanted, (2) it includes aggressive behavior, and (3) it is repeated over time (StopBullying.gov, 2021b). Bias, hate, racism, and bullying are strongly connected. According to Learning for Justice (n.d.a), "The targets of bullies are often from a group marginalized because of a certain characteristic (such as race, immigration status, sexual orientation, religion, ethnicity, gender expression/identity or size) about which others hold prejudiced assumptions." Victims of bullying experience trauma due to persecution, self-blame, low self-esteem, and isolation. Victims feel especially alone when witnesses to the bullying don't intercede on their behalf; this causes some victims to feel deserving of the injustice. However, the traumatic effects of bullying also impact those who witness bullying (the bystanders) and the bullies themselves (StopBullying.gov, 2018).

Students who are bystanders can make a positive difference by helping the victims and becoming upstanders (StopBullying.gov, 2018). *Upstanders* intervene, interrupt, or speak up when they witness bullying to stop and prevent further injustice. Teachers can prevent classroom bullying by learning to identify bullying behavior, call it out, and help students become upstanders by focusing on empathy and perspective taking through SEL. Being an upstander requires understanding the impact of what's happening to victims and bravely doing the right thing. It's not easy, but we can help students take up the task.

Statistics on bullying can help inform school stakeholders about bullying's impact and where bullying takes place. Teachers and school leaders should consider the following eye-opening statistics when incorporating bullying prevention into their SEL plans to keep the most vulnerable students safe (StopBullying.gov, 2021a):

- [In the United States], 19% of students in grades 9–12 report being bullied on school property in the 12 months prior to a survey conducted on the subject.
- The following percentages of students ages 12–18 had experienced bullying in various places at school.
    - Hallway or stairwell (43.4%)
    - Classroom (42.1%)
    - Cafeteria (26.8%)
    - Outside on school grounds (21.9%)
    - Online or text (15.3%)
    - Bathroom or locker room (12.1%)
    - Somewhere else in the school building (2.1%)
- Approximately 46% of students ages 12–18 who were bullied during the school year notified an adult at school about the bullying.

StopBullying.gov (2021a) further states, "Research indicates that persistent bullying can lead to or worsen feelings of isolation, rejection, exclusion, and despair, as well as depression and anxiety, which can contribute to suicidal behavior." This is doubly true for those students who belong to historically marginalized identities. The following list features statistics on hate-motivated bullying in U.S. schools (Admissionsly, 2020):

- 70% of LGBT students are bullied because of their sexuality. Among these, 28.9% were bullied just because of their sexual orientation. 59.5% of LGBT students felt safety issues at school due to their sexuality.
- 34.8% of students missed at least a complete day at school every month. Of the majority of LGBT students thinking of dropping out, 42% stated harassment they had gone through at school as the main reason for it.
- More than one-third of teenagers reported racial bullying at schools. 23% of Black, 23% of White, 16% of Hispanics, and 7% of Asian students report having been bullied at school. Most of the time, racial bullying is associated with compromised physical and negative emotional health.

The preceding facts present an alarming reality for students belonging to marginalized communities. Bullying prevention is an exercise in empathy, but we can only begin to express empathy when we do our best to understand what another person is experiencing. Do your best as an educator to research and know statistics like these so you understand the unique way each student may experience hate-focused bullying. This comprehension will give you the necessary complex, factual knowledge of your students to further reflect on your implicit biases and improve your SEL approach in the classroom.

Use Curriculum Resources to Combat Bullying, Bigotry, and Hate

To effectively tackle bias, bullying, and the aforementioned data and statistics, teachers need good question prompts (or essential questions) and curriculum resources for preventing and responding to bullying at their school. Use the following questions to guide classroom activities such as circle practice, small- and whole-group discussions, independent journaling, article readings, projects, or group writing exercises to launch your antibias and antibullying SEL lessons. You can reword these questions to better fit the context of the students in your class.

- "What is bullying, and what are different ways to bully someone?"
- "What can I do if I am bullying others?"
- "How do bias and bullying intersect?"
- "Why and how can I stand up to bullies even when my friends bully?"
- "In a society, what is the collective responsibility of the people to prevent and fight injustices?"
- "What is injustice, and how do we work together to combat it in our classroom?"

- "What is the difference between injustice and justice?"
- "How can I become more empathetic and take others' perspectives?"
- "What collective action can our class take to dismantle injustice in our school?"

To complement the question prompts compiled here, I also curated some antibullying resources for helping you promote antibias guidance, SEL, empathy, perspective taking, DEI, tolerance, and social justice in lessons. Many of these resources will help put historical context to topics that are relevant to your class's context. These resources are located in appendix A (page 193).

Sustain Student Emotional Growth

While you continue to focus on students' SEL, you may find some of them experience shame or guilt because of the emotions they recognize and are feeling (Mulcahy, 2018). This can also occur when students learn about their impact on others and are not fully aware that the discomfort they are feeling may be shame (Mulcahy, 2018). As peer conversations about emotions become more candid, some may even chastise their friends for what they admit to feeling. It's important that you clear up misconceptions for students as they begin understanding the role of emotions throughout their lives. Their increased understanding can positively affect them in becoming more empathic toward others—which is the goal of step 4 of the Equity and SEL Integration Framework.

The following vignette describes a student with increased emotional intelligence putting empathy in action.

> *Victor, a high school step dance coach, noticed that Nico, his student of five years, had begun to better understand emotions within himself and others. Rather than reacting like he did when he was younger, he could recognize and label what he felt with words and do something about it. This became apparent when a new student, Alex, joined the squad and appeared to be withdrawn and unwilling to engage with his fellow steppers. After a couple of days of watching Alex isolate himself from the others, Nico made it a point to introduce himself and befriend Alex. During a weekly check-in with Victor, Nico expressed empathy for Alex as his main reason for forging the friendship. He said, "I saw Alex alone for a couple of practices, and I, too, know what it's like to feel isolated from others. I chose to be a friend by helping him get out of his shell." Victor realized that, with increased emotional awareness, Nico was learning why he responded to certain people, events, words, or even triggers. Not only was he using this knowledge to protect himself emotionally, but he was also using it to help others.*

By synergizing with students and other faculty, teachers can make their classrooms into SEL havens that provide a holistic understanding of what it means to be human. Together, teachers and students can develop, grow, and create intellectual and physical spaces of compassion and inclusion. As your ability to integrate SEL into existing curricula and standards increases, you could be tempted to primarily use SEL to make your time at school easier and more manageable. I encourage you to focus on the benefits SEL has for students and continually look for ways to better understand and deal with a wide range of emotions as they come up.

Strategies for Approaching Different Emotions

Humans experience various emotions throughout the day—some last just a few moments while others remain longer and can alter our mood. The intensity of emotions varies from mild to intense, depending on the situation someone encounters or the type of person they're dealing with (David, 2016). Ignoring emotions, whether they are positive or challenging, can overpower people with low emotional intelligence, as opposed to those with high emotional intelligence. As learners' SEL acuity increases, incorporating the following important strategies into your lessons as needed can help you raise the emotional intelligence of your students.

Help Students Pay Attention to Both Difficult and Pleasant Emotions

Many students are unaware of how the human body responds to thoughts, feelings, and behaviors by alerting them that something isn't right. Ignoring emotions can harm students' physical health and can lead to stress, anxiety, anger, depression, and poor health (Centers for Disease Control and Prevention, 2018; Hendel, 2018). For example, stressful events (like losing a loved one or being bullied) might lead a young person to lose sleep or concentration or to develop high blood pressure, a decreased appetite, or fluctuating energy levels. In some extreme instances, stress can cause an ulcer in the stomach (Centers for Disease Control and Prevention, 2018). Therefore, helping students learn to cope using their emotional intelligence skills can be vital to their physical health.

Teachers can further encourage learners not to ignore their emotional states or responses to people, events, and thoughts by paying closer attention to how they express or suppress their emotions (Symmetry Counseling, 2016). Instead of ignoring their emotions, students should leverage the emotion-labeling skills they learned in step 4 (chapter 4, page 61). This way, they can continue meeting their emotions head-on and asking for help when they're stuck. Bear in mind that asking for help with emotions can be difficult for students. Some are uncomfortable, afraid, or embarrassed or see it as a sign of weakness. Whatever the case may be, we can help and empower the students to seek assistance (Mental Health America, 2021). It won't always be easy for them, but practice and encouragement can make a difference in the lives of many.

Additionally, we can make students aware that tuning into their emotions includes the happy ones, as this knowledge can help replicate relaxation, comfort, joy, inspiration, and pleasure. Once students are comfortable regularly labeling positive and negative emotions, an excellent next step is to teach them to rate the intensity of emotions. They can begin by rating the recurring ones' intensity using a simple five-point scale (1 being the mildest and 5 the most intense). Help them evaluate triggers and catalysts and look for ways to prevent the difficult emotions and recreate the positive and healthy ones (David, 2016). As you're coaching students through the rating process, remind them that people experience emotions temporarily and don't remain in the same emotional states for long because emotions (and feelings) are transient (Cavell, 2015).

Take Additional Steps to Boost the SEL of Students

In lessons, teachers' role is to compel learners to develop a dynamic relationship with the content; we teachers do this by modeling ways of putting the content into action. In this case, the content is SEL, and there's a lot we can help learners implement. Many students may think of their teachers as part of the content and curriculum because they most likely only know their teachers in their teaching role. The following are a few ways educators can increase their social-emotional connection with students and raise equity for them.

- **Be likable and relatable to students:** In her famous TED Talk, the late Rita Pierson (2013) says, "[Students] don't learn from people they don't like." Therefore, lead with empathy by using active-listening principles with your learners, looking for common ground, being easy to talk to, and being fair with everyone. Students will appreciate it even if they don't say it.
- **Model what you want to see in students:** If your students see you actively pay attention to your own emotions, and you help students develop emotional intelligence skills through step 4 of the Equity and SEL Integration Framework (chapter 4, page 61), they, too, will pay attention to their own emotional intelligence.

- **Be trustworthy:** To be trustworthy is to be honest and truthful, but it also means to be reliable (Hydo, 2017). Students begin to trust and rely on the words and examples in our lessons when they see that we live our teaching and are genuinely interested in their academic and personal success. This means embodying through our words and actions the objectives in our academic and SEL lessons. For example, when our lessons encourage students to improve their emotional intelligence personally and socially, they need to see us making similar strides. Doing so promotes trust.
- **Be present and responsive to your students' emotions and corresponding behaviors:** Knowing that we educators are paying attention builds trust and a rapport between us and students (Kerpen, 2016). Ways to show students that we're present with them include the following (Graham, 2012; Rost, 2011).
    - Responding when they address us
    - Making good eye contact
    - Making sure we don't turn our body away from them when they are speaking
    - Affirming what they say to us by repeating it and referring to it later
    - Asking clarifying questions when we don't understand
    - Providing feedback when they request it
- **Apologize when you're wrong or make a mistake:** When educators admit that they're wrong, it helps create trust and a rapport in their classrooms and shows they are willing to confidently model integrity for students. Students will notice when their teacher makes a mistake and will wait to see whether they take ownership (Pierson, 2013). When an educator fails to assume responsibility or acknowledge when they're wrong, students resent it deeply and understand that the adult is more concerned with being right than being just (Valenzuela, 2021b). Don't be that person.
- **Share your stories, and allow students to share theirs:** Sharing stories before lessons makes everyone more relatable and enables the entire class to build an empathic culture and community (Friday, 2014). Storytelling is a constant in my classroom, and adhering to the following has helped my learners better connect with me, their peers, and the content.
    - I share my passion for teaching and why I entered the profession. I have found that doing so promotes trust between me and learners because they know I love my job and take it seriously.

    - I connect stories to the content for activating prior knowledge and helping students make authentic connections. Here are a few prompts I use to guide students' reflections.
        - What is your favorite book and why?
        - Describe the attributes of a person you really admire.
        - Talk about an object that is special to you. What makes it so special?
        - How do you spend your free time?
        - What is your favorite school subject, and how did it become your favorite?
        - How do you use mathematics at home?
- **Critique work, not people:** Research shows that frequent harsh criticism from parents and guardians negatively affects how students' brains respond to emotional information (James, Owens, Woody, Hall, & Gibb, 2018). Adopting feedback protocols can create a classroom culture that respects students while students are improving and revising their work by using structured and respectful formats (Valenzuela, 2022e). In many school contexts, this takes effective modeling by teachers and consistent implementation before it becomes the norm (Valenzuela, 2021b).
- **Encourage learners to always do their best:** This may be difficult when students have learning gaps that prevent them from problem solving. Teach them about failure's part in the learning process and the importance of turning their learning challenges into assets (Waterford.org, 2019). Doing so will help build their confidence over time.

Many of the characteristics mentioned in the preceding list can appear daunting, and I'd be lying if I told you that I walked into my classroom on my first day of teaching possessing each of them. Embracing equity and raising your and your students' emotional intelligence is an ongoing journey. The first step is to acknowledge you are a role model for students, even though you might not know where to begin. You can take this as an opportunity to model being a gracious learner and reflective leader who is open to growth. A good place to start is to take a short list of SEL skills you feel teachers need in a classroom and *begin* to embody them. Read books that use reliable sources, and find time to implement what you've learned.

Summary

Undoubtedly, global issues change how we think, live, and teach students SEL strategies. I believe taking steps to help learners improve their emotional intelligence through our teaching makes us an asset these learners (especially students who have felt unsupported in the past) can begin to count on. As we work to fill our knowledge gaps about them, we can plan relevant lessons that activate SEL both explicitly and also as needed. I hope you have learned how necessary it is to prepare yourself for imparting SEL through these first five chapters. The Equity and SEL Integration Framework can be a powerful tool for taking the steps to begin or enhance this journey. To help us further raise equity for the students furthest from opportunities, part 2 of this book will show how we can use the framework for implementing trauma-informed, culturally responsive teaching and restorative justice.

Backward Design Alignment Tool

Final Product or Performance	Learning Goals and Pacing	Formative Assessments	Lessons, Teaching Strategies, and Scaffolds

Three Focus Areas for Equity and Social-Emotional Learning

The first part of this book provided you with the know-how, tools, and resources for sharpening both educators' and students' emotional intelligence, skill sets, and equity lens. I encourage you to refer to chapters 1–5 throughout your SEL teaching journey. The principles in part 1 are foundational and will prepare you for implementing the content in part 2.

The following three chapters offer an overview of three research-based approaches: (1) trauma-informed teaching, (2) culturally responsive teaching, and (3) restorative justice. These approaches will help us make the necessary pedagogical transformation to improve our social and cultural competence during our SEL-infused lessons.

We can use SEL to advance equity by establishing more collaborative and inclusive school communities where students and educators are committed partners. But, as we learned in steps 1–3 of the Equity and SEL Integration Framework, educators must concentrate on critical self-work for expanding their knowledge of both self and students and thus activating SEL equitably. Therefore, it is imperative to know how to recognize trauma, be culturally responsive, and restore justice through healing, compassion, and accountability so we can raise equity for students with diverse SEL needs.

The content in the following chapters is not meant to replace comprehensive professional learning for each of these approaches. Instead, it provides you with the foundational knowledge and rationale required for getting started. These chapters offer access to the right resources for developing the correct language, accurate data on the issues impacting students' SEL, and tools for best practices. The chapters include contributions from reputable experts, researchers, and practitioners in each of the fields. They also include actionable steps to take in the classroom and professional learning options for you to consider as you move forward in your learning.

CHAPTER 6

Implement Trauma-Informed Teaching

KEY CHAPTER TASKS

- Learn and identify when someone has experienced a traumatic event or situation.
- Become trauma informed and learn how to apply trauma-informed teaching in the classroom.
- Adjust your teaching style to accommodate students affected by trauma.
- Access resources for trauma-responsive classroom management.

Trauma informed is an equity-raising lens through which educators choose to view their students to build better rapports and relationships. Better relationships help us create classroom environments that resolve conflict, encourage discourse, and improve teaching. Trauma-informed educators are experts on their students, and they understand the impact of trauma on student learning and overall well-being (Thomas et al., 2019b).

Furthermore, these educators are deeply informed about the key factors that cause learners trauma and how those experiences may prevent students from learning in school and succeeding in life (Crosby, 2015). Having this knowledge does not mean trauma-informed educators provide therapy to students affected by trauma. Instead, it allows them to establish safe, stable, and caring environments and meaningful relationships that can serve as avenues toward healing and guidance for their students. This chapter will help you learn more about trauma, its causes, its impact on students, and trauma-informed strategies you can use to improve your SEL plan and raise equity for learners experiencing acute trauma.

Traumatic events are many and can include, but are not limited to, poverty, bullying, domestic violence, microaggressions, and racism in its various forms (implicit, overt, and systemic). Developing your understanding of trauma can begin with two different contexts: (1) physical and (2) emotional and psychological (Leonard, 2020; McMahon, 2022). *Physical trauma* relates to physical injury and bodily harm, like a sports injury, car accident, or attack. *Emotional and psychological trauma* relates to the emotional responses to events that cause significant trauma and distress, like war, the loss of a loved one, sexual assault, or murder (Leonard, 2020; Robinson, Smith, & Segal, 2021). Students (really, *all* people) who have traumatic experiences may respond in various ways, such as in anger, grief, depression, or denial, and some may completely shut down (Robinson et al., 2021).

Trauma-informed educators must understand the nuances of emotional and psychological trauma to influence classroom implementation of trauma-informed strategies and their limitations for helping students heal. Emotional trauma is a natural response to disturbing, frightening, threatening, or painful events that distress individuals. Symptoms of emotional trauma range in intensity by individual and may include self-blame, anxiety, sleep loss, depression, anger, mood swings, and obsessive and compulsive behaviors (Cascade Behavioral Health Hospital, 2021). However, when a person's nervous system gets stuck, remains in psychological shock, and cannot process their emotions or the event, it becomes psychological trauma (Robinson et al., 2021). And if the person continues to relive the event and is unable to move on, they may be experiencing post-traumatic stress disorder (PTSD).

Although some signs and symptoms of PTSD are observable, only doctors who have experience assisting people with mental illnesses (psychiatrists or psychologists) are qualified to diagnose and treat PTSD (Khoddam, 2021; Robinson et al., 2021). When psychological trauma becomes overwhelming for students, schools may need to help families get professional therapy for the students. SEL is never a substitute for professional trauma-informed treatment.

According to the Substance Abuse and Mental Health Services Administration (2020), potentially traumatic events include the following:

- Psychological, physical, or sexual abuse
- Community or school violence
- Witnessing or experiencing domestic violence
- National disasters or terrorism
- Commercial sexual exploitation

- Sudden or violent loss of a loved one
- Refugee or war experiences
- Military family-related stressors (e.g., deployment, parental loss, or injury)
- Physical or sexual assault
- Neglect
- Serious accidents or life-threatening illness

Additionally, a student's age may determine how trauma manifests; it is therefore critical to offer informed supports following a traumatic event (Smith, Robinson, & Segal, 2021). Table 6.1 provides examples of what teachers and families may encounter.

TABLE 6.1: Signs of Trauma in Students by Age

Infants under age two may:	• Fuss more or be harder to soothe • Exhibit changes in sleep or eating patterns • Appear withdrawn
Students ages two to five may:	• Cry, scream, or whine • Cling to their parent or caregiver more • Move aimlessly or freeze up • Regress to earlier childhood behaviors, such as thumb sucking or bed wetting • Show other signs of fear
Students ages six to eleven may:	• Lose interest in friends, family, or activities they used to enjoy • Experience nightmares or other sleep problems • Become moody, disruptive, or angry • Struggle with school and homework • Complain of physical problems such as headaches or stomachaches • Develop unfounded fears • Feel sad, emotionally numb, or guilty over what happened
Students ages twelve to seventeen may:	• Have flashbacks to the event, suffer from nightmares, or experience other sleep problems • Avoid reminders of the event • Abuse alcohol, drugs, or nicotine products • Act disruptively, disrespectfully, or aggressively • Complain of physical ailments • Feel isolated, guilty, or sad • Lose interest in hobbies and interests • Have suicidal thoughts

Source: Adapted from Smith et al., 2021.

Research on Trauma in Schools

All students have experience with some form of emotional pain, perhaps through fears, bullying, disappointment, or an unexpected loss. However, many of them are dealing with overwhelming traumatic difficulties both at home and in the community. Trauma isn't confined to one situation or event. It can comprise many areas, and teachers need to be aware and prepared.

Lori Sanchez, professor of education at Concordia University in Portland, Oregon, states:

> In the past, when you talked about a child experiencing trauma, you assumed abuse or neglect. . . . Now we understand that trauma can mean a lot of things—families dealing with divorce, serious illness, a natural disaster, a military deployment, and more. (Resilient Educator, 2021a)

Many students cannot cope and do not have the emotional intelligence skills to regulate their emotions or seek the help they need. The U.S. average of child abuse and neglect victims in 2015 was 683,000, or 9.2 victims per 1,000 students (Zarrabi, 2020). The following list, featuring data from a report by the Substance Abuse and Mental Health Services Administration (2020), details just how pervasive experiences of trauma are among students.

- More than two-thirds of students report at least one traumatic event by age sixteen.
- One in four high school students has been in at least one physical fight.
- One in five high school students has been bullied at school; one in six experiences cyberbullying.
- Nineteen percent of injured and 12 percent of physically ill youth have post-traumatic stress disorder.
- Fifty-four percent of U.S. families have been affected by some type of disaster.

As we can see, teachers are interacting with many students who are adversely impacted by traumatic experiences; SEL plans in schools therefore should include trauma-informed teaching strategies to serve these students appropriately. The Equity and SEL Integration Framework is designed to help us implement trauma-informed teaching.

Trauma-Informed SEL

Educators who understand trauma and its impacts can help students begin healing by collaborating with them to establish healthy relationships and safe spaces where positive interactions, acceptance, unconditional regard, and kind speech are commonplace. SEL is the vehicle many educators use for carrying out and normalizing trauma-informed pedagogy in their classrooms (Jagers, Rivas-Drake, & Borowski, 2018). Educators can tailor SEL lessons to meet the needs of students who've experienced trauma by providing them with the emotional intelligence acuity for recognizing their emotional trauma.

The good news is the emotional intelligence skills we are trying to achieve for students with the CASEL 5 have considerable overlap with trauma-informed practices and strategies, as you will see in the following section. Furthermore, the Equity and SEL Integration Framework is designed to assist us educators with improving our knowledge of students; this way, we can build our skills to raise equity for students experiencing trauma. For learners with trauma, trauma-responsive coping and healing strategies can supplement or strengthen ordinary SEL skills (Spinazzola et al., 2005). For example, trauma-informed educators may need to help students work through being angry and shutting down as part of boosting their self-awareness and self-management skills within the CASEL 5 integrated framework. Additionally, assisting traumatized students in improving relational boundaries, becoming more independent, and regulating their demeanor during interactions can easily align with social awareness and relationship skills in the CASEL 5. The emotions planner for students (figure 4.3, page 69) can also be helpful for these purposes.

We can teach students to self-regulate by collaborating with them to reach their goal of being in control. No student wants to have a meltdown in front of their friends, so being on their side and learning how to help them is key.

The following vignette describes this type of collaboration in action.

Hedreich had a student in her eighth-grade class, Anya, who regularly experienced meltdowns with seemingly no provocation. After a few trial-and-error runs, Hedreich gave Anya her own spot in the classroom. She could go there whenever she needed to as long as she did not disrupt others who were working. Getting her to that point involved a few mistakes in which Hedreich saw Anya's behavior as belligerent and disruptive. Once Hedreich saw Anya struggling with self-control and realized she was as unhappy at being disruptive as Hedreich was at having her interrupt class, Hedreich began to help Anya in her struggle.

Hedreich learned to calmly address her: "Anya, I see you getting angry. Take a few minutes and get some water. Just stay on this hall." Hedreich left the door open and could easily continue instruction while checking on Anya's well-being. Giving her space to reset was much different from a stern removal from class. Once Anya became calm, which usually was a little while after her return to class, they would talk about what had happened and what Hedreich could have changed about her role in the interaction. They also focused on what Anya could do to be more in control rather than have disruptive and unacceptable behavior.

Once their relationship became collaborative instead of adversarial, they had a basis for productive interactions, even when Anya was triggered. Hedreich began to allow Anya to work in the hall after her walks because she recognized Anya needed to be out of the situation and away from stimulation. That morphed into her having a spot in the back of class near Hedreich's desk. Anya chose the spot, and by the end of the year, she was able to go there before getting out of control. All those steps and the many little ones in between that allowed her to learn tools for self-regulation avoided calls home and visits to the principal's office. (This vignette was written by contributor Dr. Hedreich Nichols).

Educators can have traumatized students use the responsible decision-making matrix (figure 4.5, page 78) as they weigh pros and cons during the decision-making process. However, the core SEL strategies educators employ, coupled with plans for use of trauma-informed strategies, may need to vary in intensity and will require collaboration with colleagues, additional planning, and development. This is because students coping with acute stress or fear experience the fight, flight, or freeze response much more often than adults do. This is due to increased activation of the limbic system, which is the part of the brain involved in behavioral and emotional responses (van der Kolk, 2014). Creating tangible connections between SEL and trauma-informed strategies can make educators more effective with both interventions (Elias & Leverett, 2011). Now, let's look at some strategies for bridging SEL and trauma-informed practices.

Strategies for Making Trauma-Informed Improvements to SEL Plans

Although educators are unable to undo painful experiences students have had, they can help students build resilience skills and prepare for SEL by bringing trauma-informed strategies into the classroom. An important goal in trauma-informed classrooms is to be aware of the signs of trauma and have a collection of strategies for helping students and not retraumatizing them. Retraumatization can happen when a student re-experiences a previously traumatic event, either consciously or unconsciously (Online MSW Programs, 2022). This can be caused by encountering stressors that correlate with the original trauma. Stressors may include recounting traumatic experiences and experiencing smells, imagery, lighting, sounds, locations, or interactions that mimic previous traumatic ones (Alexander, 2012).

This section compiles widely used trauma-informed teaching practices from credible sources and resources for refining your trauma-informed SEL plan. I put the strategies in a logical order of execution to help you prioritize them, but don't feel compelled to follow this order precisely. Pedagogical transformation should always begin with the educators.

Develop a Trauma-Informed Team to Provide Wraparound Services

To support students who are survivors of trauma, teachers must understand trauma, know how not to retraumatize students, establish norms and protocols for recentering after triggering events, and provide access to wraparound services. Wraparound services comprise comprehensive and holistic care for students and their families experiencing severe mental health or behavioral challenges. Wraparound programs providing these services are typically collaborations between state or local government agencies and organizations that work with schools (Colburn & Beggs, 2021).

Your trauma-informed team can consist of various community members, such as teachers, school leaders, counselors, and organizations. In schools, a teaching team typically collaborates with administrators, school counselors, and providers of wraparound services dedicated to supporting student survivors of trauma. These individuals may have undergone SEL training together and are looking for ways to become trauma informed to improve their teaching of trauma survivors. The following list shows some examples of what a trauma-informed team should do to support recentering after triggering events.

- Ensure that classrooms and campuses have monitored calm-down areas free from stimulation available.
- Help students and teachers recenter and describe their moods by using tools like mood meters or fun ones like emoji and meme check-ins.
- Complete wellness check-ins after the event has passed. Consider using sentence stems or reflections to guide the conversation—for example, "After ________, I felt ________. Now, I feel ________."
- Use word lists or temperature charts for further support.
- Reassure students that they are valued members of the learning community.
- Find something praiseworthy in interactions, and recap what has been learned.

Unfortunately, teachers often have no choice but to respond to the trauma students bring from their homes and neighborhoods—and over time, it can take a toll. People who help someone with trauma can experience symptoms from the stress of exposure to their trauma. Often called *secondary traumatic stress* or *vicarious trauma* (The Write of Your L!fe, 2020), these instances of emotional duress result when someone listens to the traumatic experiences of others. Over time, those exposed may experience emotional symptoms such as grief, anxiety, and detachment from students. Behaviorally, some may have trouble sleeping and eating. Others may isolate themselves and turn to substance abuse. Trauma-informed teachers require emotional support from their colleagues and school leaders to avoid burnout and lessen the impact of secondary trauma.

Emotional support can take the form of an accessible trained professional or an informal peer support group formed so educators can check in on one another during times of work-related or non-work-related stress. Ways to check in include group texts, brief weekly meetings, and an assigned buddy system where two or more teachers agree to support one another.

Empathize With Students

Teachers can be proactive about empathizing with learners by increasing their knowledge of them (see chapter 3, page 47). To become better informed of learners' trauma without being invasive or inappropriate, especially in the most sensitive cases, we can practice empathy by listening to what they say and validating their point of view. We can also pay attention to how their moods change by viewing their interactions with others. Our own healed trauma can help us empathize with students as well. Research supports that those who have overcome traumatic childhood experiences can be more prone to empathy as adults (Dolan, 2018).

When a student is showing signs of behavior rooted in trauma, teachers can use empathetic language to validate the student's experience without making them feel vulnerable or called out for carrying trauma. This language may include the following.

- "If I understand correctly, _________."
- "I would feel _________ too in that situation."
- "It's normal for you to feel this way."
- "I'm sorry that this happened and that this is your experience."
- "I've recently experienced the same thing too."
- "Thank you for letting me know about this."

Teachers can learn more about students while being mindful not to push them to share information they are uncomfortable sharing. In extreme cases where you fear for a student's well-being or safety, contacting an emergency intervention in your school context (such as a school counselor) is the most appropriate action.

Remain Consistent and Predictable

Keep a calm, equitable, and reliable presence in the classroom through your demeanor; this can help put student survivors of trauma at ease. Be intentional and set timers during classroom activities or when you are going to do something for students (Minahan, 2019). For example, structure instructional activities similarly each day. Also, be specific about when you will do so (in five minutes, in ten minutes, tomorrow at one in the afternoon, and so forth). Last, if you need to meet with a student, don't be vague. For example, avoid saying, "We need to talk." This kind of statement can unnecessarily build anticipatory stress and cause the student to ruminate on what you could want to speak to them about. Be specific and kind. For example, say, "I would love to talk about your essay. I know we can make it better with some tweaking." This will also give them time to prepare for the conversation.

Establish a Relationship Before You Form a Learning Partnership

Teachers need to be caring, relatable, and trustworthy to their students before engaging them as learning partners. Educators should never lead with content (Resilient Educator, 2021a). To make a student coping with trauma feel safe in your classroom, you will need to build a rapport and use relationship-building strategies. Ways of connecting with students can include being friendly, using relatable and empathetic language, being courteous, finding common ground, appreciating their work, sharing stories, and making connections. Also, give them space when they need it. Providing students who are experiencing trauma with a safe space for de-stressing can make all the difference they need (The Write of Your L!fe, 2020).

Additionally, educators can make their classrooms physically, intellectually, and emotionally safer by keeping in mind some of the norms and shared agreements discussed in chapter 4 (page 61). It's important to note that those suffering from extreme fear and psychological insecurity will need to thoroughly process and examine their trauma and pain with an experienced licensed professional for healing to occur. These individuals may need extra support to feel safe, and educators may not have the tools or resources to provide this. Be patient with individuals who are still working on feeling safe even in a stable environment, and do not take their continued discomfort as meaning you have personally failed to establish a safe space.

Help Students Recenter Themselves After a Triggering Event

Unfortunately, some teachers may label behavior that doesn't appear to be compliant as "bad." However, it's essential to consider when a situation triggers a student's trauma. If the student hasn't yet developed the appropriate communication skills to describe their trauma, they may express themselves in less-than-desirable ways through their words, demeanor, facial expressions, or disposition (Ashbaugh, 2020). Some traumas can be triggered easily and quickly, such as by sights, words, light, sounds, smells, food, weather changes, specific movements, and even thoughts (Psychophysiologic Disorders Association, 2022).

We may not even pinpoint exactly why or how triggers occur, so we must look beyond the "bad" behavior by remaining calm, showing understanding, and meeting students where they are. Help your students recenter by focusing on breathing, repeating coping statements, and using positive self-talk (Ashbaugh, 2020). *Positive self-talk* refers to the monologue teachers can help students use to get through difficult situations. Students may even continue using this strategy when they encounter similar difficulties beyond school. Examples of positive self-talk include the following.

- "I am responsible for my life."
- "I have the power to do this."
- "I can change my mind."
- "I'm proud of myself for doing my best."
- "I love myself."
- "Fear can't hold me back."
- "My mistakes do not define me."

Help Students Improve Their Self-Image

Symptoms of trauma and PTSD can be challenging to cope with and can result in many students having low self-esteem (Tull, 2020). Students with abandonment or bullying experience may have negative thoughts about themselves, which negatively impact their self-worth and self-image. Trauma-informed educators can help these students learn to improve their self-image by combating negative thoughts with positive ones. Matthew Tull (2020), professor of psychology at the University of Toledo in Ohio, recommends deep breathing, self-affirmations, and mindfulness as distractors to teach students. However, he also prescribes challenging negative or impulsively anxious thoughts with the following question prompts (Tull, 2020):

- What evidence do I have for this thought?
- What evidence do I have against this thought?
- Are there times when this thought hasn't been true?
- Do I have this kind of thought when I am feeling OK as opposed to feeling sad, angry, or anxious?
- What would I tell someone else who was having this kind of thought?
- What may be an alternative explanation?

These questions can be excellent discussion prompts in circle practice and can accompany readings on self-esteem and positive self-image.

Be Patient

At times, you may feel offended or hurt by your traumatized student's distance or mood changes, or you may struggle to understand their inconsistent behavior patterns. You may even feel like you're meeting this person for the first time each day or that you can never say the right thing to them. Your other students may also resent their classmate if they have to assume more significant shares of classroom projects, tasks, or responsibilities. This is especially true if the student coping with trauma appears indifferent.

When working to establish relationships with student survivors of trauma, don't take their behavior personally, and exercise patience amid challenges. Students with PTSD cannot always control their behavior. Remember, their nervous system is effectively stuck, which puts them in a constant state of alert (Robinson et al., 2021). Because they are in a state of constant vigilance, they will feel vulnerable and unsafe when something triggers their trauma (Smith & Robinson, 2021). The good news is with love, patience, compassion, and a good support system that includes family, friends, and you, their nervous system can become unstuck (Pappas, 2018). As you learn to anticipate and manage triggers, it's vital to provide positive feedback and affirmations to students when they make strides to cope and heal. Table 6.2 (page 118) features some possible positive responses to classroom events.

Create a Calm-Down Corner

Consider creating a space in your classroom dedicated to the de-escalation of feelings. Make it free for all students to use at any time besides active learning sessions or work time. A calm-down corner (also known as a *peace corner*) is a small, dedicated wellness area decorated with some combination of pillows, rugs, beanbags, curtains, fairy lights, and so on (Lantieri, 2012). It can contain books on developing emotional

TABLE 6.2: Example Classroom Events and Possible Teacher Responses

Classroom Event	Possible Teacher Response
A student enters the classroom angrily, loudly complaining about the last class. Repeated attempts to begin class fail because the student's outbursts are causing a disruption.	Momentarily ignoring the disruption, assign an engaging, easy-to-complete warm-up activity to the whole class. Invite the student to get water and take a brief walk (for K–2 students, this walk could be replaced by time in a calm-down corner). Set time and place limits that ensure student safety. When the student returns, make eye contact and do a wellness check. If the student is calm, proceed, offering the student the opportunity to write or record a reflection. Check in with the student before class is over.
A student calls an assignment pointless and refuses to work.	Say, "OK, I hear you, [student name]. Let me get everyone started. Meanwhile, you think of which part you don't like so we can come up with a way to make the assignment more meaningful for you." Come up with an appropriate modification, and include peer input if time and disposition allow. Offer other students similar desired adaptations as well.
A student refuses to work on a group assignment, and the group complains.	Begin group conflict resolution by acknowledging frustrations on all sides. List possible reasons for the frustrations, naming emotions to build emotional intelligence. Ask group members what outcome they envision. Then try to mediate the negotiation of a contract using as much student input as possible.
A student has a meltdown involving physical behaviors like throwing books or chairs.	In a calm voice, reassure all students they are safe; quietly move the other students to safety. Activate the campus plan for violent incidents. Continue to monitor the student and speak calmly until help arrives.

intelligence, paper to draw on, soft toys, balls, and headphones with calming music or soundscapes. This area should be a welcoming space that students want to go to rather than a punitive time-out corner. You can make this a democratically designed calm-down corner by asking students how they'd like it to look and what they'd like it to include, or by asking them to submit blueprints of their ideal calm-down corner and vote for a winner.

Summary

Becoming trauma informed can provide you the know-how for helping students cope, heal, and hopefully begin to put their trauma in the past and live a peaceful life. Hopefully, you've found the prework in the Equity and SEL Integration Framework helpful for implementing the trauma-informed teaching strategies in this chapter. You must tell students they are valued, celebrate when they manage to gain control, praise what they learn in the moment, and notice how long it's been since their last outburst. Acknowledging and celebrating students will serve our classrooms well as we move into the next chapter to explore the role of culture in their lives. We will continue using the Equity and SEL Integration Framework, but now to implement culturally responsive teaching.

CHAPTER 7

Implement Culturally Responsive Teaching

KEY CHAPTER TASKS

- Define cultural responsiveness.
- Identify who belongs to marginalized groups to bridge opportunity gaps in the classroom.
- Better understand student identities.
- Help students celebrate their cultures by creating a welcoming classroom space for multiculturalism.

The term *culturally responsive teaching* (sometimes called *culturally relevant teaching*) was coined by Gloria Ladson-Billings (1994) in her seminal work, *The Dreamkeepers: Successful Teachers of African American Children*. Culturally responsive teaching is an equity-based pedagogy grounded in the idea that teachers develop cultural competence and know-how for teaching in cross-cultural or multicultural settings. It is a teaching methodology that honors and includes students' cultural references in all aspects of learning and raises equity for them. Ladson-Billings (1995) also defined *culturally responsive teaching* as a pedagogy that empowers learners to maintain their cultural integrity while achieving educational goals. Culturally responsive teaching places a high value on teaching and learning and means honoring students' cultural identities while leveling up their learning capacity. I often wonder whether educators who aren't yet grounded in the research or who haven't received formal training in culturally responsive teaching interpret it that way.

The goal of this chapter is to enhance SEL plans with culturally responsive teaching and guide teachers to remove the isolation students may feel when their cultural identities aren't valued. Students who feel the need to fit in because they may not yet have the emotional intelligence required for knowledge of self or appreciation of others will respond well to culturally responsive teaching. Culturally responsive SEL raises equity and also helps students build the confidence and self-efficacy for becoming better learners when it is combined with the prescribed step-by-step activities as well as the thinking strategies from your specific content area (such as Bloom's taxonomy, design thinking, computational thinking, the inquiry process, and others).

Culturally responsive teaching should not be confused with multicultural education or social justice education, nor does it mean solely having students see themselves represented in the curriculum. Although these items are always important, culturally responsive teaching is about creating synergy between learners and educators so that students who have historically been marginalized due to structural inequities in society and school can learn how to learn (Hammond, 2019). *Synergy* refers to transforming learning into a reciprocal process in which teachers and students give their best to create thriving learning environments together (Jack, Lin, & Yore, 2014).

These aspirational environments take time to develop, and educators need to go first by leading with empathy for perspective taking; culturally responsive teaching can help them make this transformation (Fuhrman, 2020). To begin making this pedagogical shift, it's important that we properly understand the multilayered concept of culture and its role in students' lives as well as our own. In the subsequent sections, we will work on ways of developing cultural proficiency and learning to demonstrate it in our classrooms.

Cultural Understanding

Culture refers to the characteristics and knowledge of people or a group of people. Educators who are committed to their students become aware of critical aspects of the students' cultures and backgrounds so they can enhance student-teacher dynamics in the classroom. Culture can comprise language, religion, beliefs, norms, familial and social habits and behavior, symbols, gestures, cuisine, artifacts, music, and art. To form better relationships and learning partnerships with their students, educators can commit to understanding the cultural nuances and customs that may hinder them from meaningfully connecting with the students. This is especially true when educators teach culturally and linguistically diverse learners. A breakdown in relationships with educators may lead to a breakdown in the students' academic achievement (Rucker, 2019).

Unfortunately, empowering educators with culturally responsive teaching strategies may initially seem trivial to some. But creating space in the classroom to learn, acknowledge, and honor students' multicultural assets helps teachers and students alike empathize and establish the multicultural competence required for rapports, relationships, and over time, community. Multicultural competence encompasses the following qualities (Chao, 2018):

- An intrinsic interest to acquire cultural knowledge
- Knowledge about other cultures
- Awareness of different cultural values and beliefs, and their potential biases
- The skills to respond in a culturally appropriate manner

U.S. educators shouldn't overlook culturally responsive teaching because school demographics make it highly likely that they will serve students from several culturally diverse backgrounds. Educators, therefore, need to develop multicultural competence to be culturally responsive and equitable in classrooms. The following statistics detail just how diverse U.S. schools have become (Colby & Ortman, 2015).

- Data from the U.S. Census Bureau indicate that in 2010, foreign-born individuals represented 13.3 percent of the U.S. population, comprising 42.3 million people.
- In 2014, non-Latinx White people represented 62.2 percent of the U.S. population. Multiracial individuals and racial and ethnic minorities represented 37.8 percent.
- By 2044, the percentage of foreign-born racial and ethnic minority individuals in the United States is expected to grow to more than 50 percent.
- By 2060, 20 percent of the U.S. population is expected to be foreign born.

Educators who are still on the fence about culturally responsive teaching must also consider that the United States has resettled approximately three million refugees since 1980 (Pew Research Center, 2019). The U.S. Department of State's Refugee Processing Center reports the following (Budiman, 2020).

- In 2018, more than a quarter of all refugees admitted in the United States resettled in Texas, Washington, New York, and California.
- In 2019, a total of 30,000 refugees were resettled in the United States. The main origin groups were the Democratic Republic of the Congo, Burma (Myanmar), Ukraine, Eritrea, and Afghanistan.
- In 2019, 4,900 admitted refugees were Muslims (16 percent) and 23,800 were Christians (79 percent).
- In 2021, the United States' withdrawal from Afghanistan added over 100,000 refugees, some in almost every state (Montoya-Galvez, 2021).

One can imagine the emotional and psychological trauma and isolation experienced by immigrants and refugees entering our classrooms.

Marginalization doesn't only pertain to immigrants. Marginalized groups and communities or marginalized populations are people who experience both discrimination and exclusion in social, political, and economic structures (Sevelius et al., 2020). Students belonging to marginalized groups have disadvantages that can prevent them from many opportunities. According to Charter for Compassion (2021), possible marginalized groups include but are not limited to the following.

- Immigrants, refugees, and migrants
- Women and girls
- Victims of human trafficking
- People with mental illnesses
- Children and youth
- People of differing sexual orientations (LGBTQ+ community)
- People of differing religions
- People with developmental delays
- People with physical disabilities
- Incarcerated people (and their families)
- People released from incarceration
- People of low socioeconomic status
- Unemployed people
- People of a particular ethnicity or country of origin
- People with a differing political orientation

As you can see, the list of marginalized populations is extensive and may represent many of the students teachers serve in their classrooms, some of whom belong to multiple marginalized groups. Therefore, it's not enough for schools to identify the content and skills that K–12 students need in order to become successful. Culturally responsive teaching provides educators with actionable pedagogy for raising school equity and delivering access to the experiences that will develop marginalized students' academic learning and social-emotional learning skills (Lee, 2020b).

Research on the Effectiveness of Culturally Responsive Teaching

Research shows that culturally responsive teaching produces positive outcomes for students (Gay, 2018). This is especially true for students of color when two factors are present in teaching and learning in schools. The curriculum of culturally responsive teaching draws on students' cultural backgrounds and knowledge as assets in the classroom (Gay, 2018). In a culturally responsive classroom, students encounter encouraging, positive racial attitudes and understand race and culture's roles in society (Hughes et al., 2006).

Since 1994 (Ladson-Billings, 1994), the aforementioned culturally responsive teaching practices have proven to effectively address the achievement gap for, and increase representation of, the disproportionately unbalanced racially, culturally, ethnically, and linguistically diverse students in schools (Wah & Nasri, 2019). Supporting research includes the following.

- Culturally responsive teaching can be an impactful tool for empowering students to find their way out of achievement gaps in reading and mathematics (Griner & Stewart, 2013).
- For increasing literacy skills as a social practice, researchers Susan V. Piazza, Shaila Rao, and Maria Selena Protacio (2015) examined culturally responsive pedagogy across special education, multicultural literacy education, and the teaching of English learners. A systematic review of recommendations shows that dialogue, collaboration, visual representation, explicit instruction, inquiry, and incorporation of students' cultural knowledge and lived experiences lead to more equitable learning (Piazza et al., 2015).
- In her study titled "Does Culturally Relevant Teaching Work?" Christy M. Byrd (2016) considers student perceptions of classrooms that vary in culturally relevant practices. The population sample consists of 315 sixth-grade through twelfth-grade students from across the United States of the following demographic percentages.
    - Sixty-two percent female
    - Twenty-five percent White
    - Twenty-five percent Latinx
    - Twenty-five percent African American
    - Twenty-five percent Asian

Every individual in the population sample completed surveys on their experiences of culturally responsive teaching, cultural socialization, opportunities to learn about other cultures, and racism. The findings show that elements of culturally responsive teaching are significantly associated with increased academic outcomes and ethnic-racial identity development in the surveyed students (Byrd, 2016).

- Kristine E. Larson, Elise T. Pas, Catherine P. Bradshaw, Michael S. Rosenberg, and Norma L. Day-Vines (2018) collected data from 274 teachers in eighteen schools to examine the relationship between student behaviors and self-reported teacher efficacy in using culturally responsive teaching and proactive behavior management practices. The results show teachers' use of culturally responsive teaching and proactive behavior management practices has a statistically significant association with positive student responses in the classroom (Larson et al., 2018).
- A qualitative study by Hannah Mackay and Martha J. Strickland (2018) explores how one middle school English language arts teacher built relationships with his culturally diverse students and deepened their understanding of English content through video production. The findings show that engaging students with a culturally responsive teaching approach and technology can create a collaborative dynamic between educators and students (Mackay & Strickland, 2018).

As we can see, there is strong evidence that culturally responsive teaching practices raise equity by boosting the academic achievement of socioculturally diverse learners. Now we will examine the research for incorporating the pedagogy into SEL.

Culturally Responsive SEL

As we've learned, integrating SEL into the instructional day and into academic programs is critical for continuous growth in several areas, including relationship building (Durlak et al., 2011)—and it is a real equity raiser for many students. Empathizing with others is an essential relationship-building skill that students typically learn through the CASEL 5's social awareness competency as part of SEL. Step 3 of the Equity and SEL Integration Framework uplifts this skill (Valenzuela, 2021e; see chapter 3, page 47). Students often learn empathy through the teaching of SEL-specific strategies, such as learning social cues, being in someone else's shoes, using optical illusions to understand perspective taking, and seeing the other sides of opinions (Scully, 2019). However, teachers can make SEL culturally responsive when they intentionally frame empathy and related skills, such as perspective taking, understanding, and compassion for others, to help connect students with different cultures, backgrounds, or identities.

Educators who include culturally responsive teaching in their SEL plan realize over time that a one-size-fits-all approach to SEL will not raise equity for culturally and linguistically diverse learners; it will not give them a sense of belonging to the learning community they attend (Wiglesworth et al., 2016). A one-size-fits-all approach doesn't acknowledge the learners' cultural identities or help others view them as assets to be celebrated and reflected in the curriculum. Unfortunately, this type of SEL becomes a surface-level display of polite manners and smiles, which does little for the social-emotional health of marginalized students. Now that thousands of K–12 schools and districts are applying SEL as a fundamental component of student success, many committed educators want to ensure that their SEL practices are culturally responsive and equitable for their learners who belong to historically marginalized groups (CASEL, 2021c; Seider & Graves, 2020; Taylor et al., 2017). To make SEL more culturally responsive, educators must understand what it means for someone to experience marginalization and how it can occur for students in their classrooms.

Charter for Compassion (2021) explains that people who have a marginalized identity include anyone who either feels or is underserved, disregarded, ostracized, harassed, persecuted, or excluded in a community. The word *feels* is key for raising equity for these students. It requires us to focus on the individuals who feel marginalized rather than on how others may view them.

Students who do not feel safe or supported in their school environments can develop a marginalized identity at school just as adults can do so at work (Castle, 2019). Marginalization can be subtle or obvious. The trauma and emotional pain effects are disastrous for the victimized students. Marginalized students who feel excluded and isolated from their teachers and peers can suffer mentally, emotionally, and physically and disengage from their schoolwork (De La Rosa, 2021). We actually got to see this during the COVID-19 pandemic beginning in 2020. To increase our awareness, we must consider the following harmful actions that cause students to feel marginalized at school.

- Stereotyping students as ones who act in specific ways based on their identity (such as race, gender, or sexual orientation)
- Providing inequitable access to academic opportunities (like rigorous coursework, tutoring, or other services) because of students' identity

- Bullying and threatening physical danger
- Using derogatory language and blatant disrespect
- Singling out students because of religious beliefs or cultural practices
- Isolating students by purposefully leaving them out of social activities, like games, sports, or events

As educators, we may feel a sense of hopelessness and remorse in looking at this list and seeing situations where we had the power to make equitable change and did not do so. I'm sure plenty of us have witnessed many of these actions (even between adults) but didn't have the correct language to articulate what was truly happening, which resulted in more trauma for marginalized students. The good news is we can use our past experiences as points of reference to resolve to do and be better moving forward. Educators can promote healthy relationship dynamics between their students by teaching and modeling tolerance and appreciation for cultural differences using culturally responsive SEL teaching practices (Castro-Olivo, 2014).

Strategies for Refining Cultural Responsiveness in SEL Planning

Educators who are committed to understanding culture as a concept and recognizing multicultural contexts can refocus their equity lens on empathizing with students and viewing the cultures in their classrooms as assets, not "deficiencies to overcome" (Paris & Alim, 2014, p. 87). For many of us, this takes a prolonged dedication to the inward work of the Equity and SEL Integration Framework described in chapters 1–3 before it becomes a mindset or natural behavior. I will apply what was covered in previous sections to being culturally responsive to students.

This section compiles some widely used culturally responsive teaching strategies from credible sources and resources for refining your culturally responsive SEL plan by implementing components of the Equity and SEL Integration Framework. These strategies particularly center on the framework areas dedicated to knowing what we believe and know about students. I have arranged the culturally responsive teaching strategies in a logical order to help educators prioritize them, but don't feel compelled to precisely follow this sequence. Remember that this section is not meant to *replace* comprehensive professional learning in culturally responsive teaching; rather, these strategies are meant to update or begin your SEL plan and help you take actionable steps immediately.

Understand and Get to Know Students

Being in tune with others first requires us to be in tune with ourselves. The following list features steps 1–3 of the Equity and SEL Integration Framework for connecting with others and the self but applies them to a culturally responsive teaching context.

1. Develop emotional intelligence skills around social awareness (see chapter 1, page 15) with a focus on empathy. Psychologists and authors J. Andrew Morris and Daniel Feldman (1996) connect emotional responses to empathy, stating, "Empathy depends not only on one's ability to identify someone else's emotions but also on one's capacity to put oneself in the other person's place and to experience an appropriate emotional response" (p. 442).

   Don't confuse empathy with sympathy or pity; they are not the same. Looking back at my own experience as an English learner who lived in foster care, I benefited more from teachers who worked to understand ways of helping me learn than from teachers who solely felt sorry for my circumstance. Sympathy and compassion have a time and a place, but they can become unhelpful crutches for learners. Our natural inclination to sympathize with marginalized students or those who experience misfortune tends to keep us focused on their unfortunate condition or circumstance. There's nothing wrong with that, but culturally responsive, SEL-infused teaching requires that educators show empathy by sharing in students' emotions and having appropriate emotional and academic responses for truly helping them. Appropriate emotional and academic responses are those that are rooted in high expectations for students. Appropriate academic responses always show empathy while continuing to help students strive for the best outcome as measured against normative academic standards.

2. Know what you personally believe about your students (chapter 2, page 33). This includes biases you have (whether conscious or unconscious) along with myths and misconceptions about the students and their cultures and backgrounds. You can use this new understanding of self to begin viewing their cultural identities as assets, connect better with them as people, and make instructional decisions that empower them to become strong and independent learners.

3. Improve your knowledge of students (chapter 3, page 47). Along with learning about their goals, assets, academic needs, and career goals, also take the time to learn about their multicultural assets and backgrounds, and use this awareness for cultural responsiveness in their academic and social-emotional learning. When teachers include their students in class discussions, students learn to hear their voices and begin to see themselves in the curriculum. I include students in class discussions with culturally relevant question prompts such as the following.
    - Share your favorite childhood memory (such as a holiday or event).
    - What's your favorite book and why?
    - What is the meaning of your name, and why was your name given to you?
    - What is a special skill that you possess?

   I have found learners of all ages enjoy answering these questions and listening to one another's responses. These prompts can also help some learners open up—thus helping us learn more about them over time.

Understand Culture and Multiculturalism

Remember, culture refers to the characteristics and knowledge of people or a group of people. Often, *multiple* cultures can inform the identity of a single student. Multiculturalism supports and acknowledges diverse cultures, backgrounds, races, and ethnicities and honors their societal differences (Fitzsimmons et al., 2019).

Culture is often passed down through generations of family and society and can even cross continents for multicultural families. Many of our students belong to families that identify with multiple cultures. For example, families may observe certain holidays as part of their cultural traditions. It is part of my family's culture and traditions to honor Colombia's Independence Day (July 20, 1810) to celebrate our Colombian heritage. But my siblings and I were born and raised in the United States (unlike our parents), so we also identify with being American. Thanksgiving is a cultural tradition that we love, as it signifies the official start to the holiday season (with Christmas and the New Year following).

Encourage Students to Share Their Multicultural Identities

Before students can develop cultural awareness about others, they must first learn to uncover and examine their own social and cultural identities. This knowledge is empowering because it gives them language for how they view various aspects of their multicultural identity and for when they or others ignore what they strongly identify with. Through guided self-reflection and exercises in empathy, students can use knowledge of self to better understand how to be more culturally responsive and culturally sensitive toward their classmates and other people. Interviewing students is a great way to begin learning about their interests, hobbies, and cultural assets and how they learn best (Guido, 2021). The following are a few good questions to start this work.

- What are your favorite things to do after school?
- Do you have any hobbies?
- What is something you do that makes you happy?
- What are some customs and traditions in your family?
- Do you speak a language other than English at home?
- How do you learn best—through videos, informational text, specific strategies, or other?
- What is your favorite lesson?
- What would help you learn best in class?

Learning more about your students and their cultures will also help you redesign your curriculum to be more inclusive of their cultural identities—another essential aspect of culturally responsive SEL. For fostering this exploration and impactful conversations with students, I also highly recommend adapting the "My Multicultural Self" lesson by Learning for Justice (n.d.c).

Involve Students' Parents or Caregivers

Parents and caregivers are the primary educators in the home and can provide us teachers with critical cultural context. Therefore, we should seek their input and involvement by keeping them abreast of classroom activities, discussions, and unit plans. Use informational nights, prearranged phone calls, take-home letters, and surveys to reach out in unobtrusive ways. The key here is to take the time to develop trusting relationships with students and their families (Fuhrman, 2020), which permits educators to make their curriculum and classroom practices more culturally inclusive. Despite our best efforts, we may not be able to get families involved for various reasons. These reasons are not ours to judge or moralize. Remember that our outcomes may not always match our actions. We can only do our best and collaborate with families who are able to be involved.

Communicate High Expectations and Provide Scaffolding to Students

High expectations for students begin with our beliefs and culminate with how well we communicate our expectations and scaffold (or support) students' learning. A meta-analysis of over one hundred studies shows that supported learners feel more confident, and confidence is an indicator of academic achievement (Briggs, 2014; Hansford & Hattie, 1982). In the chapter 2 section titled Effects of Implicit Bias and How to Begin the Work (page 35), I cited a study that shows teacher perceptions and beliefs of student ability have a negative impact on academic achievement (in English language arts and mathematics), particularly for Black and Latinx learners (Cherng, 2017). With teacher biases being so central to expectations of students, I encourage you to take some time on chapter 2 if you haven't already. Additionally, scaffolding culturally responsive SEL lessons (and lessons in general) will help you engage students by allowing them to make personal connections to you and the content. The following are a few scaffolds for empowering students.

- Always communicate your high expectations to students through your words, your facial expressions, and your body language. For example, do the following.
    - Always let students know that you believe in them and their ability to learn how to do something new. I like to say, "You may not know how to do it yet, but you can definitely do it once you learn how."
    - Model the appropriate problem-solving strategies and thinking routines that are relevant to your teaching content (such as Bloom's taxonomy, design thinking, computational thinking, and others). I have found that using trusted steps in problem solving is empowering for learners.
    - After providing clear instructions for their work and the tools they need (like rubrics or checklists), offer students a positive statement about their ability to perform at the desired level.
    - Display positive facial expressions—these include smiling, relaxing your jaw, and slightly lifting your eyebrows to show interest.
    - Demonstrate empowering body language, maintain eye contact, and fully face students with your body when they speak to you. I like to allow them the last word by pausing and asking if they have any further questions.

- Continually challenge students to excel at high levels, and encourage them to challenge themselves as well.
- Praise student efforts when appropriate, and always look for ways to get everyone to meaningfully contribute to class discussions.
- Have signs of your high expectations in both your voice and students' voices in the classroom.
- Write students quick notes of affirmation or appreciation when they do well and are trying their best.
- Front-load vocabulary before having students apply specific academic skill sets. This is empowering because it provides the needed context when facilitating a lesson or imparting instructions to students early, which demonstrates an investment in their preparedness and gives them a primer for the content you will cover.
- Make assessments less intimidating by offering students alternatives to demonstrating their skills and understanding; provide voice and choice over the products they create and how they transfer learning.
- Incorporate reflection for metacognition into learning activities. Teaching students to think about their thinking empowers them to know themselves as learners (Cohen at al., 2021; Parrish, 2022).

Design an Inclusive and Rigorous Curriculum

An inclusive curriculum incorporates diverse texts and narratives so that all students in a classroom feel represented and included in lessons and projects. Educators need to consider students' diverse cultural backgrounds and languages and think of creative ways to illuminate and celebrate them. The following are a few ideas for starting this endeavor.

- Invite diverse experts to be guest speakers during the various stages of the learning. This strategy is compelling when students meet adults in an expert or model role who share in their background or culture and look like them.
- Incorporate books and media (like videos, articles, and blogs) that highlight and teach about your students' cultural backgrounds and assets.
- Acknowledge your country's multiculturalism by exposing students to diverse narratives, even if your classroom is not diverse.

Adopt Collaborative Learning Pedagogy for Relationship Building Between Students and Educators

Cooperative group activities have shown to be effective for helping students develop relationship skills, provided that teachers convey clear expectations and guidelines (Wattanawongwan, Smith, & Vannest, 2021). Examples of teaching strategies and educational protocols that foster relationships through collaborative learning include the following.

- **Storytelling at the beginning of a minilesson:** Teachers can share their own related stories to inspire students and help them connect their previous knowledge to new concepts. The students should then share their own stories in either pairs or triads. This shouldn't take more than five minutes.
- **The turn-and-talk strategy:** This is an informal and low-stakes way for students to share their thoughts and ideas about their learning in their own words. To activate the strategy, students may view a video, read informational text, or view modeling by their teacher. They then pair up with a peer and share their thoughts, takeaways, and reflections for about three to five minutes.
- **Jigsaws:** Jigsaws are an effective strategy for helping learners chunk (or jigsaw) topics of knowledge into smaller parts, improve reading and writing skills, create artifacts, hone presentation skills, and improve interactions and collaboration with peers (Valenzuela, 2018). Groups of three or four students spend time in expert teams reading, developing artifacts, and debriefing. Work time varies between projects, and teachers will need to make frequent check-ins.
- **Work time in projects:** The meaning of work time varies between guided and independent practice. For this purpose, form learning centers or stations within the structure of the workshop model.
- **Feedback protocols:** Feedback protocols help students revise their work in drafts by consulting with their teacher, experts, or classmates using a structured format (Valenzuela, 2022f). Be sure to model the protocol's use for the entire class before having students implement the protocol independently. Also, be the initial timekeeper to keep everyone on task during the protocol.

Make Learning Applicable to the Real World

Some educators call the process of making learning applicable to real-world contexts *contextual teaching*. That is because it connects the learning to the community and shows students relevant applications of the content learned in class (Haryanto

& Arty, 2019). Educators can make learning applicable to the real world in several ways, but the following are a few examples.

- Engage learners in project-based learning units with intellectual challenges that solve community problems and involve industry experts.
- Involve students in community service activities that benefit others and promote understanding for those with cultural differences.
- Bring in guest expert speakers to explain the real-world uses of the content and skills students are learning.
- Have students assume the roles of experts (like community activists, engineers, and doctors) during project work.
- Make career connections to the content. This is especially powerful for helping learners of all ages discover future career options.

Account for Diverse Languages

Students' home language helps make up their cultural assets, and teachers should leverage their preexisting speaking, communication, and cognitive abilities for learning. Examples of how teachers can be more culturally responsive with effective collaborative teaching strategies for English learners include the following.

- Make group work relevant by allowing students to choose topics that matter to their specific community.
- Provide small-group instruction with an emphasis on language skills across the content areas.
- Use visuals (such as graphics, video, line graphs, charts, and emojis) for encouraging dialogue and comprehension (Bowman, 2018).
- Use a student's home language as a support for learning English.
- Have students practice conversations with sentence starters that help them begin their dialogues, such as:
    - "I like . . ."
    - "I saw . . ."
    - "I wonder . . ."
    - "I have . . ."
    - "I think . . ."
    - "I used to think . . . but now I think . . ."

Summary

By becoming culturally responsive in your teaching, you help students who previously didn't feel seen or heard become acknowledged and included as valuable school community members. Hopefully, you've found the prework in the Equity and SEL Integration Framework helpful for implementing this chapter's culturally responsive teaching strategies. As you learn more about your students, it's essential to help them view their cultural identity components as assets that can be leveraged academically. We teachers should also recognize that our lessons and our classroom day-to-day won't always go as smoothly as intended. There will be times when we have to restore justice for students who need our support. In the next chapter, we will continue using the Equity and SEL Integration Framework, but now to implement restorative justice.

Implement Restorative Practices and Restorative Justice

KEY CHAPTER TASKS

- Distinguish between restorative practices and restorative justice.
- Learn about the effectiveness of restorative practices in schools.
- Implement restorative practices and restorative justice in your SEL lessons.

As you've gleaned throughout this book, raising equity in schools through SEL may sometimes call for us to implement trauma-informed and culturally responsive teaching approaches. However, creating classrooms that are emotionally safe and conducive to learning for students requires their buy-in—which can be difficult to gain when conflicts arise between them. This chapter aims to assist you with updating your SEL plan with *restorative justice*.

Restorative justice involves practices that ensure as much restitution for victims as possible while also rehabilitating the offender to prevent them from committing future harms. Schools and teachers looking to solve student conflict in a peaceful way, in structured steps, and with long-lasting effects can benefit from adopting restorative justice practices in their classrooms. Inspired by global Indigenous traditions and values, restorative justice philosophy stresses bringing together all concerned individuals whenever wrongdoing occurs (Marsh, 2019).

Restorative Justice

According to the Restorative Justice Exchange (2021), restorative justice is a theory of justice aiming to repair harm by mediation and shared agreements instead of punishment. Restorative justice is carried out collaboratively by involving all stakeholders, restoring relationships and communities, and fostering healing for all parties involved (including the perpetrators). In schools, restorative justice helps students take better ownership of actions or behaviors and provides steps to make things right for those they negatively impacted. Restorative justice takes a communal approach in classrooms through restorative practices to assist both victims and offenders in healing, understanding, and repairing their rapport. The Oakland Unified School District Restorative Justice Team created the foundational restorative justice practices and principles that appear in figure 8.1 (Yusem, Curtis, Johnson, & McClung, n.d.).

Restorative Justice Practices

- Builds relationships
- Strives to be respectful to all
- Provides opportunity for equitable dialogue and participatory decision making
- Involves all relevant stakeholders
- Addresses harms, needs, obligations, and causes of conflict and harm
- Encourages all to take responsibility

1. **If crime hurts, justice should heal.** The focus is on repairing harm if it has occurred.
2. **Nothing about us without us.** Those impacted feel welcome and safe to speak and participate.
3. **There is simply no substitute for the personal.** Building respectful relationships is foundational and an outcome of any process.
4. **This can work. I can live with it.** Agreements are made by consensus.
5. **I am willing to do this.** Participation is voluntary.

Source: Yusem et al., n.d., p. iii. Used with permission.

FIGURE 8.1: Restorative justice practices and principles.

Although closely related, the terms *restorative justice* and *restorative practices* are not meant to be interchangeable. For clarity between the two, I would be remiss not to mention that the term *restorative practices* encompasses restorative justice. Ted Wachtel (2016), founder of the International Institute for Restorative Practices, points out the following:

> [Restorative justice is] a subset of restorative practices. Restorative justice is reactive, consisting of formal or informal responses to crime and other wrongdoing after it occurs. [Restorative practices also include] the use of informal and formal processes that precede wrongdoing, those that proactively build relationships and a sense of community to prevent conflict and wrongdoing.

As you'll read in the subsequent sections of this chapter, educators can adapt restorative practices and restorative justice to provide infrastructure and systems for supporting both victims and offenders. Additionally, these closely align and can be implemented using the Equity and SEL Integration Framework.

Research on the Effectiveness of Restorative Practices and Restorative Justice in Schools

Restorative pedagogy has established itself in schools throughout the United States and abroad (Fronius et al., 2019). Restorative practice and restorative justice aim to nurture safe learning environments that support students and make them feel welcome. If this sounds a lot like culturally responsive teaching, that's because there are parallels between culturally responsive teaching and restorative justice. Therefore, I've combined outcomes and aligned strategies in these pedagogies (and others) with SEL in this book. Teachers can use the Equity and SEL Integration Framework to assist them with knowing the best way to raise equity for students by implementing culturally responsive teaching or restorative practices.

However, there is a difference between the two approaches that educators should take the time to understand. Culturally responsive teaching develops understanding between diverse people and helps prevent and settle conflict (Finley, 2014). Restorative justice practices are also preventive of conflict; they can help make wrongs right when conflict exists and provide wraparound services to students who are returning to school after being away (We Are Teachers Staff, 2021). Additionally, restorative practices offer equitable alternatives to time out of school for offenses.

In their updated research review on restorative justice in U.S. schools, Trevor Fronius and colleagues (2019) identify the main reasons many schools and districts initially began to adopt restorative justice practices as opposed to traditional discipline methods, which are as follows.

- Zero-tolerance policies increase the number of student suspensions and expulsions with no evidence of positive impact on school safety (Losen, 2015).
- There is racial and ethnic disparity in terms of which students receive school punishments and how severe their punishments are, even when controlling for the type of offense (Lopez, 2018).
- Increasingly, school misbehavior matters are handed over to the police (particularly with programs that have police, such as school resource officers). This leads more students to get involved with official legal

systems, thus contributing to a trend toward a school-to-prison pipeline (Petrosino, Guckenburg, & Fronius, 2012). The *school-to-prison pipeline* refers to moving students from school settings to the juvenile and criminal justice systems using discipline policies (zero-tolerance policies, suspensions, expulsions, and more)—typically for minor offenses (such as fighting, smoking, and cutting school). Research and data indicate that discipline policies and practices disproportionately affect racial and ethnic minorities and students with disabilities (Evans, 2021).

- Research strongly links suspensions and other forms of school discipline to impacted students' failure to graduate (Losen, 2015).

This research shows there is a clear need for restorative justice practices in schools. Despite the rich qualitative studies on restorative justice, more research must use a control group to show how restorative justice practices lead to specific changes to population samples (Weisburd, Petrosino, & Fronius, 2014). Both programs and research on implementing restorative justice are still developing (Guckenburg, Hurley, Persson, Fronius, & Petrosino, 2015). In their updated report, Fronius and colleagues (2019) review a plethora of articles, chapters, theses, and dissertations published between 2014 and 2018. It's important to note that their systematic review references only one published experimental restorative justice study. However, the researchers use a robust sample of forty-four schools and include many controls to estimate restorative justice's impact across a broad spectrum of outcomes (Augustine et al., 2018). Furthermore, they document the following about how restorative justice practices have worked in U.S. schools and why restorative justice is of utmost importance to the education field.

- Two Oakland schools report seeing improved community building through a whole-school approach to restorative justice implementation. They also cite that the school culture and climate must embed restorative practices for restorative justice programs to flourish (Brown, 2017).
- Schools can consciously foster restorative justice by nurturing relationships between students and staff built on active listening and respect (Brown, 2017; Cavanagh, Vigil, & Garcia, 2014).
- Restorative justice has enhanced student relationships, increased community and parental engagement, improved academic achievement, and made school staff more supportive of students (Cavanagh et al., 2014).
- In an experimental study, Catherine H. Augustine and colleagues (2018) compare data between twenty-two restorative justice schools and twenty-two

> control schools. Schools that implemented restorative justice saw a 16 percent reduction in days lost to suspensions. The reduction in suspension days was statistically significant among specific student subgroups, including African American students, low-income students, female students, special needs students, and students in grades 2–5 and 10–12.

Although more experimental data are needed to further validate restorative pedagogy, its value to the places in education where it has been implemented is undeniable. A report drawing data from almost fifty expert interviews (Guckenburg et al., 2015) provides the following considerations for guiding the direction of future research.

- Examining a school's readiness to implement restorative justice
- Establishing consensus on a clear, concise, and authentic definition of restorative justice
- Examining outcome-based empirical evidence for the implementation and effectiveness of sustainable restorative justice programs to learn the conditions that can lead to replicable successes elsewhere
- Determining what kinds of training and professional learning school leaders have implemented, and observing which programs successfully enhance practitioners' ability to confidently implement restorative justice

Clearly, there is value in restorative justice and much to do to establish these programs and practices in U.S. schools—particularly where school discipline policies negatively impact racial and ethnic minorities and students with disabilities. Schools and teachers who see restorative justice's value for their students can use guidance from the subsequent sections of this chapter to begin updating their SEL plan with restorative practices.

Restorative SEL

School administrations can use restorative practices and restorative justice to redesign schools and classrooms as restorative environments where learners are validated, supported, and taught to manage conflict through dialogue, shared agreements, healing, and relationship building (We Are Teachers Staff, 2021). When conducted correctly, restorative justice practices can complement SEL programs and help raise equity for students in conflict—especially those who may be afraid to advocate for themselves. That being said, restorative justice skills we already explored in chapters 1, 3, 4, and 5 (pages 15, 47, 61, and 87, respectively) can be implemented using the

Equity and SEL Integration Framework. And although there are differences in their approaches, SEL and restorative practices share common characteristics to systematically raise equity in schools (CASEL, 2020a).

Let's take a moment to compare some of their respective research to show how the two may complement each other. Both restorative pedagogy and SEL have shown to improve school climates by strengthening student-student, staff-staff, and student-staff relationships (Augustine et al., 2018; Brown, 2017; Cavanagh et al., 2014). Research on the two programs shows that aligning them holds the promise of improving academic and social outcomes for students. For example, SEL programming is strongly linked to significant academic improvements in tandem with social-emotional skill development (Durlak et al., 2011; Mahoney et al., 2018).

Meanwhile, restorative justice programs have been shown to reduce disciplinary rates for troubled students when they provide access to better behavioral alternatives (Fronius et al., 2019). Additionally, restorative justice gives these students a voice and empowers students to settle disputes independently by bringing them together in peer-mediated groups, where they discuss grievances within structures designed to give everyone equal airtime (Davis, 2015). Furthermore, restorative justice and restorative practices in schools offer a respectful, fair disciplinary approach and a proactive strategy to create and sustain a more cohesive and inclusive schoolwide culture. For example, the Oakland Unified School District's restorative justice program focuses on committing to the learning community as a whole and models this in part by making district resources and successes available online for other districts (www.ousd.org/Page/1054).

CASEL (2020a) has created table 8.1 (page 143) for showing the alignment between restorative practices and the CASEL competencies for adults and students.

Educators who want to change how they respond to rule violations, student conflicts, and misconduct should consider restorative practices and restorative justice for their SEL plan. Restorative pedagogy expert and pioneer Ron Claassen says, "The typical response to bad behavior is punishment. Restorative justice resolves disciplinary problems in a cooperative and constructive way" (as cited in We Are Teachers Staff, 2021). It's also important to point out that restorative practices are *not* just used for conflict resolution. Schools that establish restorative justice programs indeed offer students better alternatives in dealing with their interpersonal interactions and relationships. But like SEL and the other related pedagogies mentioned in this book, restorative justice is also a proactive strategy to create a culture of inclusiveness where all students and staff feel valued and thrive (Yusem et al., n.d.).

TABLE 8.1: Alignment of Typical Objectives for SEL and Restorative Practices in Secondary Settings

	SEL	Restorative Practices
Support SEL Competencies for Adults and Students	Students and adults have frequent and consistent opportunities to cultivate, practice, reflect on, and reinforce SEL competencies.	While some practices emphasize different skills, the five SEL competencies can be taught and reinforced by implementing restorative practices.
Improve School and Classroom Climates and Strengthen Relationships	Schoolwide and classroom learning environments that promote SEL are student centered, respectful, supportive, and focused on building relationships and community.	By working together toward shared goals and addressing challenging situations, restorative practice helps facilitate successful interpersonal interactions and create a sense of community.
Affirm Culture and Identity; Promote Equity	SEL helps make both students and adults feel respected, valued, and affirmed in their individual interests, talents, social identities, cultural values, and backgrounds.	By focusing on creating spaces where students and adults feel respected, valued, and safe, restorative practice helps create equitable learning environments.
Elevate Youth Voice and Engagement	When staff honor and elevate a broad range of student perspectives and experiences, students become engaged as leaders, problem solvers, and decision makers.	Restorative practice provides students with structures to support the skills that promote student agency, thereby giving students voice and choice in how they learn.
Prepare Students for Transitions to College, Career, and Civic Life	SEL provides students with a solid foundation of skills for achieving success in postsecondary environments and in the workplace.	Restorative practice provides students with transferable and essential skills, such as teamwork, communication, and decision making, all of which will help them thrive in postsecondary environments.

Source: Adapted from CASEL, 2020a.

Research tells us learning environments where students feel safe, supported, and welcome are the best places to develop a successful restorative education, whether in person or from a distance (Darling-Hammond, Schachner, & Edgerton, 2020). Emerging research from the learning sciences also shows that supportive relationships foster positive cognitive development and help students make better decisions (Cantor, Osher, Berg, Steyer, & Rose, 2019). Positive and trusting relationships with adults and teachers are linked to improved academic achievement (Osher, Cantor, Berg, Steyer, & Rose, 2020). Restorative pedagogy can be a game changer for students who need the adults in their lives to be caring, supportive, and intentional in interactions with them.

Strategies for Implementing Restorative Justice in SEL

This section compiles widely used restorative practices from credible sources and resources for perfecting implementation of your restorative SEL plan using the Equity and SEL Integration Framework. Like in the previous part 2 chapters, I have put the strategies in a logical order to help educators prioritize them. Again, don't feel obligated to follow this sequence exactly. Remember that this section does not *replace* comprehensive professional learning in restorative practices or restorative justice. These strategies are meant to begin or update your SEL plan and help you take actionable steps immediately.

Create a Restorative Justice Program Using a Tiered Schoolwide Model

Schools looking to establish an SEL-infused restorative justice program may explore a tiered system; such a system can allow them to establish restorative practices in phases for building both staff's and students' capacity. The Oakland Unified School District (2022) implements its model restorative justice program in the following three tiers (see figure 8.2, page 145).

- **Tier 1: Community building (prevent and relate)**—The goal of this tier is to begin developing a caring and equitable community and a schoolwide culture that promotes learning and safety for all students. Tier 1 is distinguished by SEL and restorative circle practice (see chapter 4, page 61) for building relationships, establishing norms and shared agreements, and promoting restorative dialogues after harm has been done.
- **Tier 2: Restorative processes (intervene and repair)**—The goal of this tier is to address the committed harm's root causes and the offender's accountability, and to support healing for the victim, the offender, and the school community at large (for some students). Nonpunitive responses to harm and conflict mark this tier through restorative practices, including circles, mediation, or family-group conferencing.
- **Tier 3: Supported reentry (individualize and reintegrate)**—This tier aims to welcome students back into their school community following a suspension, truancy issues, expulsion, or incarceration by providing wraparound supports so that they can thrive personally and academically. This tier of restorative justice implementation provides student accountability and one-to-one support for successful reentry.

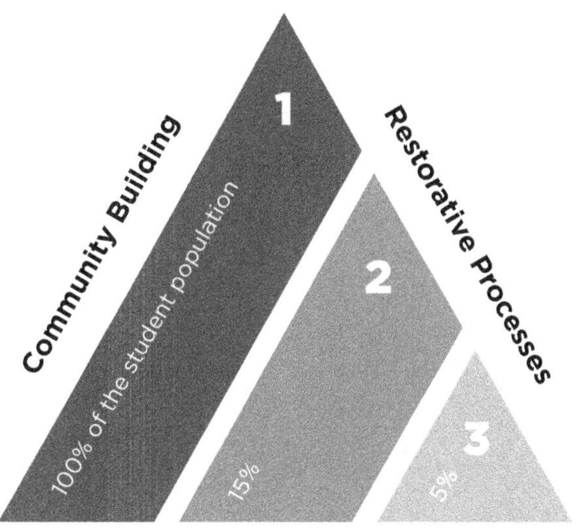

Source: Oakland Unified School District, 2022. Used with permission.

FIGURE 8.2: Graphic of the Oakland Unified School District's three-tier restorative justice program.

Implementing a tiered approach like this requires buy-in from both the faculty and support staff. Whether schools and individual teachers implement restorative justice through a tiered approach or use the Equity and SEL Integration Framework, the following are sound strategies to consider for updating SEL plans.

Use Affective Language

Affective language is effective communication that promotes honesty, empathy, and a lack of judgment between individuals (The Oxford Review Encyclopaedia of Terms, n.d.). For dialogue in restorative circle practice and daily communication to improve over time, educators will need to model affective language for students so that it eventually becomes common practice for all. There are three critical elements of affective language for bridging SEL with restorative pedagogy (CASEL, 2020a).

1. ***I* statements** help the communicator become more self-aware by focusing their comments on their own feelings, beliefs, and intentions instead of the listener's. An example of this powerful form of communication is, "I feel _________ when _________ because _________."
2. **Empathic listening** is a method of listening and questioning that helps the listener understand both the intellectual and emotional perspective of whoever is speaking to them. This skill set fosters social awareness

for relationship skills from the CASEL 5 framework. Examples include, "Thank you for sharing that with me," and "I want to make sure I understand you correctly. Did you mean ________?"

3. **Affective questions** are used for placing responsibility on the questioner to understand the impact their words and actions have on others. This element promotes social awareness for relationship skills and responsible decision making from the CASEL 5 framework. Examples include, "How were you affected by my behavior?" and "How are you currently affected?"

Use Circle Practice

You'll find the use of circle practice mentioned across several of this book's chapters. Circles can be used as a structure in several contexts, such as learning, staff meetings, after-school activities, and more. As a restorative practice, circles are group meetings in which everyone discusses a restorative justice issue. The restorative circle creates a safe space free of harm and judgment for all participants, including offenders. Participants learn to share and express their feelings and stories for connecting with others. In a classroom (or open space), everyone physically sits to form the circle. This eliminates hierarchy within the group and gives everyone equity of voice, enabling them to express themselves honestly and without fear of consequences. In restorative justice, circles are used to build trust and respect, resolve conflict, and restore relationships.

Furthermore, circle practice through norms and shared agreements offers students the opportunity to negotiate conflict by listening respectfully, empathizing with others, and expressing themselves healthily without fear of retribution (Davenport, 2018). Because all parties speak as equals and power dynamics are removed, victims can advocate for themselves and therefore receive both justice and healing. Offending students have the opportunity to take responsibility for how their actions and behavior have directly harmed a classmate, the community of classmates, and themselves. Establish some of the following norms and agreements in your classroom for best results.

- **Bring your best self to the circle:** This includes maintaining a positive disposition, a positive attitude, and complete but considerate honesty.
- **Respect the privacy of others:** Only share your own story.
- **Be mindful of airtime:** Allow others equal or ample time to express themselves.
- **Speak from the heart and only when you have the talking piece:** Share your story and speak your truth respectfully. A *talking piece* is an object

passed within the circle to indicate the speaker. When one person has the talking piece in their hands, it is generally expected that all others in the room will be quiet and listen to the speaker until they are done and pass the talking piece along.

- **Listen from the heart and respect the speaker:** Listen to others to empathize and gain perspective. This will be difficult but necessary for healing and making a wrong right.
- **Take this space to heal:** Allow yourself the opportunity to begin healing your trauma and pain by acknowledging the event and wrongdoing. Anger, resentment, and anxiety are normal emotional responses when you've been harmed. It's essential to take better control of your own thoughts, feelings, and emotions to heal. Acknowledge and honor where you are in the process.
- **Take this space to grow:** Allow yourself the opportunity to acknowledge and grow from your mistakes. Process your role in the conflict, acknowledge who you harmed, and make things right. Remember, your mistakes don't define you, and to learn, you must first fail.
- **Respect that what's shared in the circle stays in the circle:** This includes everything discussed in the circle (personal details, other people's feelings and thoughts, and so on) but excludes the learning. Do share the things you've learned so others can share in that knowledge.

Remember, social awareness relates to relationship skills, and undoubtedly, your class will give you lots of practice in this regard. The more trust and rapport you establish with students, the more willing they will be to conduct the emotions check-ins and implement SEL strategies. Your goal should be for them to use the emotions planner activity as a cognitive process they can rely on even outside of school for labeling and regulating difficult emotions regarding self and others.

No matter the topic, conduct circles using the following three simple steps.

1. **Journal independently (four to five minutes):** This step is essential for priming students for discussion by having them write their thoughts—beginning with their own experiences. A powerful norm to lift up here is that they don't share what they write with others. Instead, they formulate their thoughts about the restorative justice topic in a safe space. Open the protocol by introducing the restorative justice topic to students. Although it's not always necessary, you can supplement what you'd like

them to reflect on with either a short video or a reading to scaffold their thinking. Introduce a question prompt, and allow them a few minutes to independently write their thoughts and reflections. Here are some good prompts.

- Describe a time you showed empathy to a peer. How were you able to share in their perspective?
- What specific strategy and steps did you use to resolve a conflict with a peer last semester?

2. **Share with a peer (four to six minutes):** This step requires the facilitator to share a prompt to help students make meaning and begin conversations with a peer. The protocol norm is to do this in pairs, but if your class doesn't have an even number of students, triads work too. Other helpful norms for holding space include the following.
    - Speak from the heart.
    - Listen from the heart.
    - Listen to gain the perspective of your classmate rather than responding.
    - Share the space fairly by using a timer.

    Here are some example prompts for this activity.
    - Recall a time when a peer, teacher, or family member was empathetic toward another person. What were some of the ways that they showed empathy?
    - Think of a time when a teacher introduced a new strategy for solving peer conflicts. How did they explain and model the process in ways that allowed you and other students to understand what to do?
3. **Have an open group discussion (seven to ten minutes):** The final step is for broadening discussion and reaching consensus about how to collaboratively commence with restorative justice learning. The teacher introduces another prompt and can choose to make it a table talk with more than two peers or a whole-group discussion. Not everyone will feel comfortable sharing in the larger setting. The teacher can ease concerns for students by establishing that participation doesn't always mean speaking. Listening with the intent of gaining perspective is also engagement and learning.

Sitting in a circle structure allows everyone to see and focus on the speaker. However, implement this step how your space allows, and focus on transforming classroom discussions. The norms from step 2 also work well here, and I would add that everyone may speak more than once but should allow three others to speak before speaking again.

Prompts may include the following.

- How do we know when empathy is part of our classroom culture, and how can each of us do our part?
- What can we do to ensure that the whole class can use strategies to successfully solve peer conflict?

IMPORTANT NOTE FOR TEACHERS

During circle practice, it is important to set norms and shared agreements along with the three affective language elements covered in the section titled Use Affective Language (page 145).

As shown in figure 8.3, the same basic steps for circle practice can be implemented in virtual classroom settings.

Source: Valenzuela, 2022.

FIGURE 8.3: Virtual circle practice in three steps.

There are several types of restorative circles, all having the purpose of building community and relationships for all school stakeholders (see figure 8.4, page 150).

Talking Circles

(Community-Building Circles)

Proactively build relationships and community among a classroom or team. Talking circles may be used to have daily check-ins or meetings, set classroom norms and agreements, teach social-emotional skills, provide feedback, and discuss pertinent issues and topics.

Celebration Circles

Share and affirm accomplishments, happy news, or other positive events. These circles may be used to celebrate individuals, groups, or whole classrooms.

Peace Circles

After conflict or behavior issues, guide reflection on the actions and their impact on others; empower participants to develop a plan to make things right.

Types of Circles

Circles can be used for a variety of purposes, from setting classroom norms to resolving conflicts. These are a few different examples of types of circles, but all have one key purpose in common: building community and relationships.

Staff Circles

As part of regular team meetings or professional learning, staff circles can be used to build collaboration, set a vision, make decisions, provide feedback, and reflect on practice.

Reintegration Circles

Welcome a student back to the classroom and school following a disciplinary action, such as a suspension or expulsion. Use the circle to address outstanding issues and rebuild relationships.

Parent or Community Circles

Engage people or family and community members in circles to introduce the circle process, develop partnerships, welcome new members, hold parent-teacher conferences, and provide feedback for the school.

Healing and Support Circles

Create space for students to identify loss, express emotions, cope with trauma, and build community. These circles can be used after specific incidents in the community.

Source: Chicago Public Schools, n.d. Used with permission.

FIGURE 8.4: Types of circles.

Summary

Restoring justice through restorative practices can greatly benefit students who need assistance advocating for themselves and offenders. Using restorative practices for restorative justice and trauma-informed and culturally responsive teaching strategies can give teachers the frameworks and tools to pivot as needed as they strive to raise equity for vulnerable students. I hope you have learned how the Equity and SEL Integration Framework can be a powerful tool for implementing these strategies. To help us further raise equity for needy students, part 3 of this book will show how we can use the framework, educational technology, and the ISTE Standards for Educators (ISTE; 2017) to implement inclusive pedagogy and augment instruction.

More Equity Raisers for SEL

In part 1 of this book, we began implementing SEL with students through the Equity and SEL Integration Framework's five steps. With a solid footing in and strategies for SEL and emotional intelligence, in part 2, we took a deeper dive into equity raisers for enhancing our SEL plans with trauma-informed teaching, culturally responsive teaching, and restorative justice. To close out the book, this part will take us a step further on our equity journey by focusing on inclusive pedagogy and the effective use of educational technology. If you and your colleagues have agreed to have difficult conversations for the sake of reaching understanding and consensus for the students you serve, then the following chapters can provide needed data, language, and perspective. The goal is not to blame, shame, or alienate colleagues but rather to help them better assist students who belong to the most vulnerable groups.

In part 3, you will continue improving your SEL plan by considering students' comprehensive needs as you navigate complicated situations, such as the reentry into schools after the COVID-19 pandemic forced education to become remote.

CHAPTER 9

Add Inclusive Pedagogy to SEL Plans

KEY CHAPTER TASKS

- Learn inclusive teaching practices for your SEL lessons.
- Raise equity for marginalized students in the classroom.
- Learn how to inclusively navigate difficult conversations in the classroom.
- Understand how issues of race, sexuality, gender identity, and immigration status impact a classroom and how teachers can handle them equitably and safely for students.

Like SEL, *inclusive pedagogy* is a teaching methodology in which teachers and classmates cocreate a supportive learning environment that raises equity for all students. According to researchers Jennifer Spratt and Lani Florian (2015), teachers deliberately design student-centered, inclusive pedagogy to create welcoming and engaging classrooms for their students, including those with diverse backgrounds, learning preferences, and physical and cognitive abilities. The pedagogy draws on sound teaching and learning practices to improve learning outcomes when educators take pedagogical steps to ensure every student feels accepted and supported in the classroom (Spratt & Florian, 2015).

The list of marginalized populations presented in chapter 7 (page 124) is extensive and may represent many of the students teachers serve in their classrooms. Some students belong to multiple marginalized groups. Therefore, it's imperative to learn the intricacies of being mindful of inclusive pedagogy for raising equity gives educators actionable steps to deliver experiences that will develop marginalized students' academic learning and social-emotional learning skills (Lee, 2020b).

In this chapter about inclusivity for raising equity, we will be making more valuable connections by considering inclusive pedagogy and our students' social identities in relation to ours. Thus, we will improve the impact of our teaching practice on marginalized students and remove barriers to the students' success in our classrooms.

The History of Inclusive Pedagogy

Research supporting inclusive pedagogy dates back to the beginning of the 1900s and shows benefits to both marginalized students and other students (Eddy & Hogan, 2014; Haak, Lambers, Pitre, & Freeman, 2011). The following are some important items to consider before beginning this work.

- Feelings of alienation or exclusion can negatively impact academic performance and cause adverse health consequences for students (American Psychological Association, 2008; Blascovich, Spencer, Quinn, & Steele, 2001; Curtis, 2020; Eisenberger, Lieberman, & Williams, 2003; Matthews et al., 2015).
- Students who belong to marginalized groups due to race, social status, gender, or sexuality (among other identities) feel excluded within learning spaces (Tanner, 2013).
- Feelings of acceptance and belonging to an academic community can be predictors of academic achievement (Moallem, 2013).
- Intentional efforts to include and improve feelings of social belonging for marginalized students can increase both academic success and emotional well-being (Walton & Cohen, 2011).
- Methods such as repetition of new skills and active learning help improve academic performance for students belonging to marginalized groups (Eddy & Hogan, 2014).

There is a recurring theme in the aforementioned points: intentional inclusivity efforts can positively impact marginalized students' lives. See chapter 7's section Cultural Understanding (page 122) for a comprehensive list of historically marginalized groups learners may belong to and for definitions of what it means to be and feel marginalized.

Teachers who make this pedagogical shift strive to ensure their curriculum considers the range of students' perspectives and scaffolds in the areas most needed within SEL, academic, and career fields. Furthermore, inclusive classrooms promote mutual respect between educators and learners. Mutual respect is a prerequisite for building rapports with students and forming learning partnerships.

Inclusivity With DEI

As already expressed in previous chapters, *diversity* refers to perspective, representation, challenging conversations, and support of inclusion. *Inclusion* refers to creating environments that support diversity, are conducive to feedback, and are open to all; *equity* refers to fairly including and appreciating diverse individuals.

Many view DEI topics as divisive and deem them controversial and taboo in schools (Sawchuk, 2021; Stout & Wilburn, 2022). Many feel DEI is overdone and distracting to learning (Trump, 2021)—some feel flat-out accused and blamed when DEI efforts have them confront the privilege they don't believe they have or don't want to confront (Meckler & Natanson, 2021). I don't want to alienate or shut down readers and colleagues who feel this information isn't vital to their classroom inclusion practices (yet). Instead, I hope to make the information available to educators who may need to have consequential conversations with students about these topics; they can do so in a safe but curious classroom where important ideas are explored.

Promoting awareness, understanding, and better instructional decisions is my overall goal with the Equity and SEL Integration Framework. The aforementioned points inform how lack of inclusion adversely impacts learners socially, physically, and academically, so for students, we should educate ourselves.

By exploring pertinent data, terms, and concepts, this chapter reviews and details the need for inclusivity in classrooms around four critical items: (1) race, (2) gender identity, (3) sexual orientation, and (4) immigration status. Although these identities have always been highly politicized, and teachers are not permitted to discuss them with students in many U.S. states (thirty-six and counting), I aim to improve readers' perspective on these topics—thus improving their inclusivity practices for supporting each student (Sawchuk, 2021; Stout & Wilburn, 2022). In places where openly discussing DEI issues is illegal or unwelcome, I strongly suggest mindfulness in using this information to increase your own understanding and thus become a reliable source of information for those who depend on your awareness (Stout & Wilburn, 2022).

I hope that the knowledge in these sections invokes awareness, compassion, unity among school stakeholders, and empathy for diverse students who need more equitable inclusion at their schools. The resources in this chapter are included to help educators structure difficult conversations and provide valuable contexts between educators when permitted.

The Need for DEI and Race in SEL

The murder of George Floyd, a forty-six-year-old Black man, in Minneapolis on May 25, 2020, is a painful moment in U.S. history (Turay, 2020). His untimely death at the hands of Derek Chauvin, a forty-four-year-old White police officer, was recorded by bystanders (The New York Times, 2022). Handcuffed and pinned to the ground by Chauvin's knee, Floyd repeatedly told the former police officer he couldn't breathe and eventually succumbed to asphyxiation (The New York Times, 2022). This event sparked nationwide protests, civil unrest, and a movement toward racial equity, creating national conversations about race and police brutality (CNN, 2021; Jimenez, Chavez, & Hanna, 2020). Many educators began to reconsider their personal beliefs and practices and school DEI policies and priorities as a result (Mayberry, 2022).

School faculty and staff often have consensus on the importance of including SEL in the curriculum—but not so much on DEI as it pertains to race (Valenzuela, 2021d). Unfortunately, many don't see the connection and the role of emotions in such a highly sensitive topic as race. Given the disunity throughout the United States, I would be remiss to ignore the opinions of colleagues who don't feel DEI initiatives are beneficial in schools. Ignoring the subject that most needs discussion does little to help people work toward solutions because it disallows opportunities to reach an understanding through conversation, and it undermines opinions and viewpoints. It's important to understand why your colleagues feel the way they do. I believe disunity on race and other DEI topics occurs in spaces where not all participants have a voice because people haven't made shared agreements about how a difficult conversation should go. This results in conversations lacking unity, structure, and collegial respect, which lead some colleagues to feel blamed for racism (Meckler & Natanson, 2021). Some colleagues, parents, and critics feel that DEI hasn't been carried out correctly and it is divisive instead of inclusive (Meckler & Natanson, 2021). According to *Newsweek* writer Carly Mayberry (2022), concerns over DEI in the United States include the following.

- Public schools have spent over $20 million on DEI programs and training since the death of George Floyd.
- Some parents believe DEI training prepares teachers to indoctrinate students in how they think about, learn about, and view fairness and social justice.
- Critics feel fly-by-night consultancy companies exploited the death of Floyd by contracting with schools to deliver DEI training.
- Many parents want teachers to leave the DEI topics for them to address in the home; they want teachers to instead educate their children on reading, writing, and arithmetic so that their children are successful after school.

To make sense of what's happening in education and how I want to contribute to the profession I love, I've had to consider these concerns objectively and without judgment in my quiet moments. I have also considered that knowledge is created through action and application (Clark, Porath, Thiele, & Jobe, 2020). This book's Equity and SEL Integration Framework has resulted from action research and reflection on participants' feedback and consensus to support one another and their students. This represents a different experience from that of educators who attended a professional development session where speakers discussed DEI topics without knowing them or the context of their schools. I get it.

IMPORTANT NOTE FOR TEACHERS

The rationale and action research methods I employed to develop the Equity and SEL Integration Framework are found in appendix B (page 207).

As I discovered through action research, and as you've gleaned throughout this book, we educators must enhance our SEL plans with strategies borrowed from other pedagogies if we are truly going to raise equity for all students—especially where DEI issues are concerned. It's not enough to focus only on the CASEL 5 and ignore the context of the learners in our class. That applies SEL too generally and doesn't account for diversity, the actual needs of students, or who students are as people. The Equity and SEL Integration Framework considers that not all learners need the same lessons and scaffolds to improve their SEL, and it is therefore designed to help educators pivot in various settings and be effective in diverse learner populations.

If you are on the fence with regard to DEI-driven classroom practices, or are unsure about how to implement them effectively, know that you are important to this conversation, and your participation is vital in your school. Also, know that you don't have to agree with others when you don't, though those who value seeking the truth over being correct will value changing their minds when presented with new, fact-based information.

Educational Equity

Equity in education, or *educational equity*, is a measure of achievement, fairness, and opportunity in education. According to the Center for Public Education (2016), "Equity is achieved when all students receive the resources they need so they graduate prepared for success after high school" (p. 1). Equity in schools means school leaders, teachers, and stakeholders (including government) deliver experiences that will develop the required skills and dispositions for students who belong to racially and ethnically marginalized groups. Students belonging to oppressed racially and ethnically marginalized groups have social disadvantages that have historically prevented many of them from opportunities such as access to fair housing, policing, education, and wealth distribution (Gutierrez, Demby, & Frame, 2018).

Immediately confronting and resolving issues as they are is how healing takes place. Therefore, without a genuine focus on raising racial equity when it's required, SEL alone doesn't quite acknowledge what students need us to recognize. Often, students don't know how to convey the SEL needs that burden them. The activities within the Equity and SEL Integration Framework help us refine both the emotional intelligence skills and ways we can improve our knowledge of students to better proceed with students who need greater racial equity.

Raising racial equity requires leading with love, grace, compassion, empathy, and collaboration among various stakeholders (in and out of schools). It also requires healing both the past and present circumstances that are at the root of the inequities and the trauma that those inequities have caused. Healing doesn't always occur for students, because we, as educators, don't always treat emotional trauma as we do physical trauma. For example, if an athlete twists their ankle, it would be a mistake for them to continue playing on the injured ankle. That physical trauma needs to be acknowledged and properly cared for before play resumes. The same goes for emotional trauma. As the old adage goes, "We need to feel it to heal it!" Whether or not we choose to acknowledge it, the emotional, psychological, and physical trauma caused by racism in the United States keeps many of us divided. For healing and transcendence from the issues pertaining to racism, violence, and civil unrest in the United States to eventually occur, the adults (educators) will need to put the actual SEL needs of their students first.

By no means am I implying schools and educators are *solely* responsible for the healing that needs to occur for students. Nor should we apply racial identity discussions where they are unnecessary. But educators are with students for eight hours out of their twenty-four-hour day, five days a week, so how can SEL occur without acknowledging facts and issues pertaining to race as they come up? When a tragedy like the murder of George Floyd happens, we educators should empathize with the disappointment and anguish students and colleagues experience due to the loss of a member of their community (Costello & Duvall, 2020). Also, we shouldn't undermine the grief many feel at the greater systemic issues at play in a death like Floyd's. Unfortunately, this suggestion of systemic issues becomes a sticking point for many, and I believe it's at the core of our disunity in schools. Many don't think the same things about the root causes of racial injustices in the United States. When we disagree, that doesn't mean we can't or shouldn't empathize with the pain others at our school feel—nor does it mean we should make those people feel unwelcome when they feel the need to express their pain. Remaining empathetic isn't easy to do when emotions run high, but empathy and communication are necessary to improve our school communities.

I see how all of this can be a tremendous load for educators to carry and nearly impossible to accomplish perfectly. Equipping ourselves with good tools and frameworks can make us educators that our students and colleagues respect because we honor and respect them by seeking to empathize and understand. Schools can update SEL plans with DEI to promote understanding of race and diversity. They can do this by working together to dismantle the barriers in their respective spaces that have contributed to misunderstandings and intolerance. I urge those of us who teach Black students to consider the message that these issues, when left unresolved for decades, send to the students, their families, and their communities.

If we are genuinely working to be equitable toward our African American students, we need to empathize with their disappointment and anguish when the life of a member of their family or community is tragically lost (Costello & Duvall, 2020). The trauma and setbacks they've suffered are not easy to undo. Although we cannot magically change traumatic experiences and their consequences, we can strengthen our SEL to help students develop the emotional intelligence skills they need to begin healing. We must also accept racial discrimination is not something new for Black and Brown people. It's also not isolated or confined to one group, as we will glean in the following sections.

As we previously covered in chapter 2 (page 33), it is important that collaborative teams schoolwide collectively examine biases, establish ground rules for discussion, determine equity of voice, and identify microaggressions (see table 2.2, page 38). Derald Wing Sue (2019), professor of counseling psychology at Columbia University, notes, "While microaggressions are generally discussed from the perspective of race and racism, any marginalized group in our society may become targets: people of color, women, LGBT persons, those with disabilities, religious minorities, and so on" (p. 1). Try using circle practice (see figure 8.3, page 146) to provide structure for difficult conversations between faculty and staff members. Review the norms previously covered in chapter 2 (page 33). I encourage school leaders to implement these norms during these challenging conversations with their staff.

Strategies for Unpacking Issues Pertaining to Race

Part of unpacking the aforementioned issues is to understand them from the perspective of others (particularly those most impacted). This is a conscious decision schools need to make, and for the ones that do, data can be very useful for providing necessary perspectives and language.

George Floyd's death and its aftermath became the catalyst for increased DEI discussions in schools (Mayberry, 2022) and for those discussions' inclusion in this book and chapter. In the following section, I will momentarily return to the context of raising equity for African American students and uplift and model the types of data points we can consider for our conversations on racial injustices. I will also do the same in the context of AAPI students. African Americans, Asian Americans, and Pacific Islanders are not the only groups of students that require equity in the United States. These groups are the most widely discussed by the FBI and in the media as the targets of increased hate crimes in the United States (Mangan, 2021); however, you may not teach students from either group. To help you focus on your context, I also provide resources for supporting other marginalized groups that are impacted by racial and ethnic disparities after the following two sections.

Support African American Students in DEI Initiatives

For those who aren't African American, imagine how hurtful and traumatizing it is to daily live, feel, and experience the effects of systemic injustices (Phillips, 2020). For example, Floyd's murder was captured on film; many saw the video of Derek Chauvin with his knee on Floyd for more than nine minutes while he pleaded for his life (BBC News, 2021a). Yet many people were on edge and holding their breath as they awaited the jury's verdict because of the uncertainty that accountability would be served despite the undeniable evidence (BBC News, 2021b).

And SEL is not a panacea for trauma and inequities. We must consciously unpack the issues to better understand how to empathize and raise equity—in this case, with the effects of sustained racial discrimination.

For example, protests and civil unrest across the United States in the wake of George Floyd's death in Minneapolis police custody renewed national and worldwide attention to how African Americans are policed. Unfortunately, policing has never been consistently positive for all Americans, even before the murder of Floyd. The following are some Pew Research Center survey findings reported by Drew DeSilver, Michael Lipka, and Dalia Fahmy (2020):

- Black adults are about five times as likely as whites to say they've been unfairly stopped by police because of their race or ethnicity (44% vs. 9%).
- Nearly two-thirds of black adults (65%) say they've been in situations where people acted as if they were suspicious of them because of their race or ethnicity, while only a quarter of white adults say that's happened to them. Roughly a third of both Asian and Hispanic adults (34% and 37%, respectively) say they've been in such situations.
- Black Americans are far less likely than whites to give police high marks for the way they do their jobs. In a 2016 survey, only about a third of black adults said that police in their community did an "excellent" or "good" job in using the right amount of force (33%, compared with 75% of whites), treating racial and ethnic groups equally (35% vs. 75%), and holding officers accountable for misconduct (31% vs. 70%).

Uplifting these data points can help educators understand the pain of students and colleagues and also help mend fences without glossing over the impact of injustices on Black communities. Solutions should also move beyond empathy into action. For example, organizations like Big Brothers Big Sisters of America partner with families to help mentor youth (Big Brothers Big Sisters, n.d.). In 2018, Big Brothers Big Sisters introduced its Bigs with Badges mentoring program that connects young people with law enforcement officers and first responders to create trusting relationships and provide career guidance (Big Brothers Big Sisters, n.d.). Bigs with Badges was piloted by the Buena Park Cypress Police Department in California, which worked with local school districts (Arora, 2021).

In places with a lack of trust between students and law enforcement, I would love to see DEI programs where schools partner with local police precincts to bring officers and students together in a similar fashion. Ideally, DEI can be a community effort that brings people together to mend fences and improve relations. Imagine police officers getting to know and mentor students to develop meaningful relationships with them. Also, consider the healing that could take place for everyone involved.

Acknowledge Asian Hate in the United States

In the days before mandatory school closings in 2020 due to COVID-19, I walked into a classroom at a school where I coach to observe instruction. A student looked at me and said, "Oh no, coronavirus is in here." I wasn't harmed by the comment, but I understood the student most likely made it due to my facial features and the anti-Asian sentiment that has been documented across the media since the crisis began (Bay City News, 2020). This experience with racism made me consider how those words might have impacted my younger self and how similar situations might have been playing out differently for others in the United States. Reports of Chinese and Asian American people being unjustly harassed include incidents of racism such as microaggressions, misplaced blame for COVID-19, and name calling (AAPI Equity Alliance, 2020). More severe reported incidents involve vandalism of property and physical assault (HAAPI Employee Resource Group, 2021).

As discussions about Asian hate grew in education circles, many in the AAPI community expressed that the hatred, xenophobic (anti-immigrant) prejudice, and violence highlighted by the media since early 2020 were not new—just increased (Lee, 2021). Many Asian Americans and Pacific Islanders have suffered long-standing biases fueled by preexisting xenophobia. This xenophobia, rooted in racism and contempt toward Asian Americans, began when the earliest Asian immigrants came to the U.S. generations ago (Hackett, 2018; Zhou, 2021). To combat widespread fear about competition for jobs, the Page Act of 1875 and the Chinese Exclusion Act of 1882 were created to prevent Chinese laborers from entering the United States (Zhou, 2021). These were two of the United States' first immigration laws.

Unfortunately, Asian Americans now also shoulder the brunt of misplaced blame for the COVID-19 pandemic and continue to suffer attacks in staggering numbers (HAAPI Employee Resource Group, 2021). This misplaced blame for the pandemic goes beyond the United States and is a North American, European, and global problem (Haynes, 2021). Incidents of anti-Asian discrimination and xenophobia have been reported in Canada, Italy, Russia, Brazil, New Zealand, and other parts of the world (Haynes, 2021). In the United Kingdom, police reported a 300 percent rise in hate crimes toward Chinese, East Asian, and Southeast Asian people at the beginning of 2020 compared to the same time in 2018 and 2019 (Clements, 2021; Haynes, 2021).

Schools cannot in good conscience ignore this moment in history. We must visibly, sincerely, and continuously show concern for the inclusion of our Asian students—their emotional and physical safety may depend on it. The Center for the Study of Hate and Extremism (2021) at California State University, San Bernardino has compiled the following data on the uptick of hate crimes in sixteen heavily populated U.S. cities (Tillman, 2022). We should consider these data in providing DEI teams with critical context to protect students and have conversations that spread awareness about Asian hate.

- Reports of hate crimes against Asian Americans went up 342 percent from 2020 to 2021. This continued a pattern from the previous year, where anti-Asian crimes increased 124 percent between 2019 and 2020.

- San Francisco and New York had the highest percentage rate increases in hate crimes between 2020 and 2021, at 100 percent and 96 percent, respectively.
- Across the United States, more than ten thousand incidents of hate crimes were tracked from March 2020 to September 2021 by the Stop AAPI Hate coalition at San Francisco State University.

The safety of our AAPI students needs to be an urgent priority in schools. DEI teams can work to better understand how they may raise equity for AAPI students to strengthen their sense of belonging in the school community. Again, objectively unpacking relevant and reliable data is a first step DEI teams can take to better support AAPI students and staff.

Additionally, depending on the context in which we teach, DEI teams can begin to support students who belong to other racially and ethnically marginalized groups that have been historically and recently targeted with hate (such as Indigenous, Jewish, Muslim, and Ukrainian people). Schools need to highly prioritize targeted students' belonging and safety needs when DEI teams begin to identify materials for supporting and managing their diversity.

Curate Resources for Supporting Students From Racially and Ethnically Marginalized Groups

If educators work in spaces that are committed to raising racial equity, they can dedicate time to growing their knowledge. They can improve their conversations and their positive impact using a community professional development format. This requires excellent resources along with a structure for their use. Resources can include videos, how-to blogs, published research, and replicable classroom activities that teaching teams can adapt. Professional learning community members can work together to unpack their curated resources and become better informed about the structures and barriers that have marginalized their students, along with the effects (data) of the inequities and trauma caused. This type of data and knowledge keeps teams focused on facts and the realities affecting their students. Using this knowledge, they can work together and do their best to level the playing field for the students who are furthest from opportunities.

I created a curated document of resources for supporting students from racially and ethnically marginalized groups to get you started (https://bit.ly/3wHAoxe). You are not bound to these resources, but make sure you use sources that uplift narratives from the perspective of those experiencing the inequities. Learning from firsthand stories is essential for empathizing and ensuring that the emotional toll suffered isn't distorted.

Along with your resources, a simple structure like the text-based seminar or circle practice (see chapter 8, page 144) works well for small and grade-level collaborative DEI teams as they engage in professional learning (National School Reform Faculty, 2014).

Support LGBTQ Students in DEI Initiatives

We have seen a rise in U.S. lawmakers and school boards proposing or passing education policies to restrict teachers from addressing lesbian, gay, bisexual, transgender, and queer or questioning (LGBTQ) issues (Silva, 2022). Backers of the bills rationalize protecting "parent rights" by giving parents more say in their children's education (Silva, 2022). The direction of these bills is to prevent teaching about gender identity and sexual orientation (Block, 2022) or saying "gay" in schools, ban access to LGBTQ books in school libraries, and prevent transgender students from participating in sports according to their gender identities (Silva, 2022). Many LGBTQ students express that their values and identities are under attack and that they are feeling erased from academic spaces (Lavietes, 2022; Silva, 2022).

Educators and schools are caught in the cross fire and are under extreme pressure as they consider diversity and inclusion for LGBTQ students. On the one hand, educators don't want to suffer the consequences of breaking the law. On the other hand, many feel the dilemma is, How can we continue reinforcing gender stereotypes when they fail to promote empathy, acceptance, or respect for all (Block, 2022; Grinberg & Larned, 2018)? Moreover, the laws can be challenging to navigate because they can isolate LGBTQ students and families (Block, 2022). For example, Florida educator Paula Stephens explains that teaching about sexual orientation and gender identity isn't covered in her first-grade class, but there's talk about students' families, and some students have two moms or two dads (Block, 2022). Should these students now be excluded from conversations through no fault of their own? It's a tough spot for educators because many LGBTQ students suffer and need affirming spaces.

The Trevor Project's 2021 *National Survey on LGBTQ Youth Mental Health* captures the challenges of approximately thirty-five thousand LGBTQ youth ages 13–24 in the United States. Here's some of what the report states (The Trevor Project, 2021):

- 42% of LGBTQ youth seriously considered attempting suicide in the past year, including more than half of transgender and nonbinary youth.
- 12% of White youth attempted suicide compared to 31% of Native/Indigenous youth, 21% of Black youth, 21% of multiracial youth, 18% of Latinx youth, and 12% of Asian/Pacific Islander youth.
- 94% of LGBTQ youth reported that recent politics negatively impacted their mental health.

- 75% of LGBTQ youth reported that they had experienced discrimination based on their sexual orientation or gender identity at least once in their lifetime.
- Half of all LGBTQ youth of color reported discrimination based on their race/ethnicity in the past year, including 67% of Black LGBTQ youth and 60% of Asian/Pacific Islander LGBTQ youth.
- Transgender and nonbinary youth who reported having pronouns respected by all of the people they lived with attempted suicide at half the rate of those who did not have their pronouns respected by anyone with whom they lived.
- LGBTQ youth who had access to spaces that affirmed their sexual orientation and gender identity reported lower rates of attempting suicide. (p. 2)

As an increasing part of society is becoming more accepting of diverse sexual orientations and gender as a spectrum and not binary, the aforementioned data inform us that LGBTQ students need affirming spaces to feel emotionally and physically safe (Steinmetz, 2017). In my experience, some LGBTQ colleagues would also benefit from affirming and friendlier spaces.

During a two-week virtual professional development training in the summer of 2021, I learned the importance of more mindfully affirming the gender identity of my colleagues by addressing them with their preferred personal pronouns. During a session, a colleague, Jan (not her real name), was addressed several times with pronouns she did not identify with. I sensed Jan was hurt because she stopped actively participating in our class discussions. After the incorrect pronouns were used three times, she advocated for herself by updating her video-conferencing display name to include *she* and *her*. The minor change to her display name made others aware of her pronouns and therefore caused them to address her to her liking. I, too, updated my display name (with *he/him/his*) for the remainder of our sessions, as did some other colleagues. As a result, Jan continued to have her gender identity affirmed by our colleagues during our two weeks together. She therefore participated more in class and appeared to be more at ease.

I got to know Jan only briefly but thought about her long after the workshop ended. As I resolved to learn more and do better moving forward, I asked myself the following questions.

- "How often does Jan have to endure being incorrectly addressed before feeling compelled to advocate for herself?"
- "What was it like for Jan growing up?"

- "How did she feel in the class?"
- "Moving forward, how can I help other LGBTQ colleagues feel more included in my professional development sessions without their always having to make the first move?"
- "What about the countless students who are teased, bullied, or not confident advocating for themselves? How do they feel?"

As I considered these questions, possibilities became visible to me—I couldn't just ignore a better way to include others. I had to take action.

Meeting Jan forever transformed how I view and practice inclusivity. Although we didn't remain in contact, I reflected on what I could do moving forward to make others like Jan feel more included in my teaching spaces. I also reflected on my own challenges growing up and being excluded, teased, and bullied by some classmates for my race and physical appearance. I remember hiding from certain students to avoid being seen and harassed. I also recall feeling hopeless in elementary and middle school and ashamed of my physical attributes and life circumstance. At my lowest point, I wanted to die and contemplated suicide to escape my daily struggles. I am not attempting to equate my previous pain to Jan's or anyone else's; they're not the same. Nor could I ever know their pain with certainty. But knowing how it feels not to be included or welcome was a point of reference I used to comprehend that Jan and countless colleagues and students need me and others to be more proactive in our inclusion practices.

After diving further into the topic, I realized I had essential information and terminology to learn to better support my LGBTQ colleagues and students. I believe it's not difficult for other educators to start learning too. We can begin by trying the following items.

- Sharing our pronouns with our classes and allowing students to share theirs while ensuring students who don't want to identify themselves to classmates can opt out
- Knowing the general definitions of gender identities and sexual orientations
- Creating an affirming environment for LGBTQ students and colleagues to feel proud of themselves

It's important to acknowledge that many educators are starting to learn more about nonbinary people (those whose gender identity is not exclusively male or female) and may have trouble understanding how a student or colleague identifies or why. Drawing inspiration from what I learned about gender and sexuality, I compiled the following list of essential terms for improving DEI and belonging practices for LGBTQ students and colleagues (American Psychological Association, 2014; Grinberg, 2019).

- **Asexual:** A term that refers to someone who has no sexual feelings or desires or is not sexually attracted to others. Note that people who identify as asexual can still feel romantic attachment to others (Grinberg, 2019).
- **Bisexual:** A term that refers to someone who is sexually attracted to multiple genders (Grinberg, 2019).
- **Gay:** A term that typically refers to men who are attracted and who have a sexual orientation toward other men. It can also refer to people who are sexually attracted to someone of the same sex regardless of gender (Grinberg, 2019).
- **Gender:** A term that refers to either sex (male or female), which typically correlates to socially constructed roles in behaviors and attributes that serve as cultural indicators of individuals' personal and social identity (Grinberg, 2019; National Center for Transgender Equality, 2018).
- **Gender identity:** A term that relates to one's personal sense of their gender, which can correlate with their assigned sex at birth or differ from it. People who don't identify with male or female use the terms *transgender* or *nonbinary* (Grinberg, 2019; National Center for Transgender Equality, 2018).
- **Homophobic:** A term that refers to both having and showing dislike and prejudice for gay people (Cuncic, 2022). A study found significant physiological stress is created for a person experiencing homophobic prejudice (Mastroianni, 2021).
- **Intersex:** A term used for various situations in which a person is born with reproductive or sexual anatomy that doesn't coincide with female or male (Grinberg, 2019; National Center for Transgender Equality, 2018).
- **LGBTQ:** An acronym, the first four letters of which represent *lesbian*, *gay*, *bisexual*, and *transgender*. The *Q* can mean *questioning* for still exploring one's sexuality, or *queer* (Grinberg, 2019). It's important to note that this acronym includes sexual orientation (LGB) and gender identity (T), and that transgender is not a sexual orientation. Sometimes, it's used as an umbrella term for anyone who does not identify as heterosexual or cisgender (Youth Engaged 4 Change, n.d.).

- **LGBTQIA and LGBTQIA+:** The addition of *IA* or *IA+* to this acronym also includes individuals who identify as intersex, asexual, and more (Love Has No Labels, n.d.).
- **Queer:** An encompassing term for "people who are not heterosexual or whose personal identity and gender [does not] coincide with their birth sex" (Grinberg, 2019). Be mindful of using this term because, to many, it is offensive and considered a homophobic slur. However, it's also a self-affirming umbrella term for others who don't want to fall under restrictive labeling. Let those who identify as queer inform you whether they are comfortable with you, as an educator with a lot of power in their life (and thus, the potential to cause great harm using only words), using this term.
- **Lesbian:** A term that typically refers to "women who are attracted to and who have a sexual orientation toward other women. Some nonbinary people also identify with the term lesbian" (Grinberg, 2019).
- **Pansexual:** A term that refers to "someone who is sexually attracted to people regardless of their gender or sexual orientation" (Grinberg, 2019).
- **Preferred and personal gender pronouns:** A term that refers to the set of pronouns that reflect a person's gender identity and how they would like others to refer to them (Trans Student Educational Resources, 2020). Remember that, as language evolves, pronouns change and new pronouns emerge, so always ask someone for their pronouns (Trans Student Educational Resources, 2020).
- **Sex:** "Based on both a person's physical and biological characteristics at birth (chromosomes, hormone prevalence, and reproductive anatomy), they are assigned either male or female. However, intersex is also considered an option in some states and countries for those who share both male and female biological traits" (Grinberg, 2019).
- **Sexual orientation:** A term that refers to "one's innate sexual attraction to men, women or others who identify as non-binary" (Grinberg, 2019). These orientations include lesbian, gay, bisexual, asexual, and pansexual.

Table 9.1 (page 169) offers a guide to understanding and implementing pronouns beyond the gender binary. This information will help us better understand and use gender pronouns when addressing or referring to students and colleagues, which will allow us to increase inclusivity and properly address LGBTQ diversity in education spaces.

TABLE 9.1: Gender Pronouns

Subjective	Objective	Possessive	Reflexive	Example
She	Her	Hers	Herself	She is speaking. I listened to her. The backpack is hers.
He	Him	His	Himself	He is speaking. I listened to him. The backpack is his.
They	Them	Theirs	Themselves	They are speaking. I listened to them. The backpack is theirs.
Ze	Hir or Zir	Hirs or Zirs	Hirself or Zirself	Ze is speaking. I listened to hir. The backpack is zirs.

Source: Trans Student Educational Resources, 2020.

As we can see, supporting LGBTQ students in DEI efforts requires additional learning about various sexual orientations and gender identities. Our words matter, and referring to others in the way they identify isn't difficult and can positively impact them in ways we may not imagine. The reality schools deal with is that more students are increasingly questioning and choosing for themselves how to best represent their identity (Steinmetz, 2017). They shouldn't feel isolated at school because of it. Furthermore, harmful stigma directed toward LGBTQ youth causes them violence, discrimination, and harassment, leading to health disparities and risk for suicide, substance use, and poor sexual health (Johns, Poteat, Horn, & Kosciw, 2019). Therefore, affirming our LGBTQ students' existence is critical to helping improve their well-being by making them feel more connected to their school community (Johns et al., 2019).

Support Immigrant and Refugee Students

The inclusion of immigrant and refugee students is another complex DEI topic that many schools may need to tackle, depending on their student populations. To clarify the difference, *immigrants* leave their countries to settle in another, and *refugees* are forced to leave their countries due to restrictions or danger to their lives and well-being (Diffen, n.d.). Like the other DEI topics in this chapter, immigration in the United States has historically been difficult to talk about, no matter which immigrant group is discussed (Thompson, 2018).

I believe DEI teams need to know and consider the following information to better serve the diversity of immigrant and refugee students. According to *Atlantic* staff writer Derek Thompson (2018), three main questions pertaining to immigration cause political discord among Americans:

1. How should the United States treat [undocumented people], especially those brought to the country as children?
2. Should overall immigration levels be reduced, increased, or neither?
3. How should the U.S. prioritize the various groups—refugees, family members, economic migrants, and skilled workers among them—seeking entry to the country?

The Polarization Index (2022), which uses data science to track and measure the most divisive issues in the United States, shows that immigration is the most controversial and divisive issue in the United States as of 2022 (Gersema, 2022). In the first two decades of the 21st century, national conversations about immigration have mainly centered on how to prevent undocumented immigrants from crossing the Mexican border and what to do with Afghan and Ukrainian refugees escaping war (Gersema, 2022; Thompson, 2018). But these conversations aren't new, and history shows that people in the United States are not likely to reach a unifying consensus on what to do and feel about immigrants and refugees. DEI teams therefore must carefully navigate the day's politics to support immigrant students and understand how an influx of refugees escaping war can impact the classroom.

Often, refugees' and immigrants' cultural identities and values are positioned as inferior within the new societies they enter, which may leave them experiencing critical moments of their lives (in school or work) as outsiders. This leads to cultural marginalization, as they live within two cultures but aren't fully integrated into either of them. This is an unfortunate situation to be in through no fault of their own. It hinders their progress and allows others to avoid helping when they could. In schools that focus on DEI, acknowledging immigrant and refugee students' cultures and backgrounds creates cultural awareness between them and their peers. It also welcomes the students to school and the community by positioning their cultures as strengths and positive additions to the learning community.

Understand the Needs of Refugee Students

Refugees have left their country of origin to escape conflict, war, violence, or persecution due to race, religion, nationality, political opinion, or belonging to a particular social group (The UN Refugee Agency, n.d.). After crossing an international border to find safety in another country, they are classified as refugees (The UN Refugee

Agency, n.d.). Since 1980, the United States has resettled approximately three million refugees (Pew Research Center, 2017). The geographic origins of admitted refugees have varied over time. In 2020, the percentages of refugees admitted in the United States included the following breakdown (Monin, Batalova, & Lai, 2021).

- Thirty-five percent from Africa
- Thirty-five percent from Asia (including Near East Asia, Near South Asia, and East Asia)
- Twenty-two percent from Europe
- Eight percent from Latin America and the Caribbean

Additionally, the U.S. Department of State's Refugee Processing Center reports the following (Budiman, 2020), in addition to the content mentioned in chapter 7, page 123.

- Thousands of Haitian migrants have been seeking asylum in the United States since 2010 (Phillips, 2021). To clarify, migrants choose to move, and refugees are forced from their homes (Eldridge, n.d.).
- In 2022, due to the horrific Russian invasion of Ukraine, the United States would welcome up to 100,000 refugees. They would be resettled where Ukrainians already were—such as in the cities of Detroit, Michigan, and Harrisonburg, Virginia—so that they had a support network (Davis, 2022).

DEI teams have the task of supporting these students' integration into their chosen society while bearing in mind the traumas they may have endured (see the next section for trauma support). Being aware of the factors that contributed to students' leaving their country as refugees (war, persecution, or natural disaster) provides some context for the students' backgrounds. School communities need to understand and provide the compassionate empathy required to support the students in the coping and healing process.

To help ease immigrant students' difficult transition, DEI teams should research their country of origin, including its culture. Culture can comprise language, religion, beliefs, norms, familial and social habits and behavior, symbols, gestures, cuisine, artifacts, music, and art. Educators can commit to understanding the cultural nuances and customs that may hinder them from forming relationships and learning partnerships with their refugee students.

Because of the trauma they've endured, refugee students require more than DEI practices to feel accepted. Teachers will need to be trauma informed; they can use some of the strategies we covered in chapter 6 (page 112). The following section provides more context and a short list of widely used trauma-informed teaching practices to help refine trauma-informed SEL plans.

Support Refugee Students Using Trauma-Informed Strategies

Although I already covered trauma-informed teaching in chapter 6, I felt it important to readdress it for DEI teams in the context of supporting refugee students. Bringing trauma-informed strategies into the classroom is a universal approach for providing refugee students with emotional and psychological support. In trauma-informed classrooms, teachers must have awareness of the signs of trauma and have a tool kit of strategies to help students and not retraumatize them. SEL is an effective conduit for carrying out and normalizing trauma-informed pedagogy in teaching environments (Jagers et al., 2018).

IMPORTANT NOTE FOR TEACHERS

The trauma-informed SEL strategies in chapter 6 (page 112) can be adapted to help refugee students with their resilience skills and prepare them for SEL.

Educators can help refugee students heal by working with them to establish healthy relationships and safe spaces in schools where acceptance and kind words are the norm. Although we may not initially see how SEL and trauma-informed teaching connect, SEL lessons can provide them the emotional intelligence and emotional awareness to recognize their emotional trauma. Labeling emotions is the first step in identifying triggers and self-management strategies, including healing. See chapter 4's section titled The Importance of Understanding and Labeling Emotions (page 62).

Here's a short list of widely used trauma-informed teaching practices to help your DEI team refine trauma-informed SEL plans (Valenzuela, 2021a). These strategies, which appear in chapter 6, have been modified here to help you support refugee students.

1. **Develop a trauma-informed team:** Successfully supporting refugee students requires all hands on deck in schools. This means that school leaders, counselors, teachers, and organizations must provide wraparound services to be trauma informed and support one another.
2. **Empathize with students:** Empathy for perspective taking is a critical step to becoming trauma informed, especially if we don't have firsthand

experience with certain traumas. As teachers, we shouldn't be trauma detectives, but we can proactively become informed about three types of trauma (Allarakha, 2021; Venet, 2021).

a. *Acute trauma*—This type of trauma results from a highly distressing and extreme event threatening the sufferer's emotional or physical security. Extreme events may include accidents, rape, physical assault, war, or natural disaster.
b. *Chronic trauma*—This type of trauma occurs in people who are exposed to multiple distressing, traumatic events over a long period of time. It may result from an extended illness, bullying, sexual abuse, domestic abuse, and extreme situations, like war.
c. *Complex trauma*—This type of trauma results from exposure to multiple and varied traumatic events, typically within interpersonal relationships, making the sufferer feel trapped; this severely impacts their mind. Sufferers may be victims of childhood abuse, neglect, domestic abuse, home altercations, and repetitive, highly volatile situations, such as civil unrest and war.

This background can be helpful when encountering sensitive cases.

3. **Make them feel safe:** In extreme cases, refugees may experience danger, terror, or constant threat. Trauma can alter how many young people's brains and central nervous systems function, and it can cause them to feel unsafe (Manion, 2020). Unfortunately, these deep feelings of insecurity and fear may show up in different areas of their lives, including play, relationships, and school. Educators can make their classrooms physically, intellectually, and emotionally safer by establishing good norms and community agreements such as the following.
    - Bring your best self to class.
    - Be mindful of other people's boundaries.
    - Respect other people's privacy.
    - Be mindful of how much of everyone's time you use when speaking.
    - Speak from the heart and be open to feedback.
    - Listen from the heart and respect others when they speak.
    - Take this space to heal and grow.

4. **Remain consistent and predictable:** Students of all ages with traumatic experiences may be on high alert. Providing consistency and predictability through your demeanor, fairness (being equitable), class norms, expectations, shared agreements, use of protocols, thinking routines, pacing, accountability, and scheduling can help put them at ease. For example, I like to format instructional time similarly on most days (ten minutes for a minilesson, thirty-five minutes for work time, and ten minutes for reflection and debriefing). Samantha Bennett's (2007) adaptation of the workshop model is a helpful example of this.
5. **Know your limitations:** When psychological trauma becomes overwhelming for refugee students, we might need to assist families in seeking access to professional therapy for their children. Remember, our trauma-informed SEL plan is for helping refugee students cope and begin healing, but it isn't meant to replace professional trauma-informed treatment.

The International Rescue Committee and the National Immigration Forum are two valuable sources of information to learn more about supporting refugee students (see appendix A, page 193, of this book). Remember that learning firsthand stories is essential for empathizing and ensuring that the emotional toll suffered by victims (in this case, refugees) isn't distorted.

Summary

I hope the context, data, language, and perspective in this chapter are helpful in spaces where educators have agreed to engage in complex dialogue so they become more inclusive of their most vulnerable and diverse students. In this chapter, we explored ways DEI teams can support the following.

- African American students
- Students of diverse sexual orientations and gender identities
- Immigrant and refugee students
- AAPI students

Understanding that demographics and contexts vary from school to school, I have also provided resources for supporting students who belong to other racially and ethnically marginalized groups in this chapter. The methods of exploring relevant data and firsthand narratives and the conversation protocols provided here empower educators to work together without blaming, shaming, or alienating one another.

This way, they can focus on better assisting students who belong to the most vulnerable groups. In the final chapter of this book, we will use our gathered knowledge from previous chapters to update our SEL plans in various ways so we can raise equity for vulnerable students.

CHAPTER 10

Activate SEL Through Equity and Educational Technology

KEY CHAPTER TASKS

- Know how to implement SEL practices in distance learning.
- Know how educational technology impacts equity in the classroom and vice versa.
- Know how to use educational technology strategies to connect students.

Advances in online connection and situations that have necessitated some sort of virtual learning (such as the COVID-19 pandemic) make it impossible to leave distance learning or educational technology (edtech) out of education discussions (Gewertz, 2021). The goal of using edtech is to augment in-person and virtual lessons. Still, school leaders must listen to teachers about what has worked and hasn't worked to move forward smarter (Gewertz, 2021). Using the Equity and SEL Integration Framework can help educators learn more about students—thus providing educators insight into how the students learn best so they can make informed instructional decisions with technology.

Many teachers are teaching remotely some of the time, and many school systems are maintaining the possibility of remote teaching due to parents who want the option (Gewertz, 2021). Because of this, the subsequent sections provide tips and tools for enhancing our overall teaching with edtech as schools attempt to move forward ("work smarter, not harder," as the old adage goes). The concepts and strategies in this chapter can be applied to in-person teaching, remote teaching, and other technology-infused teaching environments. Together, schools can use historical developments in social spheres as professional learning opportunities to enhance their current and future teaching practice with effective edtech use. This chapter won't ignore the fact that distance learning doesn't work for every learner (Gewertz, 2021). You'll find in this chapter systematic, reflective, and equity-based strategies for teaching SEL along with interactive activities for engaging students in technology-infused environments, including hybrid and blended settings.

Hybrid learning is the practice of comprehensively combining in-person and virtual learning to create a customized learning experience. *Blended learning* is an instructional approach combining online learning (apps, resources, and more) with face-to-face instruction in an integrated experience. Blended learning is powerful because it gives students gradually increased ownership and control over their education by making knowledge available anytime, anywhere through technology. Schools have several blended learning models to choose from to best serve their students' needs (Blended Learning Universe, 2021).

Carefully managing all these factors with equity and consistency can help build a collaborative culture where all students and educators can maintain norms and develop social-emotional awareness in tandem with technology skills. My coaching work with schools taught me that for learning with technology to be optimal, teachers must know how to leverage the right edtech tools and teaching strategies to make their remote lessons engaging and compelling for learners (Valenzuela, 2020e).

The Need for SEL in Distance Learning

Many distance learning initiatives initially emerged as emergency academic responses to the COVID-19 pandemic beginning in March 2020 (Valenzuela, 2020e). But as educators quickly discovered, emotions were running high for everyone as they experienced a level of national trauma few ever had before, and daily life changed quickly and completely. Thus, integrating SEL into daily lessons became a high priority for teachers everywhere (Kaufman, n.d.; Walker, 2020).

At that time, students needed their teachers to lead with grace, compassion, and empathy using distance learning options designed to be engaging and relevant (Valenzuela, 2020d). However, we couldn't ignore that academic success varies by student, access to support, and family circumstances (Loeb, 2020)—SEL wasn't and isn't a panacea for students unprepared to learn online. Studies find that underprepared students who struggle to learn in person also have trouble attending class online (Loeb, 2020). Similar studies examining K–12 education settings show that in-person schooling, on average, is more effective than online schooling for most students (Ordway, 2020). Therefore, academically inclined students who have already formed good study habits are most likely to succeed in the online environment. In contrast, some experts feel students can thrive in virtual environments if the instruction is done right—meaning pedagogical approaches, technology access, and social infrastructure are prime for distance learning (Greenhow, 2020). Schools and educators need to consider that academic success will always vary by student, their access to support, and their family circumstances.

In addition to making new work for teachers, who were expected to perform instructional miracles, online teaching required additional training for teachers. And virtual classes were prone to technical issues (Thompson, 2021). In spaces where teachers were inadequately supported at the start of the COVID-19 pandemic, teaching students academics and SEL was essentially mission impossible. Knowing what we know now, we can't do this right or equitably without knowing the key issues that distract students or adequately understanding how to use technology tools to our advantage in our teaching environments. As we attempt to move forward in a smarter way, schools must listen to teachers. The following are some drawbacks of distance learning that have negatively affected many students.

- **Isolation:** Between having to learn online and not seeing their friends at school each day, some learners can easily feel isolated from their peers (Thompson, 2021).
- **Procrastination with assignments:** Learners who do not have a strong work ethic may find it easy to put off assignments when they're not tied to a set schedule (Lynch, 2020).
- **Lack of time management skills:** Students who don't know how to manage their time may have difficulty getting all their lessons done each day, which could cause them to fall behind in learning (Rinkema & Williams, 2021).
- **Lack of supervision (distractions):** Students who attend school from home and are alone or unattended during the day may dedicate more time to fun and games than to schoolwork (Lynch, 2020).
- **Disruptive work spaces:** Students who don't have a quiet space at home may have difficulty concentrating on assignments (Pinola, 2020).
- **Lack of internet and technology access:** Students need steady access to a laptop or other digital device and the internet to complete lessons each day (Valenzuela, 2020e).

A list like this can be overwhelming and make the job of educating some students online seem nearly impossible to achieve. Although providing this education can be challenging, we shouldn't feel discouraged about the unfavorable conditions we may not have immediate solutions for. Understanding that these conditions and inequities prevent students from learning in a virtual setting and cause them to experience unpleasant emotions is a big reason educators relied so heavily on SEL when we implemented distance learning (Kaufman, n.d.). SEL is a valuable asset for helping students learn to self-manage and restore peaceful emotional states, and although initiatives don't work overnight, they do work when implemented well (ASCD, 2018). Managing their sense of inner peace so they show up at their best is a valuable skill students should continue honing along with their schoolwork. Therefore, it's vital that we remain committed to SEL as many of us move back into in-person learning.

Strategies for Implementing Equity in Edtech

Though educators won't conquer every inequity or SEL need to make the distance learning environment work for every learner, they can prepare themselves with tech-savvy lessons. The following sections provide sound strategies for expertly integrating your classroom into this increasingly technological educational world. Beginning with the Equity and SEL Integration Framework, I have highlighted frameworks and strategies throughout this book. "Framework first, mindset second" is a powerful principle I use to help colleagues understand that having good general guidelines for doing something new is the prerequisite to developing second-nature expertise (Valenzuela, 2022d). Implementing equity in edtech is no different; educators must first master strategies to implement equity. As we close out this book, we will begin with the technological pedagogical content knowledge (TPACK) framework for organizing our teaching with edtech (Mishra & Koehler, 2006; PowerSchool, 2022). We will then explore edtech tools and the educator section of the ISTE Standards created by the International Society for Technology in Education (2017).

Select the Right Tools Using a Research-Based Framework

This section is for teachers who are struggling to choose among their district's varied edtech options; it is not meant to endorse specific products or edtech companies. The examples provided will include some tools I use in my classroom and others I don't that I know are popular among various school systems. Still, the ultimate goal is to have readers focus on utility before tools by considering the learning goals first and selecting the tool second.

When selecting edtech tools, teachers should lead with the learning objectives they are trying to accomplish, not the tools. Unfortunately, many supervisors expect teachers to use technology effectively to the point where their content and pedagogical knowledge falls behind. That puts teaching priorities in the wrong order. But because you're reading this book, you are undoubtedly already using teaching strategies in your classroom—so let's begin there.

For teaching with technology to be optimal, teachers require edtech that strengthens the critical thinking and social and collaborative strategies they already implement with students. If you are unsure where to start, you can ask yourself the following three questions.

1. "What evidence-based instructional strategies and educational protocols (teaching strategies) do I already use to engage my learners during lessons?"
2. "What edtech tools are the best vehicles for equitably augmenting my teaching strategies for all learners in my daily lessons?"
3. "Is there a system that can help me organize what I already do with the new edtech tools I'm learning to use?"

After answering the questions, you'll see that your goal is simply to improve what you already do in the classroom with technology. The TPACK framework was designed to address these questions as well. The TPACK framework is a model created to successfully integrate edtech into the classroom using three foundational knowledge principles: content knowledge, pedagogical knowledge, and technological knowledge. To redesign our learning environments in a way that emphasizes sustained learner engagement, collaboration, and SEL with technology, let's understand how the three types of knowledge uplifted in the TPACK framework must align in various meaningful ways (Mishra & Koehler, 2006; PowerSchool, 2022).

1. **Content knowledge:** This describes a teacher's knowledge of the subject area they teach. Content knowledge includes understanding of how critical concepts, theories, research, and knowledge exist within a particular subject area, along with best practices for teaching students within the discipline and related fields. Content knowledge also includes knowledge of the CASEL 5 and the ability to model SEL strategies to help students manage emotions and restore peaceful states so they are ready to learn.
2. **Pedagogical knowledge:** This describes a teacher's knowledge and ability in the most basic and foundational areas of teaching and learning, including

curriculum and lesson design, classroom facilitation strategies, and student assessment to plan interventions and determine instructional next steps.

3. **Technological knowledge:** This describes a teacher's knowledge and ability to adapt various technology tools and resources effectively and comfortably. Technological knowledge involves knowing how to augment different facets of instruction using technology.

As shown in figure 10.1, educators can use the TPACK framework to combine and, at times, recombine the three types of critical knowledge required for augmenting their teaching with edtech in both in-person and virtual settings. Selecting the right edtech can now be a more accessible and better-informed endeavor.

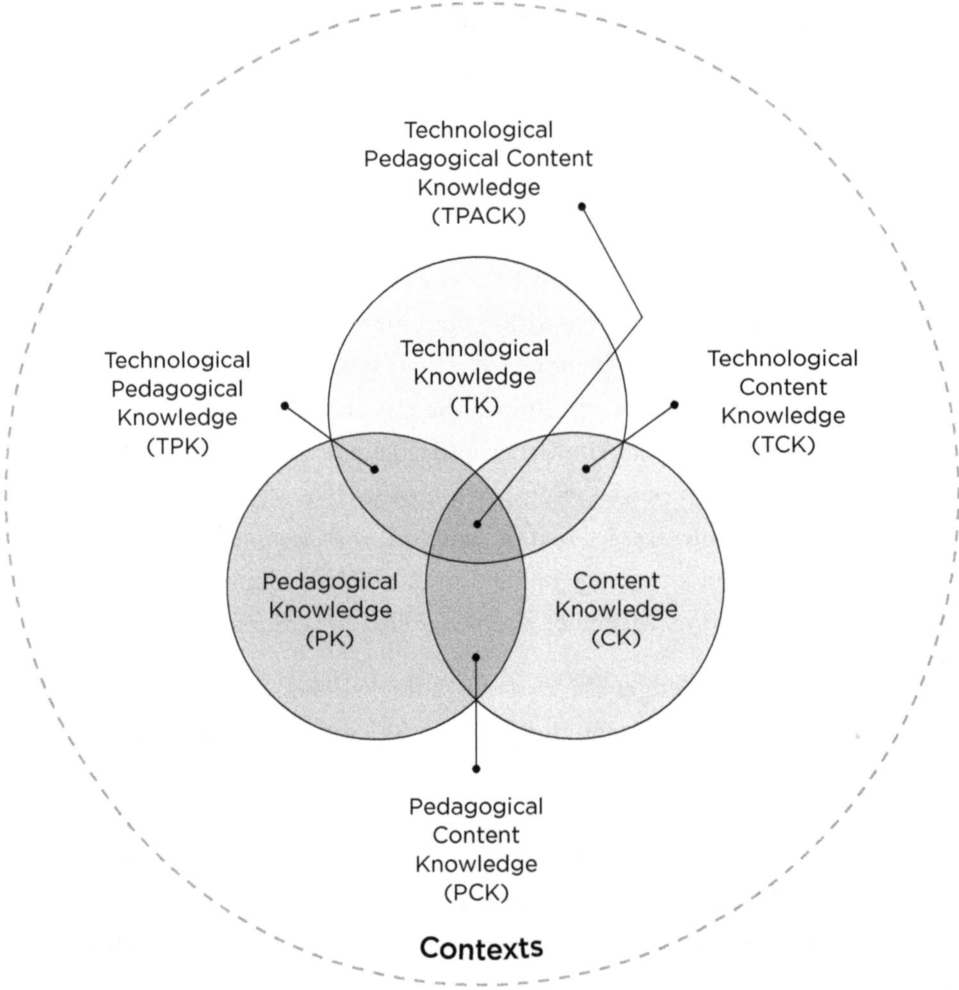

Source: © 2012 Tpack.org. Used with permission.

FIGURE 10.1: The technological pedagogical content knowledge framework.

I have organized edtech tools into the following three categories, using the TPACK framework to combine content knowledge, pedagogical knowledge, and technological knowledge in various ways to help educators make informed decisions (Valenzuela, 2020b).

1. **Learning tools for students:** These are the edtech tools and resources that educators use to teach and scaffold lessons. The tools include open educational resources. *Open educational resources* are teaching or learning materials that are made freely accessible either in the public domain or under district licenses. Teachers are allowed to adapt and share these open resources with others (Sparks, 2017).
2. **Formative assessment tools:** These are apps or tools teachers and students can use to check understanding because they can collect data about student learning. Teachers can use data provided by these edtech tools to help inform their next teaching steps, such as appropriate lessons, scaffolds, and remediation. Popular tools for remote learning include but are not limited to Nearpod, Formative, Pear Deck, and Flipgrid.
3. **Tools to transfer learning:** These are edtech tools that allow students to create authentic products, such as computational artifacts, reports, videos, digital plans, or prototypes and models. Helpful tools include Google for Education, WeVideo, Autodesk, and YouTube (Sparks, 2017).

Teachers can use the TPACK framework and these three categories as general guidelines to select the appropriate edtech tools to augment their distance, hybrid, or blended learning lessons. Although I've categorized some popular tools by utility in this section, don't forget to consider the learning goals first and select the tools second when adopting new ones.

Make Online Lessons Interactive and Perpetually Accessible

Here, I want to provide an account of how I learned to make my academic and SEL lessons engaging for students at the onset of the pandemic using edtech tools. With a few simple modifications, the tools and principles uplifted here can also apply to in-person and hybrid settings.

The COVID-19 pandemic caused me, like many teachers, to begin remotely teaching all my classes. Although virtual courses were not new to me, I wasn't sure how the experience would be fun or engaging for either me or my learners. Also, I needed to consider my learners' SEL more than before, and I was very worried and unsure how to proceed.

Knowing that I needed to present my lessons in emotionally compelling and fun formats to keep learners interested, I asked myself the following three questions.

1. "What edtech tool is suitable for making *synchronous* and *asynchronous* lessons engaging for my students?" (*Synchronous lessons* happen live, with participants meeting on an online platform. *Asynchronous lessons* involve students accessing lessons and materials independently and at their leisure.)
2. "How will I monitor both progress and completion of student work?"
3. "How can learners who were accustomed to receiving my instruction through systematic and reflective practices (like evidence-based instructional strategies and educational protocols) now get the same level of engagement through the Zoom platform?"

Teachers want to present their lessons in an emotionally compelling and fun format in synchronous and asynchronous settings. They also need to monitor both progress and completion of the work. This is a tall order. Work with your colleagues as thought partners, or engage with your collaborative team for advice.

For example, you can make your lessons interactive and accessible whether you are teaching in person or virtually with Nearpod. Using Nearpod, teachers can add interactive activities (like polls, fill-in-the-blank activities, matching pairs, and many more) to lessons. Educators can design each of these activities to fit the context of any age group and generate data about how well their students are learning the content. These data can be helpful for formative assessment. Nearpod also allows students to participate in both real-time and self-paced lessons in fun ways. Note that while there is no cost to use Nearpod's silver edition, Nearpod also offers gold, platinum, and school editions, which are not free but offer many more features for both teachers and administrators.

IMPORTANT NOTE FOR TEACHERS

Nearpod provides a student engagement platform designed to make lessons interactive and accessible with or without a facilitator; it allows teachers to launch daily lessons in both live and self-paced modes. This feature helps struggling learners because it enables them to capture the content, improve their skills, and transfer learning at their own pace. This feature can be very useful during distance learning because it supports learners who do not have access to reliable Wi-Fi or devices and are thus prevented from attending live lessons.

Students can easily use Nearpod on their parent's or guardian's phone, which is great for students who don't always have laptops or Chromebooks available. Online slide presentation alternatives for teachers whose districts may not support Nearpod are Pear Deck, Google Slides, and Keynote.

A powerful feature of Nearpod is its robust lesson library, which is packed with lessons for every grade level and content area. Included are SEL-specific lessons for helping learners develop their emotional intelligence skills.

Promote Student Collaboration in SEL Using Virtual Breakout Rooms

It is valuable to have students work together in pairs and triads to learn SEL strategies or complete an academic task or product in distance learning. Teachers sometimes feel like they lose access to this dynamic when forced to conduct lessons over video chat, but this doesn't have to be the case. Most video-conferencing software, such as Zoom (https://zoom.us), has breakout room capabilities that enable teachers to assign students to online groups. Research supporting the use of breakout rooms to improve academic and social outcomes for students shows the following.

- Using breakout rooms strategically helps keep students engaged and presents opportunities for collaborative peer learning in smaller group settings (Lowry, 2020).
- Using breakout rooms in Zoom can help develop students' collaborative skills (Agustina & Suharya, 2021).
- Along with teacher facilitation, breakout rooms support English as a second language improvement for students (Ahmed, 2021).

The following are a few examples of how teachers can blend effective teaching strategies with breakout rooms for English learners and general SEL-focused contexts.

- Make group work socially relevant by allowing students to choose topics that matter to their communities. Relevant topics may include finding solutions to environmental problems such as sustainability and climate change (Fester & Valenzuela, 2021). Critical social issues include health, education, and financial inclusion (The Global Food Fund, n.d.). Economic development and housing development are also good topics (Kingsella, 2020).
- Allow voice and choice about the types of products students create to demonstrate learning. Examples of products students can make include but are not limited to eye-catching infographics, public service announcements, videos, picture slideshows, and podcasts.

- Use visuals for encouraging dialogue and comprehension. Visible-thinking routines like *see, think, wonder* work well for this (Valenzuela, 2022a). The idea is for students to think carefully about why a visual is a certain way. Teachers introduce the following question prompts to guide students' thinking.
    - What do you see?
    - What do you think about that?
    - What does it make you wonder?
- For students learning English, provide small-group instruction in breakout rooms, emphasizing English language skill acquisition across the content areas. Vocabulary is at the core of literacy (Fisher & Frey, 2014) and is an excellent place to start. Sentence starters are also good scaffolds for English learners (Fort Worth Independent School District, n.d.).

When using breakout rooms for student collaboration, teachers have multiple platforms with different breakout features to choose from, including Zoom, GoTo Meeting, Microsoft Teams, and RingCentral. I advise using the programs your district supports.

Use the ISTE Standards for Educators to Become Leaders

The Equity and SEL Integration Framework can help us understand how our students learn best. Teaching with technology is a critical equity raiser for many of them, so we should look for sound ways of using technology in lessons. I suggest the research-informed International Society for Technology in Education Standards for keeping your academic and SEL teaching goals for technology organized. The ISTE Standards for Educators can provide the necessary guidelines for teaching equitably and engaging students socially and emotionally. Furthermore, the educator section of the ISTE Standards serves as good equity guidelines that go beyond using edtech (ISTE, 2017).

I became an ISTE member in 2017. Learning to use the ISTE Standards during the ISTE Certification process was one of the best professional learning experiences I've had. ISTE Certification for Educators is an internationally recognized credential that indicates mastery of the ISTE Standards focusing on pedagogy. I recommend ISTE Certification (ISTE, n.d.a) to educators who want to expand their equity teaching practices with technology and expand their professional learning network.

In table 10.1 (page 187), I've presented the Learner and Leader subsections of the ISTE Standards for Educators, their indicator descriptions, and their relationships to equity (ISTE, 2017).

TABLE 10.1: Connecting the ISTE Standards for Educators to Equity

ISTE Standard for Educators	Indicator Descriptions	Relationship to Equity
2.1 Learner: Educators continually improve their practice by learning from and with others and exploring proven and promising practices that leverage technology to improve student learning.	**2.1.a**: Educators set professional learning goals to explore and apply pedagogical approaches made possible by technology and reflect on their effectiveness. **2.1.b:** Educators pursue professional interests by creating and actively participating in local and global learning networks. **2.1.c:** Educators stay current with research that supports improved student learning outcomes, including findings from the learning sciences.	**2.1.a:** I incorporated the equity-based strategy In2Out (Valenzuela, 2022c) in lessons to raise equity for vulnerable learners, and I learned to integrate the edtech tool Nearpod, which proved to be an effective way for my students to have their voices heard and participate in the strategy virtually. **2.1.b:** Collaborating with like-minded educators on Twitter and Instagram to exchange ideas related to equitable practices has expanded my thinking and knowledge sources (like Nichols, 2022). **2.1.c:** To guide the action research in my equity work with schools, and the theoretical backgrounds for the equity practices in this book (for example, empathy mapping), I continuously stay abreast of the best ways to raise equity for learners in my context.
2.2 Leader: Educators seek out opportunities for leadership to support student empowerment and success and to improve teaching and learning.	**2.2.a:** Educators shape, advance and accelerate a shared vision for empowered learning with technology by engaging with education stakeholders. **2.2.b:** Educators advocate for equitable access to educational technology, digital content, and learning opportunities to meet the diverse needs of all students. **2.2.c:** Educators model for colleagues the identification, exploration, evaluation, curation, and adoption of new digital resources and tools for learning.	**2.2.a:** I engage my learners in activities for helping them create their digital profile and identity around computing. **2.2.b:** My students see people who look like them in my lessons because I uplift the accomplishments of computer science pioneers and experts who share their cultures and backgrounds. **2.2.c:** Using a town hall format and inviting colleagues to sit-in, I regularly address parents and stakeholders about the impacts of computer science skills on the students' education and future careers, and share results with colleagues (Valenzuela, 2019b).

Source for ISTE Standards: ISTE Standards for Educators (ISTE, 2017)

Educators using the ISTE Standards for guidance can use the table to reflect on their equity practices with technology. Additionally, this is a helpful practice for educators wishing to earn ISTE Certification (ISTE, n.d.a).

Align ISTE Standards to Content Standards and the CASEL 5

To complement both CASEL core competencies and academic standards, teachers can use the ISTE Standards for Educators to equitably help learners integrate the appropriate use of edtech across all technology-infused lessons. The ISTE Computational Thinking Competencies, which highlight the importance of individual teachers becoming equity leaders based on the four primary pillars for student literacy—(1) problem decomposition, (2) pattern recognition, (3) abstraction, and (4) algorithms—also reflect a healthy step-based process for understanding and applying SEL, the CASEL 5 competencies, and equity in the classroom (ISTE, 2018).

Table 10.2 (page 189) shows an easy brainstorming process for creating alignment in specific lessons between learning goals and academic standards, the CASEL 5, and ISTE Standards; educators use a few key questions to guide their thinking. Note that using ISTE Standards in alignment with academic standards and SEL competencies to develop well-composed learning goals doesn't mean that rigorous learning is sure to occur. Engaging remote lessons are the result of planning and expert facilitation on the part of teachers who can intentionally align content standards, the CASEL 5, and ISTE Standards.

Rewrite Standards and Competencies to Develop Learning Goals

Developing good learning goals for lessons is a critical practice that professional learning for teachers often neglects. Therefore, learning goals are not always well thought out in instructional design. I will briefly explain and provide examples of developing appropriate learning goals for lessons and unit plans.

The Common Core State Standards, the CASEL 5, and the ISTE Standards (as well as other academic standards) are typically broad, overarching statements with several more specific learning objectives we can interpret multiple ways (Common Core State Standards Initiative, 2022). Standards serve as guidelines and are not intended to be followed as directly expressed in lessons. Teachers must make sense of the goals and targets of a standard and how they want to see students transfer the learning by rewriting them into actionable learning goals. This rewriting practice refers to unpacking, deconstructing, or unwrapping standards (Sailor & Sellenriek, 2016).

TABLE 10.2: Key Questions for Aligning Learning Goals With Content Standards, SEL Competencies, and ISTE Standards

Content Standards	CASEL Core Competencies	ISTE Standards
What new academic concepts and skills will students be learning in this lesson?	Which of the competencies in the CASEL 5 will students be learning in this lesson? Will new emotional intelligence skills focus on better understanding themselves, their environment, or others?	What edtech tools are the best for equitably augmenting the learning for all students? What edtech tools are the best for formative assessment? What edtech tools are the best vehicles for students to use for sharing their learning?

Learning goals are vital to teaching and observing learning. They form the backbone of lessons by dictating what academic conversations teachers and learners have during minilessons and, thus, how student work is completed. Therefore, state good learning goals using student-friendly language, and represent what students will be able to accomplish in lessons and projects. The following scenario gives an example of standard alignment through social-emotional learning goals.

James, a middle school social studies teacher in an urban setting, was developing his learning goals for his upcoming service project. In the project, students would keep empathy (social awareness) at the forefront and invent a product, process, or virtual event that would bring awareness to a social problem in their community caused by COVID-19. James felt it was essential for his students to learn and demonstrate that a class can provide community service even during a crisis. His project called for students to assess their school and community for social problems by interviewing local residents, community-based organizations, and advocacy groups.

To conduct their interviews, the students would use Zoom for video conferences, and they would develop graphs to track the number of reported community issues. After settling on the problem they wished to bring awareness to, they would then use the data and feedback they received from community members to inform their final product, process, or virtual event. They would also use Flipgrid to create a short public service announcement for articulating their message and providing vital steps others could take to lessen the social issue's impact (ISTE Standard 2.6.d, Facilitator; ISTE, 2017).

Here are the learning targets a teacher might derive from the standards and competencies involved in this scenario after using table 10.2 (page 189) to guide brainstorming.

- I can explain how global emergencies (like the COVID-19 pandemic) and human activity can negatively impact the health of people in our community.
- I can help create an empathic culture in my school and community by bringing awareness to social problems that affect us.
- I can collect and analyze data to inform my decisions and design better solutions to actual problems in my community.
- I can present my conclusions to an audience using multimedia tools that more effectively convey my message.

These learning goals now become the basis of academic conversations between teachers and learners during minilessons and follow-through of James's students' work.

Summary

Technology is an integral part of effective lesson delivery, especially in this post-pandemic education world. The ISTE Standards can provide good guidelines for creatively using edtech tools to strengthen daily lessons—which should be a priority for nurturing our inner confidence as educators and raising equity for all students. Using the ISTE Standards as a supplement to the Equity and SEL Integration Framework can strengthen your teaching and learning goals by creating critical alignments with content and SEL standards (ISTE, 2017, 2018).

Epilogue

Thank you, reader, for taking the time to read and implement the advice, lessons, and ideas in this book. Undoubtedly, *Raising Equity Through SEL* envelops the many skills, attributes, attitudes, and habits that promote learning and create academic and personal success. SEL is not just about emotion management; it's also about goal setting, achievement, perseverance through difficult situations, and synergy with others.

The Equity and SEL Integration Framework can support SEL for diverse groups of students by meeting them where they are without judgment. The framework can also be used to unite colleagues. I hope the lessons in this book begin as inspiration and the strategies eventually become learned mindsets where both teachers and students support and care for one another more intentionally.

Through action research, I designed the first three steps in the Equity and SEL Integration Framework to strengthen educators' emotional intelligence as a prerequisite for assisting diverse students with their SEL. I urge school leaders to take the advice in this book and acquire sustainable professional learning for the teachers and staff in their schools without overdoing SEL. Remember, listen to teachers—they're the experts on their students' and their own needs.

To support SEL for diverse students, the Equity and SEL Integration Framework can be used to implement trauma-informed teaching, culturally responsive teaching, and restorative justice. Being effective requires collaboration, time, patience, and love. It's an investment in our teachers, our students, our country (wherever that may be), and humanity.

With gratitude,

Jorge

APPENDIX A

Additional Resources by Chapter

If you're interested in obtaining more information about the topics discussed in this book, investigate the resources included in this appendix, organized by chapter. This appendix provides access to tools (such as the backward design planning tool and the responsible decision-making matrix) and texts for further reading and engagement. Visit **go.SolutionTree.com/diversityandequity** to access live links to the resources listed in this appendix.

Chapter 1 Resources

These resources expand on the material covered in chapter 1 (page 15).

- **ISTE U online courses (www.iste.org/isteu):** ISTE U is a virtual hub of best-in-class courses to help all educators build and explore digital-age competencies. By working with leading educators and education organizations, ISTE brings you impactful, engaging courses that put pedagogy first and provide incredible learning from the moment you get started.
- **Lifelong Learning Defined workshops (www.lifelonglearningdefined.com/virtual-services):** Since its founding in 2017, Lifelong Learning Defined has become known for its commitment to enhancing the knowledge and practice of schools and educators in an array of timely education topics. Areas that Lifelong Learning Defined can help with include K–12 instructional design practices for teaching and learning, computer science and computational thinking integration, project-based learning, equity and SEL integration, and STEM education.

Chapter 2 Resources

These resources expand on the material covered in chapter 2 (page 33). I curated these resources to supplement the Equity and SEL Integration Framework and the suggested strategies with sound knowledge and guidance about relevant topics for supporting SEL and raising equity for vulnerable students.

- **"A Look at Implicit Bias and Microaggressions" (Finley, 2019):** This is an article.
- **"If They Think I Can: Teacher Bias and Youth of Color Expectations and Achievement" (Cherng, 2017):** This is an article.
- **"Our Hidden Biases" (Picture Alternatives, 2019):** This is a video by Picture Alternatives.
- **"TED Talks Live Short: Unconscious Bias" (ITVS, 2017):** This is a video by ITVS.

Chapter 3 Resources

These resources expand on the material covered in chapter 3 (page 47).

- **"Building Relationships With Empathy Maps" (Edutopia, 2021):** This video explains how to use empathy maps to make better instructional decisions with your students' strengths and needs in mind.
- **"What Is the CASEL Framework?" (CASEL, n.d.):** This is an article.
- **"Culturally Responsive Teaching Is Not a Quick Fix" (Ferlazzo, 2020):** This is an article.
- **"Essential Trauma-Informed Teaching Strategies for Managing Stress in the Classroom (and Virtual Classrooms)" (Resilient Educator, 2021b):** This is an article.
- **"Restorative Practices: A Guide for Educators" (Schott Foundation, 2014):** This is an article.

The following resources complement those mentioned in the previous list by providing historical context, accurate data, and appropriate language to the experience of various marginalized groups in the United States. Educators will find these helpful in developing needed perspectives for empathizing with students, applying their new skills, and raising equity for all students.

- **"Uncovering the Trauma of Racism" (Williams, 2019):** This is an article.
- **"A Guide to Equity and Antiracism for Educators" (Nichols, 2020):** This is an article.
- **Anti-Asian Violence Resources (HAAPI Employee Resource Group, 2021):** These resources, which have been curated by Asian American and Pacific Islander (AAPI) leaders, help individuals educate others and prevent AAPI hate.
- **"Schools Struggle to Support LGBTQ Students" (Minero, 2018):** This article includes research and practices for teachers who want to help LGBTQ students but don't know how.
- **"Supporting Students Affected by Trauma" (Desautels, 2020):** This article includes strategies for helping students access the executive functions they need to pay attention, emotionally regulate, problem solve, hold strong memory, and be creative.

Chapter 4 Resources

This resource expands on the material covered in chapter 4 (page 61).

- **SEL Starter Kit for Labeling Emotions (https://drive.google.com/drive/folders/17jdQmuuPaFMo8HMx7AtPJnu_azd0MDh6):** This starter kit includes critical resources for helping you teach students of all ages how to recognize and label emotions.

Chapter 5 Resources

These resources expand on the material covered in chapter 5 (page 87).

Resources for Embedding Social-Emotional Learning in Your Instructional Design Practices

The following are articles that can help you improve your instructional design skills for planning and facilitating lessons as needed.

- **"Understanding by Design (UbD) Framework" by Jay McTighe and Grant Wiggins (ASCD, 2012).**
- **"Visible Learning and the Science of How We Learn" (Hattie & Yates, 2014).**
- **"Visible Learning: A Synthesis of Over 800 Meta-Analyses Relating to Achievement" (Hattie, 2009).**

Resources for Reviewing Federal Statistics About Bullying in U.S. Schools

Here are some helpful sources of statistics regarding bullying in the United States.

- ***Indicators of School Crime and Safety: 2019* (Wang, Chen, Zhang, & Oudekerk, 2020):** This resource comes from the National Center for Education Statistics and the Bureau of Justice Statistics.
- ***2019 Youth Risk Behavior Surveillance System* (Centers for Disease Control and Prevention, 2020):** This resource comes from the Centers for Disease Control and Prevention.
- **"Bullying Statistics: Breakdown by the Facts and Figures" (Admissionsly, 2020):** This resource comes from Admissionsly.com, a source of reliable and unbiased information and statistics about education.

Resources for Implementing Antibullying Practices

The following are antibullying resources for helping you promote antibias guidance, SEL, empathy, perspective taking, DEI, tolerance, and social justice in lessons.

- **"Antibias Tools and Strategies" (Anti-Defamation League, 2012):** The Anti-Defamation League's tool kit includes antibias strategies, book recommendations, lesson plans, bullying prevention advice, discussion guides, and webinars for educators.
- ***A Guide for Administrators, Counselors and Teachers: Responding to Hate and Bias at School* (Learning for Justice, 2017):** This guide by Learning for Justice provides plans and protocols schools can put in place to respond to bigotry and hate.
- **"Social Justice and Bullying Lesson Plan" (Learning for Justice, 2014):** This social studies-themed grades 3–5 lesson plan by Learning for Justice deals with multiple texts on race and ethnicity, bullying, and bias and justice.
- **"Teaching Tolerance Lesson Plan" (www.learningforjustice.org/learning-plan/teaching-tolerance-lesson-plan-38):** This social studies-themed grades 9–12 lesson plan by Learning for Justice deals with multiple texts on race and ethnicity, religion, rights, activism, and social justice.

Many of these resources will help put historical context to topics that are relevant to your class's context.

Resources for Gaining General SEL Wisdom

Here are a few books that I derived SEL wisdom from. Most of them I have read multiple times and revisit annually.

- ***Emotional Intelligence 2.0* (Bradberry & Greaves, 2009):** This book by Travis Bradberry and Jean Greaves delivers a step-by-step program for increasing your emotional intelligence via four core emotional intelligence skills that enable you to achieve your fullest potential—(1) self-awareness, (2) self-management, (3) social awareness, and (4) relationship management.
- ***The Four Agreements: A Practical Guide to Personal Freedom* (Ruiz, 1997):** This offering by best-selling author Don Miguel Ruiz reveals the source of self-limiting beliefs that rob people of joy and create needless suffering. Based on ancient Toltec wisdom, the Four Agreements offer a powerful code of conduct that can rapidly transform people's lives to a new experience of freedom, true happiness, and love.
- ***The 7 Habits of Highly Effective People: Powerful Lessons in Personal Change* (Covey, 2013):** This classic book presents a principle-centered approach for solving both personal and professional problems. With penetrating insights and practical anecdotes, Stephen R. Covey reveals a step-by-step pathway for living with fairness, integrity, honesty, and human dignity—principles that give you the security to adapt to change and the wisdom and power to take advantage of the opportunities that change creates.
- ***Relentless: From Good to Great to Unstoppable* (Grover, 2013):** Coach Tim S. Grover has taken the greats—Michael Jordan and Kobe Bryant and hundreds of relentless competitors in sports, business, and every walk of life—and made them greater. In this book, he reveals what it takes to achieve total mental and physical dominance, showing you how to be relentless and achieve whatever you desire.

Chapter 6 Resources

These resources expand on the material covered in chapter 6 (page 107).

- **"Trauma-Informed Practices Benefit All Students" (Venet, 2017):** Learn how utilizing schoolwide trauma-informed practices can benefit the entire school community, including helping all students learn coping skills and self-efficacy.

- **"How Schools Are Helping Traumatized Students Learn Again" (Flannery, 2016):** Discover best practices, strategies, and tips your school can employ to foster safe, calming, and supportive learning spaces.
- **"Student Trauma: How School Leaders Can Respond" (Education Week, 2016):** Explore the latest proven strategies that can help your school make a difference in the lives of students. This guide includes a rich collection of additional resources.
- **"It's Not What's Wrong With the Children, It's What's Happened to Them" (Ng'andu, 2015):** Find a list of school-based alternatives to zero-tolerance policies that can help nurture resilience in students who have experienced adversity.
- ***Helping Traumatized Children Learn, Volume 2: Creating and Advocating for Trauma-Sensitive Schools* (Cole, Eisner, Gregory, & Ristuccia, 2013):** Understand the causes of trauma, discover how trauma manifests in schools, and learn about a framework that can help educators develop trauma-sensitive schools.

Chapter 7 Resources

These resources expand on the material covered in chapter 7 (page 121).

- **"My Multicultural Self" (www.learningforjustice.org/classroom-resources/lessons/my-multicultural-self):** This lesson plan (grades 3–5, 6–8, and 9–12) by Learning for Justice deals with addressing multicultural schools and classrooms and resolving conflict.
- **"Me and We: We Are All Similar and Different" (www.learningforjustice.org/classroom-resources/lessons/me-and-we-we-are-all-similar-and-different):** This lesson plan (grades K–2, 3–5, 6–8, and 9–12) by Learning for Justice deals with exploring and appreciating the various similarities we all share, as well as our differences.
- **"Turn and Talk" (The Teacher Toolkit, n.d.):** The turn-and-talk strategy allows all students to participate in meaningful discussion by processing their learning with a peer.
- **"Putting PBL Into Practice: The Workshop Model" (Shepard, 2018):** The workshop model is a structure to organize your lessons and class time in a way that maximizes student work and practice time and enables you to help students as needed.

- **"Discussion Protocols" (Teaching and Learning Lab, n.d.):** This repository of protocols can be used or modified to suit multiple purposes for students to discuss and provide feedback.

Chapter 8 Resources

These resources expand on the material covered in chapter 8 (page 137).

- ***Restorative Justice Implementation Guide: A Whole School Approach* (Yusem, Curtis, Johnson, & McClung, n.d.):** Restorative practices facilitators can use this guide to support their schools in creating an implementation plan to introduce restorative practices schoolwide.
- ***Restorative Practices and SEL Alignment* (CASEL, 2020a):** This is a powerful resource for showing how restorative practices and SEL can align and be implemented strategically.
- ***Chicago Public Schools Restorative Practices Guide and Toolkit* (Chicago Public Schools, n.d.):** The guidance and resources provided in this tool kit are intended to support school staff, administrators, and community partners in developing restorative school communities. In addition, each of the circle types is explained in further detail.

Chapter 9 Resources

These resources expand on the material covered in chapter 9 (page 153).

Resources for Supporting Students Belonging to Racially and Ethnically Marginalized Groups

As these resources address issues with the ever-evolving relationship we have with our collective identities, the following list by nature cannot remain evergreen. Laws and regulations change, politics change, and so, too, do the various threats and developments to our civil rights. As you review these resources, note that they are current as of 2022, but they may evolve, become outdated, or adjust their mission over time.

- **Anti-Asian Violence Resources (https://anti-asianviolenceresources.carrd.co/):** AAPI Leaders have aggregated resources for understanding and addressing anti-Asian violence in the wake of the COVID-19 pandemic.
- **"Asian Americans and Racial Identity: Dealing With Racism and Snowballs" (https://bit.ly/3aZHk1O):** This is an article by Alvin N. Alvarez and Erin F. Kimura.

- **"Asian Americans and Racism: When Bad Things Happen to 'Model Minorities'" (https://psycnet.apa.org/record/2006-09819-007):** This is an article by Alvin Alvarez, Linda Juang, and Christopher Liang.
- **"#31DaysIBPOC" (31daysibpoc.wordpress.com):** This is a collaborative blog post series.
- **"Disrupting Your Texts: Why Simply Including Diverse Voices Is Not Enough" (https://bit.ly/3b5cMM9):** This is a blog post by Tricia Ebarvia.
- **Teaching Materials on Antisemitism and Racism (www.ushmm.org/teach/teaching-materials/antisemitism-racism):** These are the collected resources on antisemitism and racism by the United States Holocaust Memorial Museum.
- **"10 Resources for Teaching Anti-Racism" (www.iste.org/explore/classroom/10-resources-teaching-legacy_of_MLK):** This is an article of compiled resources for teaching antiracism by Jerry Fingal and Samantha Mack via ISTE.
- **"A Guide to Equity and Antiracism for Educators" (www.edutopia.org/article/guide-equity-and-antiracism-educators):** This is an article by Hedreich Nichols via Edutopia.
- **"7 Steps Toward Building an Equitable School Culture" (www.edutopia.org/article/7-steps-toward-building-equitable-school-culture):** This is an article by Jessica Huang via Edutopia.
- **"11 Facts About Discrimination and Poverty in the Latino Community" (www.dosomething.org/us/facts/11-facts-about-discrimination-and-poverty-latino-community):** This is an article created by DoSomething.org.
- **"Supporting Ukrainian Refugee Students" (oecdedutoday.com/supporting-refugee-students-ukraine):** This is an article created by OECD Education and Skills Today.
- **"A Trauma-Informed Approach to Teaching the Colonization of the Americas" (www.edutopia.org/article/trauma-informed-approach-teaching-colonization-americas):** This is an article by Suzanne Methot via Edutopia.
- **"Addressing Race and Racism Head-On in the Classroom" (www.edutopia.org/article/addressing-race-and-racism-head-classroom):** This is an article by Sarah Gonser via Edutopia.
- **Anti-Defamation League (www.adl.org):** This is the landing page for the Anti-Defamation League.

- **"Bullying and Bias: Addressing Islamophobia in Schools" (islamophobia.org/research/bullying-and-bias-addressing-islamophobia-in-schools):** This is an article created by the Council on American-Islamic Relations.
- **"Important Items to Consider for Supporting Afghan Refugee Students" (https://bit.ly/3ooMN5w):** This is an article I (Jorge Valenzuela) wrote for Medium.
- **"5 Trauma-Informed Strategies for Supporting Refugee Students" (www.edutopia.org/article/5-trauma-informed-strategies-supporting-refugee-students):** This is an article I (Jorge Valenzuela) wrote for Edutopia.
- **"Educators Must 'Walk Alongside Afghans and Support Them'" (www.edweek.org/teaching-learning/opinion-educators-must-walk-alongside-afghans-and-support-them/2021/08):** This is an article by Larry Ferlazzo via edweek.org.
- **Afghan Resource Center (https://usahello.org/afghan-resource-center/):** This is a collection of methods for helping Afghan students via the organization USAHello.

Resources for Supporting LGBTQ Students

Here are resources educators can use to examine their practices and their equity lens so they become better allies of LGBTQ students and colleagues.

- **"7 LGBTQ+ Resources for Educators" (Snelling, 2022):** Jennifer Snelling created this list of organizations, curriculum resources, and tips for supporting LGBTQ students.
- **"How Educators Can Better Support LGBTQ Teachers of Color" (Tovar, 2021):** Israel Tovar provides ways that colleagues can support LGBTQ teachers from marginalized racial and ethnic groups.
- **"How to Support LGBTQ Students During Distance Learning" (McGuire, 2020):** Laura McGuire provides tips for creating LGBTQ-safe virtual spaces.
- **"Best Practices for Serving LGBTQ Students" (Learning for Justice, 2021):** Learning for Justice shares texts, ground rules, and tips for responding to myths with facts for teaching queer history.

Resources for Supporting Immigrant and Refugee Students

Here are some helpful sources of information about refugee student needs.

- **The International Rescue Committee (www.rescue.org/how-to-help):** This organization responds to the world's worst humanitarian crises and helps people whose lives and livelihoods are shattered by conflict and disaster to survive, recover, and gain control of their futures.
- **The National Immigration Forum (https://immigrationforum.org/landing_page/about):** This organization helps create the opportunities that immigrants need to succeed in building lives in the United States.
- **"Important Items to Consider for Supporting Afghan Refugee Students" (Valenzuela, 2021c):** This is an article.

Chapter 10 Resources

These resources expand on the material covered in chapter 10 (page 177).

Resources for Incorporating EdTech in the Classroom

- **Nearpod (https://nearpod.com):** This student engagement platform uses ready-to-use interactive lessons, interactive videos, gamified learning, formative assessment, and activities.
- **Pear Deck (https://www.peardeck.com):** This educational technology company offers a web-based application to K–12 schools and teachers.
- **Zoom (https://zoom.us):** Zoom is a videotelephony software program that allows participants to engage virtually.
- ***The Educator's Guide to Flipgrid* (Fahey, Moura, & Saarinen, 2019):** This is an excellent resource for teachers learning how to use Flipgrid. Savvier edtech users will find ways to incorporate Flipgrid as well as Nearpod, Zoom, and other popular education apps into some of their SEL strategies.
- **Recap (https://edshelf.com/tool/recap):** This is another powerful app for keeping students engaged by interacting socially with others.
- **"3 Ways to Make Remote Learning More Engaging" (Valenzuela, 2020d):** This is an article I wrote that includes strategies for engaging students in remote learning.

Resources for Gaining SEL-, Equity-, and Edtech-Related Information

If you're interested in furthering your reading and you want multiple resources that cover both empirical studies and pro tips, look into the following resources.

Books and Magazines

- **ISTE books (https://www.iste.org/books):** ISTE is the leading publisher of books focused on technology in education. More than one hundred titles focus on the most critical topics in edtech, including digital citizenship, inclusive learning, computer science, and more.
    - *Closing the Gap: Digital Equity Strategies for the K–12 Classroom* (Thomas, Howard, & Schaffer, 2019a).
    - *Closing the Gap: Digital Equity Strategies for Teacher Prep Programs* (Howard, Thomas, & Schaffer, 2018).
    - *Creative SEL: Using Hands-On Projects to Boost Social-Emotional Learning* (Haiken & Gura, 2023)
- **Solution Tree books and videos (https://www.solutiontree.com/products.html):** Solution Tree offers credible, research-based, and effective books, resources, and professional development on a wide range of education topics.
- ***Empowered Learner* (https://www.iste.org/empowered-learner):** This digital newsletter aims to give voice to ISTE members and leaders in edtech.
- ***AllThingsPLC Magazine* (https://www.solutiontree.com/all-things-plc-magazine.html):** *AllThingsPLC Magazine* is a must-have for emerging and veteran professional learning communities. Each issue includes professional learning community research, inspiration, fixes, how-tos, and more.

Academic Journals

- ***Journal of Research on Technology in Education* (https://www.iste.org/JRTE):** This journal publishes articles that report on original research, project descriptions and evaluations, syntheses of the literature, assessments of the state of the art, and theoretical or conceptual positions that relate to the field of educational technology in teaching and learning and inform P–16 school-based practice. Subscription is required.

- ***Journal of Digital Learning in Teacher Education* (https://www.iste.org/JDLTE):** This refereed journal provides access to the growing body of research addressing the use of digital technologies in teacher education. Articles highlight contemporary trends and effective, creative, and innovative uses of digital technologies that prepare preservice, in-service, and teacher educators for teaching in technology-rich learning environments. Digital issues are published quarterly and subscription is required.
- ***Learning, Media and Technology* (https://www.tandfonline.com/journals/cjem20):** This journal aims to stimulate debate on digital media, digital technology, and digital cultures in education. It seeks to include submissions that take a critical approach toward all aspects of education and learning, digital media, and digital technology—primarily from the perspective of the social sciences, humanities, and arts. The journal has a long heritage in the areas of media education, media and cultural studies, film and television, communications studies, design studies, and general education studies.

Websites and Blogs

- **EdSurge (https://www.edsurge.com):** This leading education news organization reports on the people, ideas, and technologies that shape the future of learning.
- **Edutopia (https://www.edutopia.org):** This website features ideas and content for transforming K–12 education so that all students can acquire and effectively apply the knowledge, attitudes, and skills necessary to thrive in their studies, careers, and adult lives.
- **Getting Smart Blog (https://www.gettingsmart.com/blog):** This blog supports innovations in learning, education, and technology.
- **ISTE Blog (https://www.iste.org/blog):** This blog features ideas, content, and resources for leading-edge educators.
- **Lifelong Learning Defined in Education (https://medium.com/lifelong-learning-defined):** I (Jorge Valenzuela) write these how-to blogs.

Podcasts

- ***SEL in Action* (www.bamradionetwork.com/genre/sel-in-action):** I (Jorge Valenzuela) host the *SEL in Action* podcast through the BAM Radio Network to address trauma and the social-emotional well-being of both students and staff. The podcast is designed to assist educators on their SEL journey with stories from all over the world that explore models, frameworks, research, and best practices in SEL and other related pedagogies. These pedagogies include culturally responsive teaching, trauma-informed teaching, restorative practices for restorative justice, and inclusive pedagogy for diversity, equity, and inclusion.
- ***SEL: Social-Emotional Well-Being* (www.bamradionetwork.com/genre/sel):** The pandemic-driven need to focus on social-emotional learning and well-being begins with teachers and school administrators. This channel curates the strategies, tactics, and practices educators are using to restore teacher and student well-being face-to-face and remotely.

APPENDIX B

Rationale and Research for the Equity and SEL Integration Framework

This appendix explains the action research methods undertaken to conceive and solidify the Equity and SEL Integration Framework and its effectiveness in classrooms. The steps in the framework are numbered in a purposeful order for educators to learn and implement. However, as you will discover, each step was determined according to the needs of students, and later, the steps were logically compiled to create the final framework.

For example, steps 1, 4, and 5 came together first because they were logical for helping educators activate SEL in lessons. Also, I did not refer to these initial unified steps as a framework until I developed steps 2 and 3. That is because this work has always been driven by data and solely based on teachers' pedagogical needs for supporting students. As you will learn, some of those needs arose due to conditions dictated by current events or school sites.

I've seen many educators independently do their best to learn to integrate critical SEL concepts and skills. As you'll see in the following sections, I've been fortunate to partner with schools where we've consistently communicated on teachers' needs, analyzed our findings, and stayed the course for creating a reliable and evergreen resource. That's where the Equity and SEL Integration Framework comes in. It starts with educators' understanding and applying the SEL core competencies and having the logical steps needed to become better trauma informed and more culturally responsive in their teaching. They will then be able to restore justice as needed while still focusing on the content they teach. The following sections will explain how the framework was developed—including one school system's use of it to guide systemic

DEI work. I'll begin with my initial mixed research methods, developed in my work with Hertford County Public Schools, that were the foundation for my integrated framework. From there, you will read about the rationale for each integration step.

Mixed Research Methods for Establishing the Framework

The framework steps are the result of examining notable research, interviewing school leaders, and gleaning survey results following my teacher professional learning sessions with a school system in North Carolina. I employed both the qualitative and quantitative methods I learned in my Old Dominion University PhD program and used in my previous published research study (Valenzuela, 2019a). The research and development process for creating the Equity and SEL Integration Framework was as follows.

1. Semistructured interviews with school leaders to develop professional development
2. Feedback surveys following professional development with educators
3. Framework development

In mid-April 2020, several instructional leaders and teachers expressed to me they needed guidance on incorporating SEL into remote lessons without disrupting their instructional focus. To be able to provide them with actionable steps in a workshop, I used intake calls as an opportunity to conduct semistructured interviews with school administrators and other site-based instructional leaders. According to researchers Melissa DeJonckheere and Lisa M. Vaughn (2019):

> Semistructured interviews are an effective method for data collection when the researcher wants: (1) to collect qualitative, open-ended data; (2) to explore participant thoughts, feelings and beliefs about a particular topic; and (3) to delve deeply into personal and sometimes sensitive issues. (pp. 2–3)

During interviews, I asked interviewees open-ended questions for eliciting their expertise on their unique school context. This allowed me to discover themes in their responses that would require my closest attention when designing the workshop. Key questions included the following.

- Did the teachers in your school system already participate in SEL training before the pandemic? If yes, what do they find the most challenging about engaging their students in SEL?

- How does SEL coincide with the school system's mission and vision, academic goals, and instructional model? Do you believe that the school-based staff (including school counselors and other support staff) share this vision?
- What specific SEL content and strategies would you like teachers in your school system to be confident implementing with students?

I relied on journaling for gathering their notable responses, quotes, and questions. In an interview, a school leader in North Carolina expressed that staff lacked understanding of how to implement SEL:

> As a staff, we understand the need for SEL at this time, and although we know the CASEL 5 competencies, we are still unclear on what that looks like in actual lessons and during the instructional day.

Another leader from the same school system expressed a similar sentiment and added that engagement was a deterrent to SEL:

> We are having a challenging time getting our students to log into their classes for remote learning at this time, and we know we have to help them with SEL. How can we make SEL engaging so we can prepare them for learning what we need to cover?

I found two recurring points early in my notes that I still see in many spaces regarding professional learning in SEL.

1. Individuals lack the knowledge to incorporate SEL in their existing lessons without feeling like they must lose their instructional focus by doing so.
2. Individuals lack the ability to use SEL for engaging students in distance learning lessons.

After learning about these pain points for educators, I based my initial workshops on these two questions.

1. How can teachers incorporate SEL in existing lessons without losing their instructional focus?
2. How can teachers leverage technology tools to augment SEL strategies during distance learning?

The following sections detail how my integration framework evolved from these beginnings.

Rationale for Step 1: Learn the Basics of the CASEL 5 and Emotional Intelligence

Answering question 1 (How can teachers incorporate SEL in existing lessons without losing their instructional focus?) is not a simple, quick fix, and it requires educators to take three vital steps, which eventually became steps 1, 4, and 5 of the framework. To help the teachers who attended the professional learning begin to understand what they were attempting to accomplish with their learners (SEL), I acquainted them with the five CASEL competencies. I stressed that an essential purpose of SEL is to help learners develop emotional intelligence skills over time by mastering various skill sets associated with each of the five competencies. By integrating SEL in everyday lessons and as needed, educators will give their learners opportunities to practice the CASEL 5 competencies and incorporate them into their schoolwork and lives.

I wanted the educators to take away how the five competencies are interconnected and purposefully color-coded (or shaded). Both self-awareness and self-management focus on skills related to self, and both social awareness and relationship skills focus on skills related to others (CASEL, 2021a). I also stressed that learners could master the responsible decision making competency by becoming more aware of their emotions and finding and implementing strategies for restoring their inner peace.

The results from the initial workshops were very encouraging. I was helping teachers who lacked the knowledge to activate SEL in their existing lessons without feeling like they had to lose their instructional focus to do so. I also assisted the teachers in using SEL to engage students in distance learning lessons and in using technology (such as breakout rooms for collaboration). The more I conducted variations of this workshop in other states and districts (outside of North Carolina), the more refined the workshop became. Teachers who attended those sessions had enthusiastic responses to the material. I would soon learn that I needed to add a layer to this work of helping teachers incorporate SEL in their existing lessons and that I was developing the underpinnings for a new framework.

Rationale for Step 2: Assess Your Unconscious Biases and Beliefs About Students

After the senseless murder of George Floyd on May 25, 2020, sparked outrage worldwide (and forever changed American education and politics), many teachers and schools began creating time to talk and check in with students and staff who were struggling with the unrest. With race and the unfair treatment of African

Americans at the forefront of discussions, some school leaders knew that silence was not an acceptable option, but they were unsure how they should hold this difficult space. I, too, felt racial equity had to be part of the work I was doing.

In response, I presented a session for ISTE's 2020 Summer Learning Academy titled "Make Remote Learning Accessible by Focusing on Equity and SEL" (Valenzuela, 2020a). I weaved racial equity, the effects of racism, and the murder of George Floyd into my presentation. I tied the topics to my strategies for activating SEL in lessons, and the feedback from participants was very positive.

To review the feedback I gathered about my presentation at the ISTE Summer Learning Academy, please see the section titled Feedback About the Integration Framework From Professional Learning Sessions (page 217).

Rationale for Step 3: Improve Your Knowledge of Your Students

As I began to conduct workshops using the newly developed framework, I saw that the demographic makeup of students was different in every academic setting. Teachers would therefore need to examine their beliefs and be empathetic regarding the issues impacting their specific student populations. For example, school leaders at independent and charter schools with little or no racial diversity requested that I make professional development sessions more relevant to their learners by having teachers examine their beliefs and misconceptions about students who are perceived to have privilege. Beliefs that teachers in those settings need to examine in preparation for equitable SEL include the following.

- These students will succeed in life no matter what.
- They love school, and that's why they get high grades.
- They are good at everything they do.
- Their innate curiosity causes them to be self-directed.
- They don't need help; they'll do fine on their own.
- Teachers in our school challenge all the students, so they will be fine in the regular classroom.
- As long as we're challenging their brains, we're servicing their needs.
- They know how to speak up for themselves.
- All their parents are extra involved.

Additionally, subsequent conversations with the North Carolina school leaders revealed a need for a more versatile framework that provided educators guidelines for equitably activating SEL within various student needs. For this school system, SEL programming needed to include racial equity, culturally and linguistically diverse learners, and academically gifted students. Being more mindful and empathetic toward students directly correlates with educators' ability to share in their feelings, which is an essential SEL skill for educators to possess when planning culturally and socially competent lessons. It is therefore critical that teachers continually improve their knowledge of students to inform teaching as they develop and implement the relevant strategies and lessons for their diverse learners. To accommodate this and help inform more personalized teaching, I added *improve your knowledge of your students* to the framework. I adjusted the steps as follows.

1. Learn the basics of the CASEL 5 and emotional intelligence.
2. Assess your unconscious biases and beliefs about students.
3. Improve your knowledge of your students.
4. Help students develop emotional intelligence skills.
5. Activate SEL in your lessons (curriculum).

With this added step, teachers then had the direction to plan relevant SEL lessons and activities for the students in their classrooms.

As opportunities to offer professional learning to educators across the United States increased, so did the reach of the Equity and SEL Integration Framework. The well-defined framework with research and actionable steps was well received during virtual workshops, and in December 2020, a school system in Maryland requested that I develop a course featuring the framework. I created my own master class (Lifelong Learning Defined, 2021a), which other education organizations, like PBLMatters (n.d.) and the Illinois Digital Educators Alliance (2021), also featured. I also partnered with ISTE to develop a jump-start guide titled *SEL in Action: Tools to Help Students Learn and Grow* to help educators begin to use the framework (Valenzuela, 2021e).

I am extremely honored and humbled to add to this growing and much-needed body of knowledge through this book and my workshops. Advancing equity through SEL in various contexts, especially to help dismantle systemic racism, is one of the most important endeavors that educational institutions will tackle throughout the following years. We need to get this right for our students and our educational system.

Rationale for Step 4: Help Students Develop Emotional Intelligence Skills

Once the teachers were familiar with the CASEL 5, I identified and demonstrated the critical strategy of labeling emotions. They could use this strategy during lessons without losing their instructional focus by spending too much time doing SEL. I introduced and modeled labeling because psychologists inform us that being able to name emotions is the important prerequisite skill required for self-managing them (David & Congleton, 2013).

Once the teachers understood the power of naming emotions, I helped them begin to determine which of the CASEL 5 would be the focus of a strategy for managing the emotions. Scenarios for labeling emotions included having students use either emojis or Plutchik's (2001) seminal wheel of emotions to identify specific emotions they were experiencing regarding the learning goals for a lesson or a product or assessment they had to complete. We also discussed scenarios in which students doing distance learning felt stressed and sad or isolated because they were separated from friends and family. Having these discussions was especially significant in 2020 during the COVID-19 pandemic, when students were feeling overwhelmingly stressed and isolated.

Rationale for Step 5: Activate SEL in Your Lessons (Curriculum)

Once teachers were familiar with the CASEL 5 and the importance of having students label emotions within the contexts of self-awareness and social awareness, students could easily see how strategies that would teach them to self-manage could be integrated into everyday lessons. Those strategies include the following.

- Focus on breathing.
- Walk away momentarily by taking counted steps.
- Count up to or down from ten.
- Express emotions and feelings to the teacher.
- Create schedules and task lists.
- Take breaks.

Because those initial workshops were virtual, I purposefully modeled how to activate SEL in lessons using the technology tools and strategies described in chapter 10 (page 180). My tools of choice were Nearpod and Zoom breakout rooms.

To answer the question, "How can teachers leverage technology tools to augment SEL strategies during distance learning?" I modeled using Zoom breakout rooms to introduce simple SEL strategies (such as those in the preceding bulleted list) as possible interventions for helping students prepare for learning and not interrupting much instructional time. The teachers were permitted time to practice in small groups of colleagues in the breakout rooms—and were encouraged to mimic using of the tech (in this case, Zoom) with their students.

Results from these initial professional learning sessions with the North Carolina school system were encouraging and let me know we were on a good path to helping teachers incorporate SEL with students. One of the school leaders created a six-item testing instrument (using both five-point Likert scale and comment sections) to determine the participants' confidence in incorporating SEL in their lessons. A *five-point Likert scale* is a type of psychometric response scale in which participants specify their level of agreement to a statement: (1) strongly disagree, (2) disagree, (3) neither agree nor disagree, (4) agree, or (5) strongly agree (Ombea, 2020). This type of feedback provides quantitative values; I used the data to measure the workshop's overall effectiveness. I also used the data to inform the next steps for improving my work. I administered the survey to the following initial SEL professional learning workshops and provided the data in figures B.1, B.2, and B.3 (page 215). Survey questions related to time management and facilitator engagement are not included to keep the focus on the effectiveness of SEL integration in lessons and educators' emotional intelligence.

The following are some comments that participants submitted in response to the request to "rate the relevance of today's agenda to your role and responsibilities."

- "SEL holds not only the student's success but teachers' and parents' as well!"
- "I know I need to learn more about emotional regulation and emotional intelligence so I can effectively model that for our students. Thanks for the rich resources!"
- "Managing emotions is something that can't be overlooked or deemed irrelevant."
- "This has been a good reawakening of key elements in the education that we provide to young people."
- "The SEL lesson plan covers all aspects of a child, which ultimately impacts student achievement."
- "Today's agenda began with allowing us to realize we have to be aware of our own emotions before we can assist someone else."

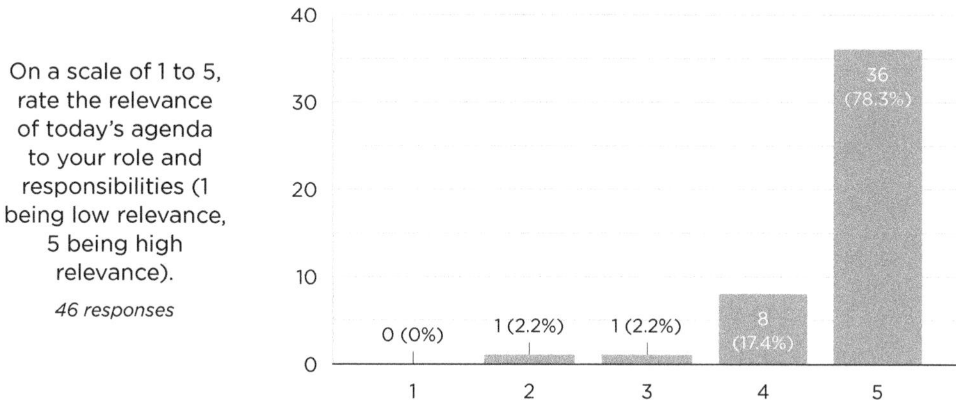

FIGURE B.1: Survey results following initial SEL integration professional learning sessions—Relevance.

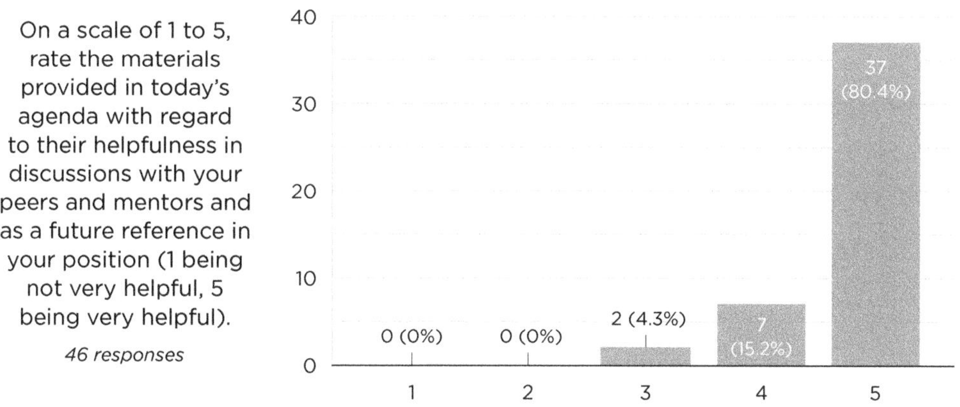

FIGURE B.2: Survey results following initial SEL integration professional learning sessions—Materials.

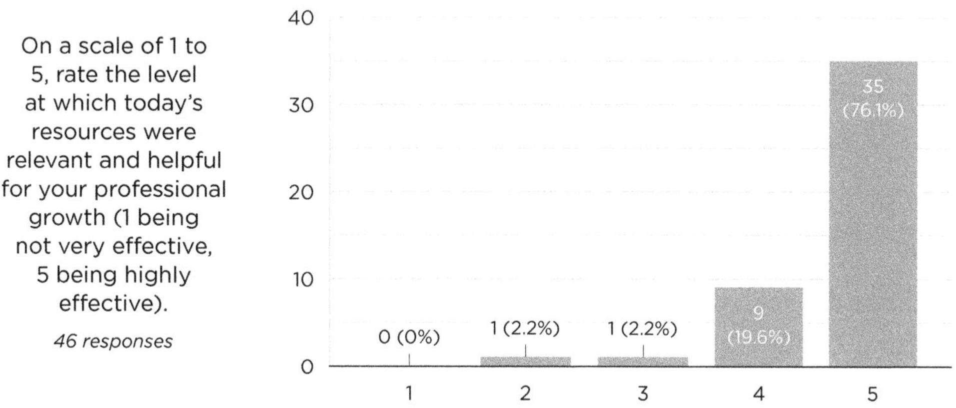

FIGURE B.3: Survey results following initial SEL integration professional learning sessions—Resources.

The following are some comments that participants submitted in response to the request to "rate the materials provided in today's agenda with regard to their helpfulness in discussions with your peers and mentors and as a future reference in your position."

- "Very good and necessary information."
- "The information provided was great! It is very important but often forgotten about."
- "I need to do a deep dive into emotional intelligence, and these are just the tools I need to do that!"
- "I liked the placement of SEL and [facilitator's] activities on the lesson plan."
- "Both staff and students are going to need so much emotional support when we all return to the classroom."
- "The reading and working with other teachers were very helpful."

The following are some comments that participants submitted in response to the request to "rate the level at which today's resources were relevant and helpful for your professional growth."

- "Students don't learn as well when they are emotionally distraught."
- "'This makes me more self-aware of the things I do and do not do."
- "Resources will help me in meeting the SEL needs of my students."
- "The article focused on helping educators build emotional intelligence was a great read. I will review it and the linked resources to better my emotional intelligence and enhance my instruction."
- "Prying into emotions is a sensitive topic because you never know what can be discovered."
- "Great articles were provided for our reading about SEL."
- "Jorge's resources are amazing and will be a big part of the SEL training and lesson planning."

The final item in the workshop survey was a response to the prompt, "In today's meeting, I really benefited most from . . ."

- "Understanding how to tie the SEL into your daily lesson plan."
- "The articles regarding social-emotional learning."
- "The emotional intelligence part."

- "Breakout session and group shares."
- "Seeing how we have to incorporate this in our classrooms with fidelity."
- "SEL strategies. I would like a copy of those strategies or least a way to access them at a later time."
- "Learning more about SEL and the different routes to take when dealing with emotions."
- "The different types of learning skills for coping with SEL."
- "How SEL is now going to be embedded into the lesson plans!"
- "[Feeling] that teachers need to know how to deal with their own emotions effectively so that they can teach their students. This was an awesome session. If teachers would only connect with their students, it would make for a better learning environment."
- "Working in my breakout session because it allowed us to discuss what we already do in the classroom and discuss some new strategies and ideas to implement in the classroom."
- "Reading the article and seeing how SEL is included in lesson plans."

Feedback About the Integration Framework From Professional Learning Sessions

A few articles I wrote uplifting some of the Equity and SEL Integration Framework practices caught the attention of several organizations that offer educators conferences. These organizations included ISTE, who invited me to be a featured speaker at their Summer Learning Academy in 2020. I had never discussed these topics with such a large audience before (fifteen thousand people registered), and I wanted to ensure that my message was accurate and helpful to the educators in attendance.

To prepare for the ISTE Summer Learning Academy, I requested that several educators and other experts on SEL, culturally responsive teaching, and racial equity provide me feedback using the critical friends protocol. This protocol is a simple-to-use structured feedback protocol for improving a piece of work (Valenzuela, 2022f).

I broke feedback I received from the critical friends protocol into five categories: (1) *I like*, (2) *I wonder*, (3), *I have (ideas for making it better)*, (4) *this glows* (referring to things done right), and (5) *this could grow* (referring to areas that need improvement or revision). This feedback included the following.

1. I like:
    - "I really like the way you introduce the fence conversation as an entry point to discuss sensitive topics and explain the Every Student Succeeds Act (ESSA) to inform audiences." (The fence here is a metaphor for barriers that cause inequities and disadvantages for those who can't see or get on the other side.)
    - "I like the language you used to say that you, too, are a learner, and you empathize through personal experience. The narrative is already in your experience ('I,' 'my,' 'my family,' 'anyone that knows me') and makes you relatable."
    - "I really like how you got meta for a sec when you delivered the SEL segment on self-awareness and self-management because it made me stop and think about that topic and how I manage it in my settings."
    - "I like your acknowledging the elephant in the room up front regarding hot topics like racial inequity. You did very well with these high-emotion issues."
    - "I like the flow and organization of the presentation; it is very clear that you are telling a story linking SEL to current times, technology, and society."
2. I wonder:
    - "What if you trimmed some of the personal stories to make time since you highlighted who you are in the intro?"
    - "Is there a way to better connect the section of culturally responsive teaching to online engagement? I feel like I missed it (maybe that's just me?)."
    - "I wonder if you can find a specific video to tie in SEL with equity within the classroom. Check out Civics for All. They may do this already."
3. I have (ideas for making it better):
    - "Maybe change the wording of *minorities* to *marginalized groups*, unless ESSA specifically states the word *minorities*?"
    - "Your presentation mentioned various pedagogies (culturally responsive teaching, restorative justice, and others) that you just showed on the one slide but didn't dive into necessarily. I am wondering what if you scaled back on project-based learning stuff at the end a bit and instead pointed to resources to buy you time?"

- "I wonder, for the pedagogy listed, if you can provide examples within the professional development (short samples from each): trauma-informed teaching, restorative justice, and others."

4. This glows:
    - "Starting the presentation speaking on social justice and George Floyd sets the precedent for the importance of this work."
    - "The Michael Jordan story was a great example to use when referring to equity and inclusion and SEL, especially when it came to self-awareness and self-confidence involving work. This is what we want educators to do by using stories of those alive—especially a man of color." (The Michael Jordan story referred to here is a lesson in always being in tune with your emotions—which is something I learned from watching him play basketball and apply to my work.)
    - "The personal story helped give a narrative to equity and inclusion and SEL work you did with yourself and your students."
    - "Going over steps 2 and 3 of your SEL article was really great. Place that table in the PDF you will share with participants after with maybe a blank template they can try themselves."
5. This could grow:
    - "Try to tie equity and inclusion with SEL verbally before sharing the article and SEL."
    - "Create a PDF with pedagogical resources from the slide if you decide not to use Nearpod. You can use a Google Form to get the answers from participants as they work through the presentation with you. The form will compile all responses on a spreadsheet for you."
    - "Be mindful of when you have participants writing something—there was some lag with timing of changing slides and writing responses."

I used their feedback to refine my message and content delivery—mainly in examples I provided to have teachers help their students through the trauma and difficult processing of emotions brought on by racial tensions in the United States. Additionally, I wanted the session to be transformative by providing the attendees with good steps to begin advancing racial equity through SEL. For this purpose, I offered them resources for starting the necessary work within themselves and for helping impacted students. Highlighted resources in the session included materials for restorative justice, culturally responsive teaching, and trauma-informed teaching—along with my advice for seeking out reputable professional development and relevant literature.

Truthfully, at the time, I wasn't sure how the session would be received, but I had strong convictions about what I designed for that night. The two-thousand-plus educators in attendance let me know exactly how they felt both in the Zoom chat box and on Twitter using the hashtag for the event, *#ISTEsla20*. Ellen Watson's (2020) systematic research review investigating the use of social media hashtags for K–12 professional learning reveals that hashtag data can show connections between individuals, content, and positive impact in classroom practices.

This feedback was very encouraging because I knew my SEL work was now more relevant and more impactful to educators everywhere. I knew this because ISTE draws an international education crowd. After that, I became more reputable as an SEL expert and began keynoting and presenting my SEL workshops to educators across the United States in public and independent (private and charter) schools and universities.

I did receive harsh criticism from some in my private Twitter messages for including race in an educational presentation. That taught me early on that although resistance and intimidation come with this territory, this "good trouble" is a small price to pay for helping students and teachers progress in their SEL work.

Shortly after ISTE's Summer Learning Academy, the district in North Carolina expressed a need to continue SEL work while intentionally becoming more culturally responsive and better equipped to have difficult conversations involving race and politics. As this was the school system's first time embarking on systemically tackling race, we had several intake calls to discuss and clearly define the district's DEI goals as part of preplanning for upcoming professional development sessions. Given the racial tensions and civil unrest throughout the United States, we began formulating goals centered on systemic equity, cultural and social competence, critical conversations, and how we could tie all of those to our previous SEL work.

Because we were attempting to cover several heavy topics, we agreed that we needed to immediately create a safe space for holding difficult but critical conversations—first among the administrative staff to align with a collective vision for DEI practices throughout the school system. I found my discussions with district leaders extremely beneficial at this time. I learned about the actual needs, which added examining one's beliefs as a step for formulating the framework. This was due to the insight the district superintendent shared during one of our semistructured interviews. During our interview, I recorded the following comment he shared:

> I was in a workshop recently on racial equity and learned that in addition to holding space for difficult conversations, it's important for people to examine their beliefs about others. That's because they can unconsciously . . . hold prejudice against them. It would be great if we as a staff would do that type of work together in a workshop.

The other school leaders and I agreed with his recommendations for having educators examine their personal beliefs. We also decided that we needed to identify the required steps for cultivating a shared vision that would activate SEL in lessons; we would use reliable and sound practices meant to jump-start equity and maintain it at the forefront of what educators did with students. For a brand-new workshop, our objectives therefore became to acknowledge and validate one another's thoughts and feelings about the day's current events (civil unrest) and to understand how implicit bias impacted students and how SEL could help everyone with emotion management.

Our first session to expand our SEL work with the aforementioned DEI focus included eighteen participants, who were a mix of principals and central-office administrators. The survey I administered after the workshop provided the following responses to four prompts: (1) *I saw*, (2) *I wonder*, (3) *I have*, and (4) *I need to know*.

1. I saw . . .
    - "The beginning of timely and important conversations."
    - "The learning circle as a way to build communities."
    - "How our biases can affect student achievement."
    - "The need for my staff to have this experience."
    - "How important it is to examine our own implicit biases and implement SEL strategies and activities into our lesson plans."
    - "The true essence of dealing with individual biases."
    - "A lot of adults engaged in self-reflection."
    - "The extreme importance of having crucial conversations with the staff."
    - "The impact of unconscious bias on our society."
    - "That we truly needed to see both the contrasts and similarities of equity and equality."
    - "The need to address equality for all students."
    - "Good instructional practices modeled."

2. I wonder . . .
    - "How will our staff receive and implement this information? Will they feel overwhelmed or value it?"
    - "How will teachers deliver these types of lessons?"
    - "How will our educational system look without teacher biases?"
    - "How do we go about changing and training all staff to not think about the biases and negative thoughts associated with our students to better educate them? It will definitely require more than one training."
    - "Will systemic racism end in our lifetime?"
    - "How will the students respond to these activities?"
    - "What would it look like to address all disparities during remote learning?"
    - "What would happen if every teacher made it their personal responsibility to ensure equity for all students in their classroom?"
    - "How can we use this more?"
    - "Will staff be able to see within themselves and find their implicit bias?"
    - "How will our teachers reflect when they get this material?"
    - "How will we use the training to get our teachers to incorporate this daily in their lesson delivery and interactions with our students?"
    - "How many people will talk about this at home?"
    - "If my people would love [themselves] more, and trust each other more, would racism have such a devastating impact on our society?"
    - "How receptive will teachers be to receive this training with an open mindset, in addition to incorporating it into the lesson design?"
    - "How will our staff absorb and respond to this information?"
    - "How do you get everyone to talk more?"
3. I have . . .
    - "Kept the effects of bias on the educational system at the forefront of teachers' minds through professional development sessions and citing examples within classrooms."
    - "To help end systemic racism; it begins with us and me!"
    - "[Learned] that learning circles will help keep students engaged."

- "To download the materials that were shared and look for other related topics."
- "[Been] processing how to lend my understanding to my colleagues in a concise manner."
- "[A thought that] I will need to do the sessions in three groups due to the size of my staff. I will check with other principals for their thoughts."
- "An idea of how I want to share with my staff."
- "Hope that this series of training will make a difference in the overall outcomes we see in our students at year's end."
- "To work hard as a school leader to enhance my understanding so that I can impactfully translate this knowledge and guidance to our teachers."
- "Decided to include SEL in an upcoming academically and intellectually gifted professional development. Academically and intellectually gifted students definitely struggle with social-emotional needs, and for many identified academically and intellectually gifted students, remote learning is extremely stressful."
- "[Thought] about the importance of having tough conversations, but it doesn't make me feel any more comfortable having them."
- "[Considered] teaching our parents to use learning circles also with their students."

4. I need to know . . .
    - "About myself to help others."
    - "More about implementing this activity."
    - "How we as educators can be part of changing mindsets that display systemic racism and refuse to change for the betterment of the nation. That is, what is happening now happened in the past and also will continue in the future."
    - "Have there been previous sessions with this group on this topic?"
    - "When my staff will have an opportunity to view this information."
    - "More of the concerns as [they pertain] to areas where we are not serving our students as well as we should in this area."
    - "That I can have crucial conversations that are effective and meaningful."

These data suggest that the school leaders in the workshop found the inclusion of implicit bias for examining their own beliefs about students relevant to the school system's ongoing SEL work and necessary for equitable teaching. The data also uncovered that using the circle practice strategy (Davenport, 2018) in the workshop helped build community and created the right space for holding difficult conversations; that strategy could be a valuable structure for allowing individuals to comfortably speak their truth. Circles have various uses in education, including academic, SEL, restorative, or reflective purposes. I found this all extremely encouraging because aligning these items to our previous SEL work now provided this particular district a framework with steps and DEI practices that help advance equity through social-emotional learning.

Following this session, the Equity and SEL Integration Framework became solidified and included the following four steps.

1. Understand the CASEL 5.
2. Assess your own unconscious biases.
3. Help students develop emotional intelligence skills.
4. Activate SEL in your lessons and curriculum.

But this work hadn't yet reached its zenith.

There is still so much to do to raise equity for students through SEL and other critical pedagogy (such as restorative justice). I am very grateful to have had the opportunity to develop the Equity and SEL Integration Framework along with so many colleagues and thought partners. I hope the education community views this book as an evergreen resource that anyone can pick up and take something positive from, no matter where they are in their equity journey.

References and Resources

AAPI Equity Alliance. (2020, September 17). *New report shows rising racism against Asian-American youth.* [Press Release]. Accessed at aapiequityalliance.org/new-report-shows-rising-racism-against-asian-american-youth on May 20, 2022.

Academy to Innovate HR. (2022). *Diversity, equity, inclusion and belonging (DEIB): A 2022 overview* [Blog post]. Accessed at www.aihr.com/blog/diversity-equity-inclusion-belonging-deib on May 19, 2022.

Admissionsly. (2020, November 21). *Bullying statistics: Breakdown by the facts and figures.* Accessed at admissionsly.com/bullying-statistics on December 15, 2021.

Agustina, E., & Suharya, T. (2021). Zoom breakout room for students' collaborative skill enhancement in history learning during COVID-19 outbreak. *International Journal of Research in Counseling and Education*, *5*(1), 33. doi.org/10.24036/00430za0002

Ahmed, K. M. (2021, April). *The impact of utilizing breakout rooms in ESL distance learning from students perspectives.* Accessed at www.researchgate.net/publication/350771174_The_Impact_of_Utilizing_Breakout_Rooms_in_ESL_Distance_Learning_from_Students_Perspectives on June 2, 2022.

Alexander, P. C. (2012). Retraumatization and revictimization: An attachment perspective. In M. P. Duckworth & V. M. Follette (Eds.), *Retraumatization: Assessment, treatment, and prevention* (pp. 191–220). New York: Routledge.

Allarakha, S. (2021, February 8). *What are the 3 types of trauma?* Accessed at www.medicinenet.com/what_are_the_3_types_of_trauma/article.htm on May 29, 2022.

Altman, A. (2020, June 4). Why the killing of George Floyd sparked an American uprising. *TIME.* Accessed at time.com/5847967/george-floyd-protests-trump on December 15, 2021.

American Psychological Association. (2008). *Stereotype threat widens achievement gap.* Accessed at www.apa.org/research/action/stereotype on December 15, 2021.

American Psychological Association. (2014). *What does transgender mean?* Accessed at www.apa.org/topics/lgbtq/transgender on December 15, 2021.

America's Story from America's Library. (n.d.). *Tennessee Valley Authority.* Accessed at www.americaslibrary.gov/es/tn/es_tn_tva_1.html on December 20, 2021.

Anderson, G. (2020, October 23). *The emotional toll of racism.* Accessed at www.insidehighered.com/news/2020/10/23/racism-fuels-poor-mental-health-outcomes-black-students on April 18, 2022.

Anirudh. (2014, June 5). *10 major accomplishments of Martin Luther King Jr.* Accessed at learnodo-newtonic.com/martin-luther-king-jr-accomplishments on December 15, 2021.

Anti-Defamation League. (2012, October 18). *Anti-bias tools and strategies.* Accessed at www.adl.org/resources/tools-and-strategies/anti-bias-tools-strategies on July 6, 2022.

Arora, C. (2021, May 21). *Bigs with badges: Police-student mentorship program exposes kids to LE careers.* Accessed at www.police1.com/police-jobs-and-careers/articles/bigs-with-badges-police-student-mentorship-program-exposes-kids-to-le-careers-wQmGqww4LYvx2V1O on May 19, 2022.

Ashbaugh, R. (2020, September 23). *6 ways to self-soothe when you're feeling triggered.* Accessed at solidfoundationstherapy.com/6-way-to-self-soothe-when-youre-feeling-triggered on December 15, 2021.

Association for Supervision and Curriculum Development. (2012). *Understanding by Design (UbD) framework by Jay McTighe and Grant Wiggins* [White paper]. Accessed at files.ascd.org/staticfiles/ascd/pdf/siteASCD/publications/UbD_WhitePaper0312.pdf on July 6, 2022.

Association for Supervision and Curriculum Development. (2018, October 4). *5 tips for successful SEL implementation.* Accessed at www.ascd.org/el/articles/five-tips-for-successful-sel-implementation on May 31, 2022.

Association for Supervision and Curriculum Development. (2022). *Professional learning.* Accessed at www.ascd.org/services on May 2, 2022.

Augustine, C. H., Engberg, J., Grimm, G. E., Lee, E., Wang, E. L., Christianson, K., et al. (2018). *Can restorative practices improve school climate and curb suspensions? An evaluation of the impact of restorative practices in a mid-sized urban school district.* Santa Monica, CA: RAND. Accessed at www.rand.org/pubs/research_reports/RR2840.html on December 15, 2021.

Baikie, K. & Wilhelm, K. (2005). Emotional and physical benefits of expressive writing. *Advances in Psychiatric Treatment, 11*(1), 338-346.

Barber, C. E., & Vega, L. D. (2011). Conflict, cultural marginalization, and personal costs of filial caregiving. *Journal of Cultural Diversity, 18*(1), 20–28.

Barkley, S. (2019, February 10). *The impact of knowing and being known* [Blog post]. Accessed at barkleypd.com/blog/knowing-your-students on April 14, 2022.

Bass, K. (2020, June 25). *House passes George Floyd Justice in Policing Act* [Press release]. Accessed at bass.house.gov/media-center/press-releases/house-passes-george-floyd-justice-policing-act on December 15, 2021.

Bastos, F. (2022). *The benefits of journaling for your mental health and how to start it.* Accessed at mindowl.org/the-benefits-of-journaling-for-your-mental-health-and-how-to-start-it on April 5, 2022.

Bay City News. (2020, March 19). *Website launches to document anti-Asian hate crimes in wake of COVID-19.* Accessed at www.nbcbayarea.com/news/coronavirus/website-launches-to-document-anti-asian-hate-crimes-in-wake-of-covid-19/2258297 on May 20, 2022.

BBC News. (2021a, April 1). *Derek Chauvin trial: New footage shows George Floyd pleading with officers.* Accessed at www.bbc.com/news/world-us-canada-56594099 on May 18, 2022.

BBC News. (2021b, April 20). *George Floyd: US city on edge as jury deliberates Chauvin verdict.* Accessed at www.bbc.com/news/world-us-canada-56806961 on May 18, 2022.

Bennett, S. (2007) *That workshop book: New systems and structures for classrooms that read, write, and think.* Portsmouth, NH: Heinemann.

Berman, M., Sullivan, J., Tate, J., & Jenkins, J. (2020, June 8). Protests spread over police shootings. Police promised reforms. Every year, they still shoot and kill nearly 1,000 people. *The Washington Post.* Accessed at www.washingtonpost.com/investigations/protests-spread-over-police-shootings-police-promised-reforms-every-year-they-still-shoot-nearly-1000-people/2020/06/08/5c204f0c-a67c-11ea-b473-04905b1af82b_story.html on December 15, 2021.

Bernstein, L. (2020, June 9). *America has 18,000 police agencies, no national standards; experts say that's a problem.* Accessed at wjla.com/news/nation-world/america-has-18000-police-agencies-no-national-standards-experts-say-thats-a-problem on December 15, 2021.

Big Brothers Big Sisters. (n.d.). *Bigs with badges.* Accessed at bbbs-sac.org/bigs-with-badges on May 19, 2022.

Blackburn, B. (2018, December 13). *Productive struggle is a learner's sweet spot.* Accessed at www.ascd.org/el/articles/productive-struggle-is-a-learners-sweet-spot on February 3, 2021.

Blad, E. (2022, June 23). *There's pushback to social-emotional learning. here's what happened in one state.* Education Week. Retrieved September 13, 2022, from www.edweek.org/education/theres-pushback-to-social-emotional-learning-heres-what-happened-in-one-state/2020/02

Bland, D. J. (2020, December 21). *What is an empathy map?* [Blog post]. Accessed at www.accenture.com/us-en/blogs/software-engineering-blog/what-is-an-empathy-map on April 17, 2022.

Blascovich, J., Spencer, S. J., Quinn, D., & Steele, C. (2001). African Americans and high blood pressure: The role of stereotype threat. *Psychological Science, 12*(3), 225–229. doi.org/10.1111/1467-9280.00340

Blended Learning Universe. (2021). *Blended learning models.* Accessed at www.blendedlearning.org/models on December 15, 2021.

Block, M. (2022, March 29). *How Florida teachers plan to deal with "Don't Say Gay" rules.* Accessed at www.npr.org/2022/03/29/1089533801/how-florida-teachers-plan-to-deal-with-dont-say-gay-rules on May 23, 2022.

Bowen, R. S. (2017). *Understanding by Design.* Nashville, TN: Vanderbilt University Center for Teaching. Accessed at cft.vanderbilt.edu/understanding-by-design on June 17, 2022.

Bowman, J. D. (2018, June 20). *Making the most of visual aids.* Accessed at www.edutopia.org/article/making-most-visual-aids on May 11, 2022.

Bradberry, T., & Greaves, J. (2009). *Emotional intelligence 2.0.* San Diego, CA: TalentSmart.

Brandt, A. (2019, October 2). To heal from trauma, you have to feel your feelings [Blog post]. *Psychology Today.* Accessed at www.psychologytoday.com/us/blog/mindful-anger/201910/heal-trauma-you-have-feel-your-feelings on December 15, 2021.

Briggs, S. (2014, July 5). *Why self-esteem hurts learning but self-confidence does the opposite.* Accessed at www.opencolleges.edu.au/informed/features/self-efficacy-and-learning on December 15, 2021.

Brown, L. (2018, February 21). *People with true integrity have these 19 awesome traits.* Accessed at hackspirit.com/people-true-integrity-13-special-traits on December 15, 2021.

Brown, M. A. (2017). Being heard: How a listening culture supports the implementation of schoolwide restorative practices. *Restorative Justice: An International Journal, 5*(1), 53–69.

Budiman, A. (2020, August 20). *Key findings about U.S. immigrants.* Accessed at www.pewresearch.org/fact-tank/2020/08/20/key-findings-about-u-s-immigrants on December 15, 2021.

Burton, L. (2016, September 20). *ISTE student standards promote equity in education.* Accessed at www.iste.org/explore/ISTE-Standards-in-Action/ISTE-student-standards-promote-equity-in-education on December 15, 2021.

Byrd, C. M. (2016). Does culturally relevant teaching work? An examination from student perspectives. *SAGE Open, 6*(3). Accessed at journals.sagepub.com/doi/10.1177/2158244016660744 on December 15, 2021.

Campellone, J., & Turley, R. K. (2021). Understanding the teen brain. *University of Rochester Medical Center health encyclopedia.* Accessed at www.urmc.rochester.edu/encyclopedia/content.aspx?contenttypeid=1&contentid=3051 on December 15, 2021.

Cantor, P., Osher, D., Berg, J., Steyer, L., & Rose, T. (2019). Malleability, plasticity, and individuality: How children learn and develop in context. *Applied Developmental Science, 23*(4), 307–337.

Carratala, S., & Maxwell, C. (2020, May 7). *Health disparities by race and ethnicity* [Fact sheet]. Washington, DC: Center for American Progress. Accessed at www.americanprogress.org/article/health-disparities-race-ethnicity on December 15, 2021.

Carson, C. (n.d.). *American civil rights movement.* Accessed at www.britannica.com/event/American-civil-rights-movement on December 15, 2021.

Cascade Behavioral Health Hospital. (2021). *Symptoms, signs and effects of psychological trauma.* Accessed at www.cascadebh.com/behavioral/trauma/signs-symptoms-effects on December 15, 2021.

Castle, B. (2019, December 30). *What is marginalization and what can you do about it?* [Blog post]. Accessed at www.inhersight.com/blog/guide/marginalization on December 15, 2021.

Castro-Olivo, S. M. (2014). Promoting social-emotional learning in adolescent Latino ELLs: A study of the culturally adapted Strong Teens program. *School Psychology Quarterly, 29*(4), 567–577.

Causey, J., Huie, F., Lang, R., Ryu, M., & Shapiro, D. (2020). *Completing college 2020: A national view of student completion rates for 2014 entering cohort.* Herndon, VA: National Student Clearinghouse Research Center.

Cavanagh, T., Vigil, P., & Garcia, E. (2014). A story legitimating the voices of Latino/Hispanic students and their parents: Creating a restorative justice response to wrongdoing and conflict in schools. *Equity & Excellence in Education, 47*(4), 565–579.

Cavell, T. (2015, May 15). *Fact #8: Emotions are subjective and temporary.* Accessed at drtimcavell.com/fact-8-emotions-subjective-temporary on December 15, 2021.

Center for Public Education. (2016, January). *Educational equity: What does it mean? How do we know when we reach it?* Accessed at www.nsba.org/-/media/NSBA/File/cpe-educational-equity-research-brief-january-2016.pdf on December 16, 2021.

Center for the Study of Hate and Extremism. (2021). *Report to the nation: Anti-Asian prejudice and hate crime—City data chart (June 1, 2021).* Accessed at www.csusb.edu/hate-and-extremism-center on May 20, 2022.

Centers for Disease Control and Prevention. (2016). *Understanding school violence* [Fact sheet]. Accessed at www.cdc.gov/violenceprevention/pdf/school_violence_fact_sheet-a.pdf on April 18, 2022.

Centers for Disease Control and Prevention. (2018). *Coping with a disaster or traumatic event.* Accessed at emergency.cdc.gov/coping/index.asp on December 15, 2021.

Centers for Disease Control and Prevention. (2020). *2019 Youth Risk Behavior Surveillance System (YRBSS)*. Accessed at www.cdc.gov/healthyyouth/data/yrbs/index.htm on July 6, 2022.

Chao, M. M. (2018, July 17). *Mindset matters: From cultural mindset to multicultural competence*. Accessed at globalnetwork.io/perspectives/2018/07/mindset-matters-cultural-mindset-multicultural-competence on December 16, 2021.

Charter for Compassion. (2021). *Marginalized populations: Treatment of people*. Accessed at charterforcompassion.org/charter-tool-box-a-framework-for-getting-started/marginalized-populations-treatment-of-people on December 16, 2021.

Cherng, H. Y. S. (2017). If they think I can: Teacher bias and youth of color expectations and achievement. *Social Science Research*, *66*, 170–186. doi.org/10.1016/j.ssresearch.2017.04.001

Cherry, K. (2020a, September 18). *How does implicit bias influence behavior? Explanations and impacts of unconscious bias*. Accessed at www.verywellmind.com/implicit-bias-overview-4178401 on April 9, 2022.

Cherry, K. (2020b, May 7). *The 6 major theories of emotion*. Accessed at www.verywellmind.com/theories-of-emotion-2795717 on December 16, 2021.

Cherry, K. (2020c, March 9). *What is cognition?* Accessed at www.verywellmind.com/what-is-cognition-2794982 on December 16, 2021.

Cherry, K. (2021, August 16). *8 basic psychology facts you need to know*. Accessed at www.verywellmind.com/psychology-basics-4157186 on December 16, 2021.

Cherry, K. (2022, February 25). *Emotions and types of emotional responses: The three key elements that make up emotion*. Accessed at www.verywellmind.com/what-are-emotions-2795178 on April 2, 2022.

Chicago Public Schools. (n.d.). *Chicago Public Schools restorative practices guide and toolkit*. Chicago: Author. Accessed at blog.cps.edu/wp-content/uploads/2017/08/CPS_RP_Booklet.pdf on May 12, 2022.

Children's Defense Fund. (2020). *The State of America's Children 2020*. Washington, DC: Author. Accessed at www.childrensdefense.org/wp-content/uploads/2020/02/The-State-Of-Americas-Children-2020.pdf on April 18, 2022.

Childs, S. (2020, October 23). Five mindsets to help leaders approach DEI conversations with their team. *Forbes*. Accessed at www.forbes.com/sites/forbeshumanresourcescouncil/2020/10/23/five-mindsets-to-help-leaders-approach-dei-conversations-with-their-team/?sh=43aee02c8682 on April 11, 2022.

Clark, J. S., Porath, S., Thiele, J., & Jobe, M. (2020). *Action research*. Manhattan, KS: New Prairie Press eBooks. Accessed at newprairiepress.org/ebooks/34 on June 21, 2022.

Clarke, A., Sorgenfrei, M., Mulcahy, J., Davie, P., Friedrich, C., & McBride, T. (2021). *Adolescent mental health: A systematic review on the effectiveness of school-based interventions*. London: Early Intervention Foundation. Accessed at www.eif.org.uk/report/adolescent-mental-health-a-systematic-review-on-the-effectiveness-of-school-based-interventions on June 17, 2022.

Clements, L. (2021, March 9). *COVID in Wales: Racist incidents 'take your breath away.'* Accessed at www.bbc.com/news/uk-wales-56323775 on May 20, 2022.

CNN. (2021, May 21). *How George Floyd's death reignited a movement*. Accessed at www.cnn.com/2021/05/21/us/gallery/george-floyd-protests-2020-look-back/index.html on May 13, 2022.

Cohen, R. K., Opatosky, D. K., Savage, J., Stevens, S. O., & Darrah, E. P. (2021). *The metacognitive student: How to teach academic, social, and emotional intelligence in every content area*. Bloomington, IN: Solution Tree Press.

Colburn, L., & Beggs, L. (2021). *The wraparound guide: How to gather student voice, build community partnerships, and cultivate hope*. Bloomington, IN: Solution Tree Press.

Colby, S. L., & Ortman, J. M. (2015). *Projections of the size and composition of the U.S. population: 2014 to 2060*. Washington, DC: U.S. Census Bureau. Accessed at www.census.gov/content/dam/Census/library/publications/2015/demo/p25-1143.pdf on December 16, 2021.

Cole, S. F., Eisner, A., Gregory, M., & Ristuccia, J. (2013). *Helping traumatized children learn, volume 2: Creating and advocating for trauma-sensitive schools*. Boston: Massachusetts Advocates for Children. Accessed at traumasensitiveschools.org/wp-content/uploads/2013/11/HTCL-Vol-2-Creating-and-Advocating-for-TSS.pdf on July 6, 2022.

Collaborative for Academic, Social, and Emotional Learning. (n.d.). *What is the CASEL framework?* Accessed at casel.org/fundamentals-of-sel/what -is-the-casel-framework on July 6, 2022.

Collaborative for Academic, Social, and Emotional Learning. (2020a). *Restorative practices and SEL alignment*. Accessed at schoolguide.casel.org/resource/restorative-practices-and-sel-alignment on December 15, 2021.

Collaborative for Academic, Social, and Emotional Learning. (2020b). *SEL framework: What are the core competence areas and where are they promoted?* Accessed at casel.s3.us-east-2.amazonaws.com/CASEL-SEL-Framework-11.2020.pdf on December 15, 2021.

Collaborative for Academic, Social, and Emotional Learning. (2021a). *The CASEL guide to schoolwide SEL essentials: A printable compilation of key activities and tools for school teams*. Accessed at schoolguide.casel.org/resource/the-casel-guide-to-schoolwide-sel-essentials on December 15, 2021.

Collaborative for Academic, Social, and Emotional Learning. (2021b). *Collaborating States Initiative*. Accessed at casel.org/collaborative-state-initiative on December 15, 2021.

Collaborative for Academic, Social, and Emotional Learning. (2021c). *What does the research say?* Accessed at casel.org/fundamentals-of-sel/what-does-the-research-say on December 15, 2021.

Common Core State Standards Initiative. (2022). *English language arts standards » Anchor standards » College and career readiness anchor standards for speaking and listening*. Accessed at www.corestandards.org/ELA-Literacy/CCRA/SL on April 20, 2022.

Connaughton, A. (2021, October 13). *Americans see stronger societal conflicts than people in other advanced economies*. Accessed at www.pewresearch.org/fact-tank/2021/10/13/americans-see-stronger-societal-conflicts-than-people-in-other-advanced-economies on May 17, 2022.

Connor, C. M., Morrison, F. J., Fishman, B. J., Giuliani, S., Luck, M., Underwood, P. S., et al. (2011). Testing the impact of child characteristics × instruction interactions on third graders' reading comprehension by differentiating literacy instruction. *Reading Research Quarterly, 46*(3), 189–221.

Connor, C. M., Morrison, F. J., Fishman, B. J., Schatschneider, C., & Underwood, P. (2007). Algorithm-guided individualized reading instruction. *Science, 315*(5811), 464–465.

Cook-Cottone, C. (2013). Dosage as a critical variable in yoga therapy research. *International Journal of Yoga Therapy, 23*(2), 11–12.

Costello, D., & Duvall, T. (2020, May 12). How did Breonna Taylor die? What to know about the Louisville woman shot by police. *Courier Journal.* Accessed at www.courier-journal.com/story/news/local/2020/05/12/breonna-taylor-case-what-know-louisville-emt-killed-cops/3110066001 on December 16, 2021.

Covey, S. R. (2013). *The 7 habits of highly effective people: Powerful lessons in personal change.* New York: Simon & Schuster.

Crosby, S. D. (2015). An ecological perspective on emerging trauma-informed teaching practices. *Children & Schools, 37*(4), 223–230. doi.org/10.1093/cs/cdv027

Cuncic, A. (2022, February 8). *What is homophobia?* Accessed at www.verywellmind.com/what-is-homophobia-5077409 on May 26, 2022.

Curtis, C. (2020, October 13). *Isolated students may struggle to stay mentally healthy.* Accessed at www.edutopia.org/article/isolated-students-may-struggle-stay-mentally-healthy on May 13, 2022.

Darling-Hammond, L., & Cook-Harvey, C. M. (2018). *Educating the whole child: Improving school climate to support student success.* Palo Alto, CA: Learning Policy Institute.

Darling-Hammond, L., Schachner, A., & Edgerton, A. K. (2020). *Restarting and reinventing school: Learning in the time of COVID and beyond.* Palo Alto, CA: Learning Policy Institute.

Davenport, M. (2018, August 16). *Using circle practice in the classroom.* Accessed at www.edutopia.org/article/using-circle-practice-classroom on December 16, 2021.

David, S. (2016, November 10). 3 ways to better understand your emotions. *Harvard Business Review.* Accessed at hbr.org/2016/11/3-ways-to-better-understand-your-emotions on December 16, 2021.

David, S., & Congleton, C. (2013, November). Emotional agility. *Harvard Business Review.* Accessed at hbr.org/2013/11/emotional-agility on December 16, 2021.

Davis, E., Jr. (2022, May 25). What to know about Ukrainian refugees in the U.S. *U.S. News & World Report.* Accessed at www.usnews.com/news/national-news/articles/2022-05-25/explainer-what-to-know-about-ukrainian-refugees-in-the-u-s on May 29, 2022.

Davis, M. (2015, October 29). *Restorative justice: Resources for schools* [Blog post]. Accessed at www.edutopia.org/blog/restorative-justice-resources-matt-davis on December 16, 2021.

Day, H. T. [@HeatherTDay]. (2020, May 9). *There is a difference between a person who hurts you by making a mistake, and a person who hurts you by continuing a pattern. Mistakes can be forgiven. Patterns should be broken* [Tweet]. Accessed at twitter.com/heathertday/status/1259141101660901377 on April 7, 2022.

DeJonckheere, M., & Vaughn, L. M. (2019). Semistructured interviewing in primary care research: A balance of relationship and rigour. *Family Medicine and Community Health, 7*(2), 1–8. https://doi.org/10.1136/fmch-2018-000057

De La Rosa, S. (2021, June 28). *How can schools re-engage "missing" students ahead of fall?* Accessed at www.k12dive.com/news/how-can-schools-re-engage-missing-students-ahead-of-fall/602476 on May 9, 2022.

Desautels, L. (2020, January 23). *Supporting students affected by trauma.* Accessed at www.edutopia.org/article/supporting-students-affected-trauma on July 6, 2022.

DeSilver, D., Lipka, M., & Fahmy, D. (2020, June 3). *10 things we know about race and policing in the U.S.* Accessed at www.pewresearch.org/fact-tank/2020/06/03/10-things-we-know-about-race-and-policing-in-the-u-s on December 17, 2021.

Dhaliwal, T. K., Chin, M. J., Lovison, V. S., & Quinn, D. M. (2020, July 20). *Educator bias is associated with racial disparities in student achievement and discipline* [Blog post]. Accessed at www.brookings.edu/blog/brown-center-chalkboard/2020/07/20/educator-bias-is-associated-with-racial-disparities-in-student-achievement-and-discipline on April 18, 2022.

Diffen. (n.d.). *Immigrant vs. refugee.* Accessed at www.diffen.com/difference/Immigrant_vs_Refugee on May 29, 2022.

Divecha, D., & Brackett, M. (2020). Rethinking school-based bullying prevention through the lens of social and emotional learning: A bioecological perspective. *International Journal of Bullying Prevention, 2,* 93–113. doi.org/10.1007/s42380-019-00019-5

Dolan, E. W. (2018, November 20). *People who experience traumatic events as children are more empathetic as adults.* Accessed at www.psypost.org/2018/11/people-who-experience-traumatic-events-as-children-are-more-empathetic-as-adults-52640 on December 17, 2021.

Drake, B., & Kiley, J. (2019, July 18). *Americans say the nation's political debate has grown more toxic and "heated" rhetoric could lead to violence.* Accessed at www.pewresearch.org/fact-tank/2019/07/18/americans-say-the-nations-political-debate-has-grown-more-toxic-and-heated-rhetoric-could-lead-to-violence on April 26, 2022.

Duncan, A. (2010, July 14). *Equity and education reform: Secretary Arne Duncan's remarks at the annual meeting of the National Association for the Advancement of Colored People (NAACP)* [Speech]. U.S. Department of Education. Accessed at www.ed.gov/news/speeches/equity-and-education-reform-secretary-arne-duncans-remarks-annual-meeting-national-association-advancement-colored-people-naacp on December 20, 2021.

Durlak, J. A., Weissberg, R. P., Dymnicki, A. B., Taylor, R. D., & Schellinger, K. B. (2011). The impact of enhancing students' social and emotional learning: A meta-analysis of school-based universal interventions. *Child Development, 82*(1), 405–432.

Eddy, S. L., & Hogan, K. A. (2014). Getting under the hood: How and for whom does increasing course structure work? *CBE: Life Sciences Education, 13*(3), 453–468.

Edsys. (2018, May 14). *15 best pedagogical strategies for innovative learning.* Accessed at www.edsys.in/best-pedagogical-strategies on December 17, 2021.

Education Week. (2016). *Student trauma: How school leaders can respond.* Accessed at www.edweek.org/leadership/student-trauma on July 6, 2022.

Edutopia. (2016, November 1). *Critique protocol: Helping students produce high-quality work* [Video]. www.edutopia.org/video/critique-protocol-helping-students-produce-high-quality-work

Edutopia. (2018a, February 4). *Creating a dedicated space for reflection* [Video]. www.edutopia.org/video/creating-dedicated-space-reflection

Edutopia. (2018b, February 5). *A daily support system for students* [Video]. www.edutopia.org/video/daily-support-system-students

Edutopia. (2021, August 25). *Building relationships with empathy maps* [Video]. www.edutopia.org/video/building-relationships-empathy-maps

Eisenberger, N. I., Lieberman, M. D., & Williams, K. D. (2003). Does rejection hurt? An FMRI study of social exclusion. *Science, 302*(5643), 290–292.

Eldridge, A. (n.d.). *What's the difference between a migrant and a refugee?* Accessed at www.britannica.com/story/whats-the-difference-between-a-migrant-and-a-refugee on May 29, 2022.

EL Education. (n.d.). *Ron Berger.* Accessed at eleducation.org/about/staff/ron-berger on June 13, 2022.

Elias, M. J., & Leverett, L. (2011). Consultation to urban schools for improvements in academics and behavior: No alibis. No excuses. No exceptions. *Journal of Educational and Psychological Consultation, 21*(1), 28–45.

Ellis, C. (2019, January 30). *Why emotion plays a critical role in decision making*. Accessed at www.thedrum.com/news/2019/01/30/why-emotion-plays-critical-role-decision-making on December 15, 2021.

Erdman, C. (2021, April 5). History in its entirety: How whitewashed history education leaves much of history, students out. *The Badger Herald*. Accessed at badgerherald.com/features/2021/04/05/history-in-its-entirety-how-whitewashed-history-education-leave-much-of-history-students-out on April 11, 2022.

Evans, A. C. (2021, June 14). *The school-to-prison pipeline: Definition, examples and implications*. Accessed at study.com/academy/lesson/the-school-to-prison-pipeline-definition-examples-implications.html on May 11, 2022.

Fahey, S., Moura, K., & Saarinen, J. (2019). *The educator's guide to Flipgrid: Version 4*. Accessed at static.flipgrid.com/docs/Flipgrid_eBook_2nd_edition.pdf on July 6, 2022.

Ferlazzo, L. (2020, March 10): Culturally responsive teaching is not a quick fix. *Education Week*. Accessed at www.edweek.org/teaching-learning/opinion-culturally-responsive-teaching-is-not-a-quick-fix/2020/03 on July 6, 2022.

Fester, J., & Valenzuela, J. (2021). *Environmental science for grades 6-12: A project-based approach to solving the earth's most urgent problems*. Portland, OR: International Society for Technology in Education.

Finley, T. (2013, June 24). *Rethinking whole class discussion* [Blog post]. Accessed at www.edutopia.org/blog/rethinking-whole-class-discussion-todd-finley on April 20, 2022.

Finley, T. (2014, August 14). *Relationship building through culturally responsive classroom management* [Blog post]. Accessed at www.edutopia.org/blog/relationship-building-culturally-responsive-classroom-todd-finley on December 20, 2021.

Finley, T. (2019, March 25). *A look at implicit bias and microaggressions*. Accessed at www.edutopia.org/article/look-implicit-bias-and-microaggressions on July 6, 2022.

Fisher, D., & Frey, N. (2014). Content area vocabulary learning. *The Reading Teacher, 67*(8), 594–599. doi.org/10.1002/trtr.1258

Fitzsimmons, S., Vora, D., Martin, L., Raheem, S., Pekerti, A., & Lakshman, C. (2019, December 2). What makes you "multicultural." *Harvard Business Review*. Accessed at hbr.org/2019/12/what-makes-you-multicultural on December 20, 2021.

Flannery, M. E. (2016, November 3). *How schools are helping traumatized students learn again*. Accessed at www.nea.org/advocating-for-change/new-from-nea/how-schools-are-helping-traumatized-students-learn-again on July 6, 2022.

Florian, L. (2015). Conceptualising inclusive pedagogy: The inclusive pedagogical approach in action. In J. M. Deppeler, T. Loreman, R. Smith, & L. Florian (Eds.), *Inclusive pedagogy across the curriculum* (pp. 11–24). Bingley, England: Emerald.

Fort Worth Independent School District. (n.d.). *Examples of sentence stems*. Accessed at www.fwisd.org/Page/14628 on June 2, 2022.

Freidel, F., & Sidey, H. (2006). *Franklin D. Roosevelt: The 32nd president of the United States*. Accessed at www.whitehouse.gov/about-the-white-house/presidents/franklin-d-roosevelt on December 20, 2021.

Friday, M. J. (2014, July 11). *Why storytelling in the classroom matters* [Blog post]. Accessed at www.edutopia.org/blog/storytelling-in-the-classroom-matters-matthew-friday on December 20, 2021.

Froehle, C. (2016, April 14). *The evolution of an accidental meme*. Accessed at medium.com/@CRA1G/the-evolution-of-an-accidental-meme-ddc4e139e0e4 on December 20, 2021.

Fronius, T., Darling-Hammond, S., Persson, H., Guckenburg, S., Hurley, N., & Petrosino A. (2019, March). *Restorative justice in U.S. schools: An updated research review*. Washington, DC: WestEd Justice and Prevention Research Center. Accessed at www.wested.org/wp-content/uploads/2019/04/resource-restorative-justice-in-u-s-schools-an-updated-research-review.pdf on December 20, 2021.

Fuhrman, R. (2020, September 15). *Learning to recognize and celebrate students' cultural experiences*. Accessed at www.edutopia.org/article/learning-recognize-and-celebrate-students-cultural-experiences on December 20, 2021.

Gawande, A. (2011). *The checklist manifesto: How to get things right*. London: Profile Books.

Gay, G. (2018). *Culturally responsive teaching: Theory, research, and practice* (3rd ed.). New York: Teachers College Press.

Gear Patrol. (2020, June 1). *A directory of brands and retailers that have spoken out against racism*. Accessed at www.gearpatrol.com/briefings/a733181/brands-standing-against-racism on December 20, 2021.

Gersema, E. (2022, May 3). *Increasing discord over abortion, LGBTQ+ issues keep polarization levels high*. Accessed at news.usc.edu/199165/increasing-discord-over-abortion-lgbtq-issues-keep-polarization-levels-high on May 29, 2022.

Gershenson, S., Holt S. B., & Papageorge, N. (2015). *Who believes in me? The effect of student-teacher demographic match on teacher expectations* (Upjohn Institute Working Paper 15-231). Kalamazoo, MI: W. E. Upjohn Institute for Employment Research. doi.org/10.17848/wp15-231

Gewertz, C. (2021, June 1). Forbidding remote learning: Why some schools won't offer a virtual option this fall. *Education Week*. Accessed at www.edweek.org/leadership/forbidding-remote-learning-why-some-schools-wont-offer-a-virtual-option-this-fall/2021/06 on May 31, 2022.

The Global Food Fund. (n.d.). *The issues*. Accessed at globalgoodfund.org/fellowship/issues on June 2, 2022.

The Glossary of Education Reform. (2013, December 13). *Backward design*. Accessed at www.edglossary.org/backward-design on December 20, 2021.

Gonser, S. (2020, July 24). *How to start talking about race in the early elementary classroom*. Accessed at www.edutopia.org/article/how-start-talking-about-race-early-elementary-classroom on December 20, 2021.

Gonzalez, J. (2017, September 10). *Culturally responsive teaching: 4 misconceptions*. Accessed at www.cultofpedagogy.com/culturally-responsive-misconceptions on December 20, 2021.

Good, K., & Shaw, A. (2022, February 14). Why kids are afraid to ask for help. *Scientific American*. Accessed at www.scientificamerican.com/article/why-kids-are-afraid-to-ask-for-help on April 10, 2022.

Grafwallner, P. (2021). *Not yet . . . and that's OK: How productive struggle fosters student learning*. Bloomington, IN: Solution Tree Press.

Graham, S. (2012). [Review of the book *Teaching and Researching Listening*, by Rost, M.]. *International Journal of Applied Linguistics*, *22*(3), 420–423. doi.org/10.1111/ijal.12003

Gray, D., Brown, S., & Macanufo, J. (2010). *Gamestorming: A playbook for innovators, rulebreakers, and changemakers*. Sebastopol, CA: O'Reilly.

Greenberg, M. (2017, August 29). 3 negative thinking patterns to avoid: What to do instead [Blog post]. *Psychology Today*. Accessed at www.psychologytoday.com/us/blog/the-mindful-self-express/201708/3-negative-thinking-patterns-avoid-what-do-instead on December 20, 2021.

Greenhow, C. (2020, June 4). *Ask the expert: Online learning vs. classroom learning*. Accessed at msutoday.msu.edu/news/2020/ask-the-expert-online-learning-vs-classroom-learning on December 20, 2021.

Greenwald, A. G., & Banaji, M. R. (1995). Implicit social cognition: Attitudes, self-esteem, and stereotypes. *Psychological Review, 102*(1), 4–27.

Grinberg, E., & Larned, V. (2018, October 3). *This is what happens when gender roles are forced on kids*. Accessed at www.cnn.com/2017/09/20/health/geas-gender-stereotypes-study/index.html on May 24, 2022.

Grinberg, E. (2019, June 14). *Pride + progress: What the "Q" in LGBTQ stands for, and other identity terms explained*. Accessed at www.cnn.com/interactive/2019/06/health/lgbtq-explainer on December 15, 2021.

Griner, A. C., & Stewart, M. L. (2013). Addressing the achievement gap and disproportionality through the use of culturally responsive teaching practices. *Urban Education, 48*(4), 585–621. doi.org/10.1177/0042085912456847

Groshell, Z. (2019, October 21). *What is instructional design and does it matter for K–12 education?* Accessed at https://educationrickshaw.com/2019/10/21/what-is-instructional-design-and-does-it-matter-for-k-12-education on December 20, 2021.

Gross, J. J. (1998). Sharpening the focus: Emotion regulation, arousal, and social competence. *Psychological Inquiry, 9*(4), 287–290. https://doi.org/10.1207/s15327965pli0904_8

Gross, J. J. (2002). Emotion regulation: Affective, cognitive, and social consequences. *Psychophysiology, 39*(3), 281–291. https://doi.org/10.1017/S0048577201393198

Gross, J. J. (2015). The extended process model of emotion regulation: Elaborations, applications, and future directions. *Psychological Inquiry, 26*(1), 130–137. https://doi.org/10.1080/1047840X.2015.989751

Grothaus, M. (2015, January 29). Why journaling is good for your health (and 8 tips to get better). *Fast Company*. Accessed at www.fastcompany.com/3041487/8-tips-to-more-effective-journaling-for-health on April 5, 2022.

Grover, T. (2013). *Relentless: From good to great to unstoppable*. New York: Scribner.

Guckenburg, S., Hurley, N., Persson, H., Fronius, T., & Petrosino, A. (2015, October). *Restorative justice in U.S. schools: Summary findings from interviews with experts*. San Francisco: WestEd. Accessed at www.wested.org/resources/restorative-justice-in-schools-report on December 20, 2021.

The Guest House. (2020, October 28). *Trauma affects our ability to feel safe*. Accessed at www.theguesthouseocala.com/trauma-affects-our-ability-to-feel-safe on December 15, 2021.

Guido, M. (2021, October 6). *Culturally responsive teaching: Examples, strategies and activities for success* [Blog post]. Accessed at www.prodigygame.com/main-en/blog/culturally-responsive-teaching/#list on December 15, 2021.

Gumper, K. (2020). *Social emotional learning: Building empathy*. Accessed at www.selpractices.org/blog/68-social-emotional-learning-building-empathy on April 17, 2022.

Guo, Y. (2012). Exploring linguistic, cultural, and religious diversity in Canadian schools: Pre-service teachers' learning from immigrant parents. *Journal of Contemporary Issues in Education*, *7*(1). doi.org/10.20355/c5qc78

Gutierrez, M. P., Demby, G., & Frame, K. (2018, April 11). *Housing segregation in everything* [Video]. www.npr.org/sections/codeswitch/2018/04/11/601494521/video-housing-segregation-in-everything

Haak, D. C., Lambers, J. H. R., Pitre, E., & Freeman, S. (2011). Increased structure and active learning reduce the achievement gap in introductory biology. *Science*, *332*(6034), 1213–1216. https://doi.org/10.1126/science.1204820

HAAPI Employee Resource Group. (2021). *Anti-Asian violence resources*. Accessed at https://anti-asianviolenceresources.carrd.co on December 20, 2021.

Hackett, A. (2018, April 11). Xenophobic prejudice doesn't just affect immigrants—it harms U.S.-born people of color too. *Pacific Standard*. Accessed at https://psmag.com/social-justice/xenophobic-remarks-dont-just-affect-immigrants-they-harm-u-s-born-people-of-color-too on May 20, 2022.

Haiken, M., & Gura, M. (2023). *Creative SEL: Using hands-on projects to boost social-emotional learning*. Portland, OR: International Society for Technology in Education.

Hammond, Z. (2014). *Culturally responsive teaching and the brain: Promoting authentic engagement and rigor among culturally and linguistically diverse students*. Thousand Oaks, CA: Corwin Press.

Hansford, B. C., & Hattie, J. (1982). The relationship between self and achievement/performance measures. *Review of Educational Research*, *52*(1), 123–142. https://doi.org/10.2307/1170275

Harvard Graduate School of Education. (2017, May 9). *Starting the conversation: High-quality discussion protocols to prompt collaborative, responsive learning*. Accessed at www.gse.harvard.edu/news/uk/17/05/starting-conversation on April 10, 2022.

Haryanto, P. C., & Arty, I. S. (2019). The application of contextual teaching and learning in natural science to improve student's HOTS and self-efficacy. *Journal of Physics: Conference Series*, *1233*(1), 012106. https://doi.org/10.1088/1742-6596/1233/1/012106

Hattie, J. (2009). *Visible learning: A synthesis of over 800 meta-analyses relating to achievement*. London: Routledge.

Hattie, J., & Yates, G. (2014). *Visible learning and the science of how we learn*. New York: Routledge.

Hattie, J., & Zierer, K. (2017). *10 mindframes for visible learning: Teaching for success*. New York: Routledge.

Hayes, A. (2021). *What is the National Housing Act?* Accessed at www.investopedia.com/terms/n/national-housing-act.asp on December 16, 2021.

Haynes, S. (2021, March 22). "This isn't just a problem for North America." The Atlanta shooting highlights the painful reality of rising anti-Asian violence around the world. *TIME*. Accessed at https://time.com/5947862/anti-asian-attacks-rising-worldwide on May 19, 2022.

Heiskala, C. (2018, March 2). *Restorative circles may play a role in preventing school shootings*. Accessed at www.linkedin.com/pulse/restorative-circles-may-play-role-preventing-school-christy/?published=t on April 28, 2022.

Hendel, H. J. (2018, February 27). Ignoring your emotions is bad for your health. Here's what to do about it. *TIME*. Accessed at time.com/5163576/ignoring-your-emotions-bad-for-your-health on December 20, 2021.

Howard, G. R. (1999). *We can't teach what we don't know: White teachers, multiracial schools*. New York: Teachers College Press.

Howard, N. R., Thomas, S., & Schaffer, R. (2018). *Closing the gap: Digital equity strategies for teacher prep programs*. Portland, OR: International Society for Technology in Education.

Hudson, L. D. (2022). Mental health of children and young people since the start of the pandemic. *Clinical Child Psychology and Psychiatry*, *27*(1), 3–5.

Hughes, D., Rodriguez, J., Smith, E. P., Johnson, D. J., Stevenson, H. C., & Spicer, P. (2006). Parents' ethnic-racial socialization practices: A review of research and directions for future study. *Developmental Psychology*, *42*(5), 747–770.

Hydo, G. (2017, February 28). *Are you trustworthy: Nine tips to becoming a trustworthy person*. Accessed at https://gretchenhydo.com/2017/02/are-you-trustworthy-nine-tips-to-becoming-a-trustworthy-person on December 20, 2021.

Illinois Digital Educators Alliance. (2021). *SEL master class with Jorge Valenzuela*. Accessed at https://ideaillinois.org/event-4158307 on December 20, 2021.

International Society for Technology in Education. (n.d.a). *ISTE Certification*. Accessed at www.iste.org/professional-development/iste-certification on June 3, 2022.

International Society for Technology in Education. (n.d.b). *The ISTE Standards*. Accessed at www.iste.org/iste-standards on June 21, 2022.

International Society for Technology in Education. (n.d.c). *Be Bold with Us*. Accessed at www.iste.org/about/about-iste on December 23, 2021.

International Society for Technology in Education. (2017). *ISTE Standards: Educators*. Accessed at www.iste.org/standards/iste-standards-for-teachers on December 23, 2021.

International Society for Technology in Education. (2018). *ISTE Computational Thinking Competencies*. Accessed at www.iste.org/standards/iste-standards-for-computational-thinking on December 23, 2021.

ITVS. (2017, January 18). *TED Talks live short: Unconscious bias* [Video]. www.youtube.com/watch?v=rspZv2a0Pp8

Jack, B. M., Lin, H.-S., & Yore, L. D. (2014). The synergistic effect of affective factors on student learning outcomes. *Journal of Research in Science Teaching*, *51*(8), 1084–1101. https://doi.org/10.1002/tea.21153

Jagers, R. J., Rivas-Drake, D., & Borowski, T. (2018, November). *Equity and social and emotional learning: A cultural analysis* (Frameworks Brief). Chicago: Collaborative for Academic, Social, and Emotional Learning.

James, K. M., Owens, M., Woody, M. L., Hall, N. T., & Gibb, B. E. (2018). Parental expressed emotion-criticism and neural markers of sustained attention to emotional faces in children. *Journal of Clinical Child and Adolescent Psychology*, *47*(1), S520–S529.

James, M. (2016, September 1). React vs respond: What's the difference? [Blog post]. *Psychology Today*. Accessed at www.psychologytoday.com/us/blog/focus-forgiveness/201609/react-vs-respond on April 2, 2022.

Jimenez, O., Chavez, N., & Hanna, J. (2020, May 28). *As heated protests over George Floyd's death continue, Minnesota governor warns of "extremely dangerous situation."* Accessed at www.cnn.com/2020/05/27/us/minneapolis-protests-george-floyd/index.html on May 13, 2022.

Johns, M. M., Poteat, V. P., Horn, S. S., & Kosciw, J. (2019). Strengthening our schools to promote resilience and health among LGBTQ youth: Emerging evidence and research priorities from *The State of LGBTQ Youth Health and Wellbeing* symposium. *LGBT health, 6*(4), 146–155. https://doi.org/10.1089/lgbt.2018.0109

Johnson, P. (2018, August). *Religion equity in schools: Protecting students and their civil rights* [Newsletter]. Accessed at www.idra.org/resource-center/religion-equity-in-schools-protecting-students-and-their-civil-rights on April 18, 2022.

K12 Computer Science. (2016). *Equity in computer science education.* Accessed at https://k12cs.org/equity-in-computer-science-education on December 20, 2021.

Kaufman, T. (n.d.). *5 tips for supporting students socially and emotionally during distance learning.* Accessed at www.understood.org/en/articles/5-tips-for-supporting-students-socially-and-emotionally-during-distance on May 31, 2022.

Kerpen, D. (2016, March 24). This surprisingly simple trick can make you a better listener. *Fast Company.* Accessed at www.fastcompany.com/3058200/this-surprisingly-simple-trick-can-make-you-a-better-liste on December 20, 2021.

Khoddam, R. (2021, March 3). How trauma affects the body [Blog post]. *Psychology Today.* Accessed at www.psychologytoday.com/us/blog/the-addiction-connection/202103/how-trauma-affects-the-body on May 7, 2022.

Kingsella, M. (2020, October 9). *Economic development begins with pro-housing policy.* Accessed at www.upforgrowth.org/news/economic-development-begins-pro-housing-policy on June 2, 2022.

Koehler, M. J., Mishra, P., Kereluik, K., Shin, T. S., & Graham, C. R. (2014). The technological pedagogical content knowledge framework. In J. M. Spector, M. D. Merrill, J. Elen, & M. J. Bishop (Eds.), *Handbook of research on educational communications and technology* (pp. 101–111). New York: Springer. https://doi.org/10.1007/978-1-4614-3185-5_9

Ladson-Billings, G. (1994). *The dreamkeepers: Successful teachers of African American children.* San Francisco: Jossey-Bass.

Ladson-Billings, G. (1995). Toward a theory of culturally relevant pedagogy. *American Educational Research Journal, 32*(3), 465–491.

Lantieri, L. (2012). Cultivating the social, emotional, and inner lives of children and teachers. *Reclaiming Children and Youth, 21*(2), 27–33.

Larson, K. E., Pas, E. T., Bradshaw, C. P., Rosenberg, M. S., & Day-Vines, N. L. (2018). Examining how proactive management and culturally responsive teaching relate to student behavior: Implications for measurement and practice. *School Psychology Review, 47*(2), 153–166.

Lavietes, M. (2022, February 20). *From book bans to "Don't Say Gay" bill, LGBTQ kids feel "erased" in the classroom.* Accessed at www.nbcnews.com/nbc-out/out-news/book-bans-dont-say-gay-bill-lgbtq-kids-feel-erased-classroom-rcna15819 on May 24, 2022.

Learning for Justice. (n.d.a). *Bullying basics professional development.* Accessed at www.learningforjustice.org/professional-development/bullying-basics on December 20, 2021.

Learning for Justice. (n.d.b). *Color blindness professional development.* Accessed at www.learningforjustice.org/professional-development/color-blindness on May 18, 2022.

Learning for Justice. (n.d.c). *My multicultural self lesson.* Accessed at www.learningforjustice.org/classroom-resources/lessons/my-multicultural-self on May 10, 2022.

Learning for Justice. (2014). *Social justice and bullying lesson plan.* Accessed at www.learningforjustice.org/learning-plan/social-justice-and-bullying-lesson-plan on July 6, 2022.

Learning for Justice. (2017). *A guide for administrators, counselors and teachers: Responding to hate and bias at school.* Montgomery, AL: Southern Poverty Law Center. Accessed at www.learningforjustice.org/sites/default/files/2017-07/Responding%20to%20Hate%20at%20School%202017.pdf on July 6, 2022.

Learning for Justice. (2021, November). Section III: Instruction. In *Best practices for serving LGBTQ students.* Montgomery, AL: Southern Poverty Law Center. Accessed at www.learningforjustice.org/magazine/publications/best-practices-for-serving-lgbtq-students/section-iii-instruction on July 6, 2022.

Lee, A. M. I. (n.d.). *What is the Every Student Succeeds Act (ESSA)?* Accessed at www.understood.org/en/school-learning/your-childs-rights/basics-about-childs-rights/every-student-succeeds-act-essa-what-you-need-to-know on December 20, 2021.

Lee, K. (2020a, July 3). Convictions of violent cops who kill Black people prove elusive. Dallas is becoming an exception. *Los Angeles Times.* Accessed at www.latimes.com/world-nation/story/2020-07-03/la-na-police-convictions-dallas on December 20, 2021.

Lee, L. (2020b, June 15). *The value of culturally responsive teaching in distance learning.* Accessed at www.edutopia.org/article/value-culturally-responsive-teaching-distance-learning on December 20, 2021.

Lee, Z. (2021, March 25). *Anti-Asian sentiment in America is not new* [Blog post]. Accessed at www.nationalpartnership.org/our-impact/blog/general/anti-asian-sentiment-in-america-is-not-new.html on May 19, 2022.

Lenzen, M. (2005, April 1). Feeling our emotions. *Scientific American.* Accessed at www.scientificamerican.com/article/feeling-our-emotions on December 20, 2021.

Leonard, J. (2020, June 3). *What is trauma? What to know.* Accessed at www.medicalnewstoday.com/articles/trauma on May 7, 2022.

Lifelong Learning Defined. (2021a). *Master class with Jorge Valenzuela.* Accessed at www.lifelonglearningdefined.com/master-class on December 20, 2021.

Lifelong Learning Defined. (2021b). *Project plan template.* Accessed at https://drive.google.com/file/d/1_IH6tY6bWR7_kFW2BEscVO7q3Vf4xLkv/edit on July 6, 2022.

Livingston, M. (2020, June 16). *These are the major brands donating to the Black Lives Matter movement.* Accessed at www.cnet.com/how-to/companies-donating-black-lives-matter on December 15, 2021.

Loeb, S. (2020, March 20). How effective is online learning? What the research does and doesn't tell us. *Education Week.* Accessed at www.edweek.org/technology/opinion-how-effective-is-online-learning-what-the-research-does-and-doesnt-tell-us/2020/03 on December 20, 2021.

Lopez, G. (2018, April 5). Black kids are way more likely to be punished in school than White kids, study finds. *Vox.* Accessed at www.vox.com/identities/2018/4/5/17199810/school-discipline-race-racism-gao on May 11, 2022.

Losen, D. J. (Ed.). (2015). *Closing the school discipline gap: Equitable remedies for excessive exclusion.* New York: Teachers College Press.

Love Has No Labels. (n.d.). *Glossary*. Accessed at https://lovehasnolabels.com/resources/glossary?gclid=CjwKCAjwyryUBhBSEiwAGN5OCAyUiBu0rQA11IXFRJsmaBaMRUEMGAEeEqaCcjLnxK82gB4nZwTvthoClaEQAvD_BwE#lgbt on May 26, 2022.

Lowry, G. (2020). *Breakout rooms can increase student engagement in online tutorials*. Accessed at https://otl.uoguelph.ca/teaching-learning-resources/sotl-snapshots/remote-teaching-and-teaching-technology/breakout-rooms on June 2, 2022.

Lynch, M. (2020, December 3). *I'll get to it tomorrow: Procrastination in online learning*. Accessed at www.thetechedvocate.org/ill-get-to-it-tomorrow-procrastination-in-online-learning on May 31, 2022.

Mackay, H., & Strickland, M. J. (2018). Exploring culturally responsive teaching and student-created videos in an at-risk middle school classroom. *Middle Grades Review*, *4*(1), 1–15.

Mahoney, J. L., Durlak, J. A., & Weissberg, R. P. (2018, November 26). *An update on social and emotional learning outcome research*. Accessed at https://kappanonline.org/social-emotional-learning-outcome-research-mahoney-durlak-weissberg on December 20, 2021.

Mangan, D. (2021, August 30). *Hate crimes against Asian and Black people rise sharply in the U.S., FBI says*. Accessed at www.cnbc.com/2021/08/30/fbi-says-hate-crimes-against-asian-and-black-people-rise-in-the-us.html on May 18, 2022.

Manion, L. (2020, September 21). *What safety means as a trauma survivor* [Blog post]. Accessed at www.nami.org/Blogs/NAMI-Blog/September-2020/What-Safety-Means-as-a-Trauma-Survivor on May 29, 2022.

Manitoba Accessibility Office. (2021). *The Accessibility for Manitobans Act: Barriers and solutions*. Accessed at https://accessibilitymb.ca/types-of-barriers.html on December 20, 2021.

Marsh, C. (2019, November 1). *Honoring the global Indigenous roots of restorative justice: Potential restorative approaches for child welfare*. Accessed at https://cssp.org/2019/11/honoring-the-global-indigenous-roots-of-restorative-justice on May 11, 2022.

Mastroianni, B. (2021, June 23). *How stress from homophobia affects the mind and body of LGB people*. Accessed at www.healthline.com/health-news/how-stress-from-homophobia-affects-the-mind-and-body-of-lgb-people on May 26, 2022.

Matthews, T., Danese, A., Wertz, J., Ambler, A., Kelly, M., Diver, A., et al. (2015). Social isolation and mental health at primary and secondary school entry: A longitudinal cohort study. *Journal of the American Academy of Child & Adolescent Psychiatry*, *54*(3), 225–232. https://doi.org/10.1016/j.jaac.2014.12.008

Mayberry, C. (2022, January 24). Public schools have spent $21M on diversity inclusion programs since George Floyd's death. *Newsweek*. Accessed at www.newsweek.com/public-schools-have-spent-21m-diversity-inclusion-programs-since-george-floyds-death-1672323 on May 15, 2022.

McGuire, L. (2020, September 18). *How to support LGBTQ students during distance learning*. Accessed at www.edutopia.org/article/how-support-lgbtq-students-during-distance-learning on July 6, 2022.

Mcilroy, T. (2022, April 5). *The stages of emotional development in early childhood*. Accessed at https://empoweredparents.co/emotional-development-stages on April 25, 2022.

McMahon, M. (2022, May 20). *What is physical trauma?* Accessed at www.wise-geek.com/what-is-physical-trauma.htm on May 7, 2022.

Meckler, L., & Natanson, H. (2021, May 3). As schools expand racial equity work, conservatives see a new threat in critical race theory. *The Washington Post.* Accessed at www.washingtonpost .com/education/2021/05/03/critical-race-theory-backlash on May 13, 2022.

Mental Health America. (2021). *Helpful vs harmful: Ways to manage emotions.* Accessed at www .mhanational.org/helpful-vs-harmful-ways-manage-emotions on December 15, 2021.

Meyer, C. (2012, April 25). *Emotions vs. feelings* [Blog post]. Accessed at https://emotionaldetective .typepad.com/emotional-detective/2012/04/emotions-vs-feelings.html on December 20, 2021.

Minahan, J. (2019, October 1). *Trauma-informed teaching strategies.* Accessed at www.ascd.org /el/articles/trauma-informed-teaching-strategies on June 21, 2022.

Miner, K. (2010, November 5). *Restorative justice circles provide a feeling of importance.* Accessed at https://circle-space.org/2010/11/05/restorative-justice-circles-provide-a-feeling-of-importance on April 28, 2022.

Minero, E. (2018, April 19). *Schools struggle to support LGBTQ students.* Accessed at www.edutopia .org/article/schools-struggle-support-lgbtq-students on July 6, 2022.

Mishra, P., & Koehler, M. J. (2006). Technological pedagogical content knowledge: A framework for teacher knowledge. *Teachers College Record, 108*(6), 1017–1054.

Mitchell, B., & Franco, J. (2018, March 20). *HOLC "redlining" maps: The persistent structure of segregation and economic inequality.* Accessed at https://ncrc.org/holc on December 15, 2021.

Moallem, I. (2013). *A meta-analysis of school belonging and academic success and persistence* [Unpublished doctoral dissertation]. Loyola University Chicago. Accessed at https://ecommons.luc.edu/luc _diss/726 on December 20, 2021.

Mogahed, D., & Chouhoud, Y. (2017). *American Muslim poll: Muslims at the crossroads.* Washington, DC: Institute for Social Policy and Understanding (ISPU). 1–16.

Monin, K., Batalova, J., & Lai, T. (2021, May 13). *Refugees and asylees in the United States.* Accessed at www.migrationpolicy.org/article/refugees-and-asylees-united-states-2021 on May 29, 2022.

Montoya-Galvez, C. (2021, September 16). *Where Afghan refugees are expected to be resettled, by state.* Accessed at www.cbsnews.com/news/afghan-refugees-resettled-by-state on December 15, 2021.

Morris, J. A., & Feldman, D. C. (1996). The dimensions, antecedents, and consequences of emotional labor. *The Academy of Management Review, 21*(4), 986–1010. Accessed at doi.org/10.2307/259161

Mulcahy, D. (2018). *Affective practices of learning at the museum: Children's critical encounters with the past.* Taylor & Francis. Accessed at www.taylorfrancis.com/chapters/edit/10.4324/9781351250962 -13/affective-practices-learning-museum-dianne-mulcahy-andrea-witcomb on July 18, 2022.

National Center for Education Statistics. (2020). *Race and ethnicity of public school teachers and their students.* Accessed at https://nces.ed.gov/pubs2020/2020103/index.asp on April 7, 2022.

National Center for Transgender Equality. (2018, October 5). *Understanding non-binary people: How to be respectful and supportive.* Accessed at transequality.org/issues/resources/understanding-non -binary-people-how-to-be-respectful-and-supportive on December 20, 2021.

National Park Service. (n.d.). *The Civilian Conservation Corps.* Accessed at www.nps.gov/articles /the-civilian-conservation-corps.htm on December 20, 2021.

National School Reform Faculty. (2014, Spring). *Text-based seminar protocol.* Accessed at www .nsrfharmony.org/wp-content/uploads/2017/10/TextBasedSeminar-N.pdf on December 20, 2021.

Nedd, A. (2017, September 11). 10 times Dr. K made everyone cry on *This Is Us*. *Cosmopolitan.* Accessed at www.cosmopolitan.com/entertainment/tv/a12217518/10-times-dr-k-made-everyone-cry-on-this-is-us on December 20, 2021.

The New York Times. (2022, May 19). How George Floyd died, and what happened next. *The New York Times.* Accessed at www.nytimes.com/article/george-floyd.html on May 13, 2022.

Ng'andu, J. (2015, January 22). *It's not what's wrong with the children, it's what's happened to them.* Accessed at www.edutopia.org/blog/not-whats-wrong-whats-happened-jennifer-ngandu on July 6, 2022.

Nichols, H. (2020, June 5). *A guide to equity and antiracism for educators.* Accessed at www.edutopia.org/article/guide-equity-and-antiracism-educators on July 6, 2022.

Nichols, H. [@Hedreich]. (2022, June 1). *#blackteachersmatter. Anyone have similar statistics for other populations? @JorgeDoesPBL @T_F_Berger @sarahdateechur @thewongways @turnerhj* [Tweet]. Accessed at https://twitter.com/Hedreich/status/1531970642173624320?s=20&t=h07C-UW5lCZE6xGL_NfZxA on June 3, 2022.

Oakland Unified School District. (2022). *Restorative justice*. Accessed at www.ousd.org/restorativejustice on May 11, 2022.

Office of Communications. (2019, February 21). *Children and parents: Media use and attitudes report 2018.* Accessed at www.ofcom.org.uk/research-and-data/media-literacy-research/childrens/children-and-parents-media-use-and-attitudes-report-2018 on December 20, 2021.

Olorunnipa, T., & Witte, G. (2020, October 8). Born with two strikes: How systemic racism shaped Floyd's life and hobbled his ambition. *The Washington Post.* Accessed at www.washingtonpost.com/graphics/2020/national/george-floyd-america/systemic-racism/ on May 17, 2022.

Ombea. (2020, August 27). *5-point Likert scale: The key to easily understanding your audience.* Accessed at www.ombea.com/us/resources/articles/5-point-likert-scale-the-key-to-easily-understanding-your-audience on June 4, 2022.

Online MSW Programs. (2022). *Supporting survivors of trauma: How to avoid re-traumatization.* Accessed at www.onlinemswprograms.com/resources/how-to-be-mindful-re-traumatization on May 8, 2022.

Ordway, D.-M. (2020, March 11). *Online schools: Students' performance often falls behind kids at other public schools.* Accessed at https://journalistsresource.org/studies/society/education/virtual-schools-parents-choice-performance-research on December 20, 2021.

Osher, D., Cantor, P., Berg, J., Steyer, L., & Rose, T. (2020). Drivers of human development: How relationships and context shape learning and development. *Applied Developmental Science, 24*(1), 6–36.

The Oxford Review Encyclopaedia of Terms. (n.d.). *Affective communication: Definition and explanation*. Accessed at https://oxford-review.com/oxford-review-encyclopaedia-terms/affective-communication on May 11, 2022.

Pappas, M. (2018, April 16). *7 steps to help you get unstuck, and move forward in healing from trauma.* Accessed at www.survivingmypast.net/7-steps-help-get-unstuck-move-forward-healing-trauma on December 20, 2021.

Paris, D., & Alim, H. S. (2014). What are we seeking to sustain through culturally sustaining pedagogy? A loving critique forward. *Harvard Educational Review, 84*(1), 85–100.

Parrish, N. (2022). *The independent learner: Metacognitive exercises to help K–12 students focus, self-regulate, and persevere.* Bloomington, IN: Solution Tree Press.

PBLMatters. (n.d.). *Equity and SEL integration master class*. Accessed at www.pblmatters.org/camp-pbl-facilitators.html on December 20, 2021.

PBLWorks. (2015). *Project design: Overview and student learning guide*. Accessed at my.pblworks.org/resource/document/project_design_overview_and_student_learning_guide on February 23, 2022.

Peek, S. (2021, July 28). *What is a decision matrix? Definition and examples*. Accessed at www.businessnewsdaily.com/6146-decision-matrix.html on April 28, 2022.

Peixoto, J. M., & Moura, E. P. (2020). Health empathy map: Creation of an instrument for empathy development. *Revista Brasileira de Educação Médica, 44*(1), e029. https://doi.org/10.1590/1981-5271v44.1-20190151.ing

Pennebaker, J. W. (1997). *Opening up: The healing power of expressing emotions*. New York: Guilford Press.

Penn Today. (2020, September 16). *Rebranding the NFL: How the league shifted its message on racial justice*. Accessed at https://penntoday.upenn.edu/news/rebranding-nfl-how-league-shifted-its-message-racial-justice on December 20, 2021.

Peterson, H. (2020, June 5). *Walmart CEO in email condemns racial violence and pledges $100 million to address systematic racism*. Accessed at www.businessinsider.com/walmart-ceo-email-condemns-racial-violence-pledges-100-million-donation-2020-6 on December 20, 2021.

Petrosino, A., Guckenburg, S., & Fronius, T. (2012). "Policing schools" strategies: A review of the evaluation evidence. *Journal of MultiDisciplinary Evaluation, 8*(17), 80–101.

Pew Research Center. (2019, June 19). *Public highly critical of state of political discourse in the U.S.* Washington, DC: Author. Accessed at www.pewresearch.org/politics/2019/06/19/public-highly-critical-of-state-of-political-discourse-in-the-u-s/ on April 25, 2022.

Phillips, A. (2021, September 24). Why are there thousands of Haitian migrants at the Texas border? *The Washington Post*. Accessed at www.washingtonpost.com/politics/2021/09/21/haiti-migrants-texas-border on May 29, 2022.

Phillips, L. (2020, July 27). *Black mental health matters*. Accessed at https://ct.counseling.org/2020/07/black-mental-health-matters on May 17, 2022.

Piazza, S. V., Rao, S., & Protacio, M. S. (2015). Converging recommendations for culturally responsive literacy practices: Students with learning disabilities, English language learners, and socioculturally diverse learners. *International Journal of Multicultural Education, 17*(3), 1–20.

Picture Alternatives. (2019, November 12). *Our hidden biases* [Video]. YouTube. www.youtube.com/watch?v=ZWgVs4qj1ho&t=58s on July 6, 2022.

Pierson, R. (2013, May). *Every kid needs a champion* [Video]. TED Conferences. Accessed at www.ted.com/talks/rita_pierson_every_kid_needs_a_champion?language=en

Pinola, M. (2020, August 17). How to set up a remote learning space for your kids [Blog post]. *The New York Times*. Accessed at www.nytimes.com/wirecutter/blog/remote-learning-space-set-up on May 31, 2022.

Plutchik, R. (2001). The nature of emotions: Human emotions have deep evolutionary roots, a fact that may explain their complexity and provide tools for clinical practice. *American Scientist, 89*(4), 344–350.

The Polarization Index. (2022). *Where does America stand on these issues?* Accessed at https://thepolarizationindex.com/issues on May 29, 2022.

Positive Action. (2020, August 6). *Responsible decision making: An introductory guide* [Blog post]. Accessed at www.positiveaction.net/blog/responsible-decision-making on April 28, 2022.

Powell, W., & Kusuma-Powell, O. (2011). *How to teach now: Five keys to personalized learning in the global classroom.* Alexandria, VA: Association for Supervision and Curriculum Development.

PowerSchool. (2022, April 20). *The TPACK framework explained (with classroom examples)* [Blog post]. Accessed at www.powerschool.com/blog/the-tpack-framework-explained-with-classroom-examples on May 31, 2022.

Prothero, A., & Blad, E. (2021, December 13). Schools face fears of "critical race theory" as they scale up social-emotional learning. *Education Week.* Accessed at www.edweek.org/leadership/schools-face-fears-of-critical-race-theory-as-they-scale-up-social-emotional-learning/2021/12 on June 5, 2022.

The Proud Diplomat. (2018, June 10). *Tackling loneliness in the LGBTQ+ community.* Accessed at www.theprouddiplomat.com/facts/2018/6/10/tackling-loneliness-in-the-lgbtq-community on April 17, 2022.

Psychology Today Staff. (2020). Emotion regulation. *Psychology Today.* Accessed at www.psychologytoday.com/us/basics/emotion-regulation on December 20, 2021.

Psychophysiologic Disorders Association. (2022). *Symptoms: Your pain is real. The solution is, too.* Accessed at https://ppdassociation.org/symptoms on December 20, 2021.

Pugh, S. (1981). Concept selection: A method that works. In *Proceedings of International Conference on Engineering Design* (pp. 497–506). Zürich, Switzerland: Heurista.

Race Forward. (2020). *What is racial equity? Understanding key concepts related to race.* Accessed at www.raceforward.org/about/what-is-racial-equity-key-concepts?csi=1 on June 21, 2022.

Raising Children Network. (2021) *Brain development in pre-teens and teenagers.* Accessed at https://raisingchildren.net.au/pre-teens/development/understanding-your-pre-teen/brain-development-teens on December 20, 2021.

Ramdhani, S., & Jamari, J. (2018). The modeling of a conceptual engineering design system using the decision-matrix logic. *MATEC Web of Conferences, 159,* 1–6. https://doi.org/10.1051/matecconf/201815902022

ReachOut Schools. (2022). *Why it's important to understand students' needs and interests.* Accessed at https://schools.au.reachout.com/articles/why-its-important-to-understand-student-needs-and-interests on April 14, 2022.

Rebora, A. (2019, November 1). *Turn & talk / Zaretta Hammond on coaching and culturally responsive teaching.* Accessed at www.ascd.org/el/articles/zaretta-hammond-on-coaching -and-culturally-responsive-teaching on June 21, 2022.

Reiners, B. (2022, May 31). *16 unconscious bias examples and how to avoid them in the workplace.* Accessed at https://builtin.com/diversity-inclusion/unconscious-bias-examples on April 9, 2022.

Resilient Educator. (2021a). *Trauma-informed strategies to use in your classroom.* Accessed at https://resilienteducator.com/classroom-resources/trauma-informed-strategies on December 20, 2021.

Resilient Educator. (2021b, June 8). *Essential trauma-informed teaching strategies for managing stress in the classroom (and virtual classrooms).* Accessed at https://resilienteducator.com/classroom-resources/trauma-informed-teaching-tips on July 6, 2022.

Restorative Justice Exchange. (2021). *Why restorative justice?* Accessed at https://restorativejustice.org/restorative-justice/about-restorative-justice/tutorial-intro-to-restorative-justice/#sthash.eHkMRsQm.dpbs on December 15, 2021.

Riddle, T., & Sinclair, S. (2019). Racial disparities in school-based disciplinary actions are associated with county-level rates of racial bias. *Proceedings of the National Academy of Sciences of the United States of America, 116*(17), 8255–8260. https://doi.org/10.1073/pnas.1808307116

Rinkema, E., & Williams, S. (2021, February 26). Remote learning makes time management even harder. *Education Week*. Accessed at www.edweek.org/teaching-learning/opinion-remote-learning-makes-time-management-even-harder/2021/02 on May 31, 2022.

Robinson, L., Smith, M., & Segal, J. (2021, November). *Emotional and psychological trauma.* Accessed at www.helpguide.org/articles/ptsd-trauma/coping-with-emotional-and-psychological-trauma.htm on May 7, 2022.

Rogers, J., Franke, M., Yun, J. E., Ishimoto, M., Deira, C., Cooper Gellar, R., Berryman, A., & Brenes, T. (2017). *Teaching and learning in the age of trump: Increasing stress and hostility in America's high schools.* IDEA. Accessed at idea.gseis.ucla.edu/publications/teaching-and-learning-in-age-of-trump on September 13,2022

Rogers, K. (2019, October 29). *US teens use screens more than seven hours a day on average—and that's not including school work.* Accessed at www.cnn.com/2019/10/29/health/common-sense-kids-media-use-report-wellness/index.html on December 20, 2021.

Rost, M. (2011). *Teaching and researching listening.* New York: Longman.

Rucker, N. W. (2019, December 10). *Getting started with culturally responsive teaching.* Accessed at www.edutopia.org/article/getting-started-culturally-responsive-teaching on December 20, 2021.

Ruiz, D. M. (1997). *The four agreements: A practical guide to personal freedom.* San Rafael, CA: Amber-Allen.

Rummler, O. (2020, June 10). *The major police reforms enacted since George Floyd's death.* Accessed at www.axios.com/police-reform-george-floyd-protest-2150b2dd-a6dc-4a0c-a1fb-62c2e999a03a.html on December 20, 2021.

Safir, S. (2017, August 1). *Getting to know students deeply* [Blog post]. Accessed at www.edutopia.org/blog/getting-know-students-deeply-shane-safir on April 13, 2022.

Sailor, J., & Sellenriek, D. (2016, June 29). *Moving from content standards to student-friendly learning targets, part 1* [Blog post]. Accessed at https://blog.masteryconnect.com/four-steps-unpacking-standards on December 20, 2021.

Samuels, T. (2019, January 4). *Grounding techniques with five senses: Moving on from trauma.* Accessed at https://terrisamuels.com/a-grounding-techniques-with-five-senses-moving-on-from-trauma on May 9, 2022.

Santos, J. M. D. (2019, July 24). *The importance of checklists in the workplace* [Blog post]. Accessed at https://bridge24.com/blog/the-importance-of-checklists-in-the-workplace on April 28, 2022.

Sawchuk, S. (2021, August 25). Local school boards are banning critical race theory. Here's how that looks in 7 districts. *Education Week.* Accessed at www.edweek.org/leadership/local-school-boards-are-also-banning-lessons-on-race-heres-how-that-looks-in-7-districts/2021/08 on May 13, 2022.

Schott Foundation. (2014). *Restorative practices: A guide for educators*. Accessed at http://schottfoundation.org/restorative-practices on July 6, 2022.

Schultz, M. (2015, March 6). *The importance of getting to know your students*. Accessed at www.bamradionetwork.com/the-importance-of-getting-to-know-your-students on April 14, 2022.

Scully, K. (2019, August 13). *20+ strategies for teaching empathy*. Accessed at www.thepathway2success.com/20-strategies-for-teaching-empathy on December 20, 2021.

Seider, S., & Graves, D. (2020, January 9). *Making SEL culturally competent*. Accessed at www.edutopia.org/article/making-sel-culturally-competent on December 20, 2021.

Sevelius, J. M., Gutierrez-Mock, L., Zamudio-Haas, S., McCree, B., Ngo, A., Jackson, A., et al. (2020). Research with marginalized communities: Challenges to continuity during the COVID-19 pandemic. *AIDS and Behavior, 24*(7), 2009–2012. https://doi.org/10.1007/s10461-020-02920-3

Shea, C. (2017, October 23). *5 reasons why inner peace is important* [Blog post]. Accessed at www.lifesjourneyblog.com/blog-posts/finding-inner-peace/561-5-reasons-why-inner-peace-is-important on April 27, 2022.

Shepard, M. (2018, April 23). *Putting PBL into practice: The workshop model*. Accessed at www.pblworks.org/blog/putting-pbl-practice-workshop-model on July 6, 2022.

Sieck, W. (2021, September 20). *Cultural competence: What, why, and how*. Accessed at www.globalcognition.org/cultural-competence on April 11, 2022.

Silva, D. (2022, May 21). *Students say restrictive new education laws are scary and frustrating*. Accessed at www.nbcnews.com/news/us-news/students-say-restrictive-new-education-laws-are-scary-frustrating-rcna29599 on May 23, 2022.

Simms, M. C., McDaniel, M., Fyffe, S. D., & Lowenstein, C. (2015, October). *Structural barriers to racial equity in Pittsburgh: Expanding economic opportunity for African American men and boys*. Washington, DC: Urban Institute. Accessed at www.urban.org/sites/default/files/alfresco/publication-pdfs/2000518-Structural-Barriers-to-Racial-Equity-in-Pittsburgh-Expanding-Economic-Opportunity-for-African-American-Men-and-Boys.pdf on December 20, 2021.

Skiba, R. J., Michael, R. S., Nardo, A. C., & Peterson, R. L. (2002). The color of discipline: Sources of racial and gender disproportionality in school punishment. *The Urban Review, 34*(4), 317–342.

Sklad, M., Diekstra, R., de Ritter, M., Ben, J., & Gravesteijn, C. (2012). Effectiveness of school-based universal social, emotional, and behavioral programs. Do they enhance students' development in the area of skill, behavior, and adjustment? *Psychology in the Schools, 49*(9), 892–909.

Smith, M., & Robinson, L. (2021, November). *Helping someone with PTSD*. Accessed at www.helpguide.org/articles/ptsd-trauma/helping-someone-with-ptsd.htm on December 20, 2021.

Smith, M., Robinson, L., & Segal, J. (2021, November). *Helping children cope with traumatic events*. Accessed at www.helpguide.org/articles/ptsd-trauma/helping-children-cope-with-traumatic-stress.htm on December 21, 2021.

Smith, R. (2019, August 28). *Advancing racial equity in career and technical education enrollment*. Accessed at www.americanprogress.org/issues/education-k-12/news/2019/08/28/473876/advancing-racial-equity-career-technical-education-enrollment on December 20, 2021.

Snelling, J. (2022, May 31). *7 LGBTQ+ resources for educators*. Accessed at www.iste.org/explore/classroom/7-lgbtq-resources-educators on July 6, 2022.

Spangler, T. (2020, June 11). Apple commits $100 million to racial equity and justice causes. *Variety*. Accessed at https://variety.com/2020/digital/news/apple-100-million-racial-equity-injustice-1234631693 on December 20, 2021.

Sparks, S. D. (2017, April 12). Open educational resources (OER): Overview and definition. *Education Week*. Accessed at www.edweek.org/teaching-learning/open-educational-resources-oer-overview-and-definition/2017/04 on June 1, 2022.

Spinazzola, J., Cook, A., Ford, J., Lanktree, C., Blaustein, M., Cloitre, M., DeRosa, R., Hubbard, R., Kagan, R., Liautaud, J., Mallah, K., Olafson, E., & van der Kolk, B. (2005). Complex Trauma in Children and Adolescents. *Psychiatric Annals*. *35*(1). 10.3928/00485713-20050501-05. 390-398.S

pratt, J., & Florian, L. (2015). Inclusive pedagogy: From learning to action. Supporting each individual in the context of "everybody." *Teaching and Teacher Education*, *49*, 89–96.

Staats, C. (2014). *State of the science: Implicit bias review 2014*. Columbus, OH: Kirwan Institute for the Study of Race and Ethnicity. Accessed at https://kirwaninstitute.osu.edu/sites/default/files/pdf/2014-implicit-bias-review.pdf on December 20, 2021.

Steinhauser, K. (2020, March 16). *Everyone is a little bit biased*. Accessed at www.americanbar.org/groups/business_law/publications/blt/2020/04/everyone-is-biased on April 8, 2022.

Steinmetz, K. (2017, March 26). Beyond "he" or "she": The changing meaning of gender and sexuality. *TIME*. Accessed at https://time.com/magazine/us/4703292/march-27th-2017-vol-189-no-11-u-s on May 23, 2022.

StopBullying.gov. (2018, October 23). *Bystanders to bullying*. Accessed at www.stopbullying.gov/prevention/bystanders-to-bullying on December 20, 2021.

StopBullying.gov. (2021a, September 9). *Facts about bullying*. Accessed at www.stopbullying.gov/resources/facts on December 20, 2021.

StopBullying.gov. (2021b, November 5). *What is bullying*. Accessed at www.stopbullying.gov/bullying/what-is-bullying on December 20, 2021.

Stout, C., & Wilburn, T. (2022, February 1). *CRT map: Efforts to restrict teaching racism and bias have multiplied across the U.S.* Accessed at www.chalkbeat.org/22525983/map-critical-race-theory-legislation-teaching-racism on May 13, 2022.

Substance Abuse and Mental Health Services Administration. (2020). *Understanding child trauma*. Accessed at www.samhsa.gov/child-trauma/understanding-child-trauma on December 20, 2021.

Sue, D. W. (2019). *Microaggression: More than just race*. Accessed at www.uua.org/files/pdf/m/microaggressions_by_derald_wing_sue_ph.d._.pdf on December 20, 2021.

Sue, D. W. (2020). *Tool: Recognizing microaggressions and the messages they send.* Accessed at https://sites.google.com/site/cacmnow/university-of-california-microaggression-lisy on December 23, 2021.

Sullivan, K. (2021, January 24). Here are the 30 executive orders and actions Biden signed in his first three days. *CNN*. Accessed at www.cnn.com/2021/01/22/politics/joe-biden-executive-orders-first-week/index.html on December 20, 2021.

Sullivan, L. (2020, March 13). *What does equity mean in the Next Generation Science Standards?* [Blog post]. Accessed at https://ctsciencecenter.org/blog/what-does-equity-mean-in-the-next-generation-science-standards on December 20, 2021.

Symmetry Counseling. (2016, November 22). *Emotions, neither good nor bad.* Accessed at www.symmetrycounseling.com/uncategorized/emotions-neither-good-bad on December 20, 2021.

Tanner, K. D. (2013). Structure matters: Twenty-one teaching strategies to promote student engagement and cultivate classroom equity. *CBE: Life Sciences Education, 12*(3), 322–331. https://doi.org/10.1187/cbe.13-06-0115

Taylor, R. D., Oberle, E., Durlak, J. A., & Weissberg, R. P. (2017). Promoting positive youth development through school-based social and emotional learning interventions: A meta-analysis of follow-up effects. *Child Development, 88*(4), 1156–1171.

The Teacher Toolkit. (n.d.). *Turn and talk.* Accessed at www.theteachertoolkit.com/index.php/tool/turn-and-talk on July 6, 2022.

Teaching and Learning Lab. (n.d.). *Discussion protocols.* Accessed at www.gse.harvard.edu/sites/default/files/Protocols_Handout.pdf on July 6, 2022.

Tesfaye, A. (2022). *BIPOC students and bias in higher education: The necessity of unlearning biases to optimize outcomes for BIPOC students.* Accessed at www.packback.co/stories/bipoc-students-and-bias-in-higher-education-the-necessity-of-unlearning-biases-to-unify-teaching-practices-and-optimize-outcomes-for-bipoc-students on April 9, 2022.

Thomas, S., Howard, N. R., & Schaffer, R. (2019). Closing the gap: Digital equity strategies for the K–12 classroom. Portland, OR: International Society for Technology in Education.

Thomas, M., Howell, P. B., Crosby, S., Brkic, E., Clemons, K., McKinley, L., et al. (2019b). Teacher candidates' emerging perspectives on trauma informed teaching. *Kentucky Teacher Education Journal, 6*(1). Accessed at https://digitalcommons.murraystate.edu/ktej/vol6/iss1/2 on December 20, 2021.

Thomas, M. S., Crosby, S., & Vanderhaar, J. (2019c). Trauma-informed practices in schools across two decades: An interdisciplinary review of research. *Review of Research in Education, 43*(1), 422–452. https://doi.org/10.3102/0091732X18821123

Thompson, D. (2018, February 2). How immigration became so controversial. *The Atlantic.* Accessed at www.theatlantic.com/politics/archive/2018/02/why-immigration-divides/552125 on May 29, 2022.

Thompson, S. (2021, December 28). *Top 5 advantages and disadvantages of online classes for higher education* [Blog post]. Accessed at https://corp.kaltura.com/blog/advantages-disadvantages-online-classes on May 31, 2022.

Thoreson, R. (2022, February 17). *Florida advances "Don't say Gay" bill: Censoring discussions jeopardizes children's rights.* Accessed at www.hrw.org/news/2022/02/17/florida-advances-dont-say-gay-bill?gclid=CjwKCAjw4ayUBhA4EiwATWyBrgMn8VONNMwd2NupWSy8Fl9LGSzDKgg-Xqfl6yBOt4IQ1RkF6FXStBoCON4QAvD_BwE on May 23, 2022.

Tillman, R. (2022, February 15). *Report: Hate crimes rose 44% last year in study of major cities.* Accessed at www.ny1.com/nyc/all-boroughs/news/2022/02/14/hate-crime-increase-2021-asian-american- on May 20, 2022.

Tovar, I. (2021, May 10). *How educators can better support LGBTQ teachers of color.* Accessed at www.edutopia.org/article/how-educators-can-better-support-lgbtq-teachers-color on July 6, 2022.

Trans Student Educational Resources. (2020). *Gender pronouns.* Accessed at https://transstudent.org/graphics/pronouns101 on December 20, 2021.

Treadwell, H. M. (2013). *Beyond stereotypes in Black and White: How everyday leaders can build healthier opportunities for African American boys and men.* Santa Barbara, CA: Praeger.

The Trevor Project. (2021). *National survey on LGBTQ youth mental health 2021.* West Hollywood, CA: Author. Accessed at www.thetrevorproject.org/wp-content/uploads/2021/05/The-Trevor-Project-National-Survey-Results-2021.pdf on May 26, 2022.

Trump, C. (2021, August 20). Diversity, equity, and inclusion efforts on college campuses distract from education. *Washington Examiner.* Accessed at www.washingtonexaminer.com/opinion/op-eds/diversity-equity-and-inclusion-efforts-on-college-campuses-distract-from-education on May 13, 2022.

Tull, M. (2020, December 16). *People with PTSD can improve a negative self-image.* Accessed at www.verywellmind.com/self-supportive-statements-2797592 on December 20, 2021.

Turay, I., Jr. (2020, July 9). Is the George Floyd killing a pivotal moment in the nation's history? *Dayton Daily News.* Accessed at www.daytondailynews.com/news/local/the-george-floyd-killing-pivotal-moment-the-nation-history/zcc5KsFUBAyHS5Mf8LKbtK on May 13, 2022.

Tzu, L. (1996). *Tao te ching* (A. Waley, Trans.). London: Wordsworth Editions.

The University of Texas at San Antonio Libraries. (2021). *HOLC redlining maps of San Antonio.* Accessed at https://digital.utsa.edu/digital/collection/p16018coll12 on December 20, 2021.

The UN Refugee Agency. (n.d.). *What is a refugee?* Accessed at www.unhcr.org/en-us/what-is-a-refugee.html on May 29, 2022.

Urofsky, M. I. (2022). *Jim Crow law.* Accessed at www.britannica.com/event/Jim-Crow-law on December 20, 2021.

USA Facts. (2021, September 17). *Black students are more likely to be punished than White students.* Accessed at https://usafacts.org/articles/black-students-more-likely-to-be-punished-than-white-students on April 7, 2022.

U.S. Census Bureau. (2020). *Quarterly residential vacancies and homeownership.* Accessed at www.census.gov/housing/hvs/files/currenthvspress.pdf on December 20, 2021.

U.S. Department of Education. (2015). *Every Student Succeeds Act (ESSA).* Accessed at www.ed.gov/essa?src=rn on December 20, 2021.

Valenzuela, J. (2018, May 1). *Embed literacy into STEM projects.* Accessed at www.iste.org/explore/Computer-Science/Embed-literacy-into-STEM-projects on May 11, 2022.

Valenzuela, J. (2019a). Attitudes towards teaching computational thinking and computer science: Insights from educator interviews and focus groups. *Journal of Computer Science Integration, 2*(2), 2.

Valenzuela, J. (2019b, May 20). *Education coach Jorge Valenzuela talking to parents and stakeholders about CS and PBL* [Video]. YouTube. www.youtube.com/watch?v=26oqwkpMbs4&t=59s

Valenzuela, J. (2020a, July 21). *Make Remote Learning Accessible by Focusing on Equity & SEL–#ISTEsla20 Wk 2 Day 2* [Conference presentation]. Accessed at https://fishbowlteaching.com/2020/07/make-remote-learning-accessible-by-focusing-on-equity-sel-istesla20-wk-2-day-2 on June 17, 2022.

Valenzuela, J. (2020b, October 21). *3 ways to ensure IT and edtech plans promote learning.* Accessed at www.iste.org/explore/3-ways-ensure-it-and-edtech-plans-promote-learning on December 20, 2021.

Valenzuela, J. (2020c, September 9). *3 ways to integrate computer science in other classes.* Accessed at www.edutopia.org/article/3-ways-integrate-computer-science-other-classes on May 2, 2022.

Valenzuela, J. (2020d, April 23). *3 ways to make remote learning more engaging.* Accessed at www .iste.org/explore/learning-during-covid-19-2 on December 23, 2021.

Valenzuela, J. (2020e, July 17). *2 simple ways to improve online instruction.* Accessed at www .edutopia.org/article/2-simple-ways-improve-online-instruction on December 23, 2021.

Valenzuela, J. (2021a, October 14). *5 trauma-informed strategies for supporting refugee students.* Accessed at www.edutopia.org/article/5-trauma-informed-strategies-supporting-refugee -students on December 23, 2021.

Valenzuela, J. (2021b, January 8). *5 ways to become a more confident educator.* Accessed at medium.com/lifelong-learning-defined-for-peak-performance-in/5-ways-to-become-a-more -confident-educator-f0ec4194fe2e on December 20, 2021.

Valenzuela, J. (2021c, September 27). *Important items to consider for supporting Afghan refugee students.* Accessed at https://medium.com/lifelong-learning-defined-for-peak-performance-in /important-items-to-consider-for-supporting-aghan-refugee-students-9dbaeabd6a63 on July 6, 2022.

Valenzuela, J. (2021d, May 25). *Preparing staff for diversity, equity, and inclusion initiatives.* Accessed at www.edutopia.org/article/preparing-staff-diversity-equity-and-inclusion-initiatives on December 20, 2021.

Valenzuela, J. (2021e). *SEL in action: Tools to help students learn and grow.* Portland, OR: International Society for Technology in Education. Accessed at https://my.iste.org/s/store#/store /browse/detail/a1w1U000002ayPuQAI on September 8, 2022.

Valenzuela, J. (2021f, November 5). *A simple tool to help teachers regulate their emotions.* Accessed at www.edutopia.org/article/simple-tool-help-teachers-regulate-their-emotions on April 2, 2022.

Valenzuela, J. (2021g, June 25). *A tool to help students make good decisions.* Accessed at www .edutopia.org/article/tool-help-students-make-good-decisions on April 27, 2022.

Valenzuela, J. (2022a, March 3). *Boosting critical thinking across the curriculum.* Accessed at www .edutopia.org/article/boosting-critical-thinking-across-curriculum on June 2, 2022.

Valenzuela, J. (Host). (2022b, April 26). It's been an SEL school year: How much did it make a difference? [Audio podcast episode]. In *SEL in Action.* Accessed at www.bamradionetwork .com/track/its-been-an-sel-school-year-how-much-did-it-make-a-difference on June 5, 2022.

Valenzuela, J. (2022c, April 1). *A protocol to encourage robust classroom discussions.* Accessed at www .edutopia.org/article/protocol-encourage-robust-classroom-discussions on April 10, 2022.

Valenzuela, J. (2022d, January 20). *A simple, effective framework for PBL.* Accessed at www.edutopia .org/article/simple-effective-framework-pbl on May 31, 2022.

Valenzuela, J. (2022e, February 18). *A simple tool for aligning instruction and assessment.* Accessed at www.edutopia.org/article/simple-tool-aligning-instruction-and-assessment on April 13, 2022.

Valenzuela, J. (2022f, May 16). *Using frequent feedback cycles to guide student work.* Accessed at www .edutopia.org/article/using-frequent-feedback-cycles-guide-student-work on June 2, 2022.

van der Kolk, B. (2014). *The body keeps the score: Brain, mind, and body in the healing of trauma.* New York: Penguin.

Venet, A. S. (2017, October 16). *Trauma-informed practices benefit all students*. Accessed at www.edutopia.org/article/trauma-informed-practices-benefit-all-students on July 6, 2022.

Venet, A. S. (2021, August 3). *What I wish teachers knew about "what I wish my teacher knew."* Accessed at https://unconditionallearning.org/tag/trauma-informed-teaching on May 29, 2022.

Vollrath, D. (2020, January 14). *A de-escalation exercise for upset students*. Accessed at www.edutopia.org/article/de-escalation-exercise-upset-students on April 20, 2022.

Vygotsky, L. S. (1978). *Mind in society. The development of higher psychological processes*. Cambridge, MA: Harvard University Press.

Wachtel, T. (2016). *What is restorative practices?* International Institute for Restorative Practices. Accessed at www.iirp.edu/restorative-practices/what-is-restorative-practices on May 11, 2022.

Wah, Y. L., & Nasri, N. B. M. (2019). A systematic review: The effect of culturally responsive pedagogy on student learning and achievement. *International Journal of Academic Research in Business and Social Sciences*, *9*(5), 588–596.

Walker, T. (2016, March 9). *Isolation of Black and Latino students in high-poverty schools is growing*. Accessed at www.nea.org/advocating-for-change/new-from-nea/isolation-black-and-latino-students-high-poverty-schools-growing on April 18, 2022.

Walker, T. (2020, April 15). *Social-emotional learning should be priority during COVID-19 crisis*. Accessed at www.nea.org/advocating-for-change/new-from-nea/social-emotional-learning-should-be-priority-during-covid-19 on May 31, 2022.

Walton, G. M., & Cohen, G. L. (2011). A brief social-belonging intervention improves academic and health outcomes of minority students. *Science*, *331*(6023), 1447–1451. https://doi.org/10.1126/science.1198364

Wang, K., Chen, Y., Zhang, J., & Oudekerk, B. A. (2020). *Indicators of school crime and safety: 2019* (NCES 2020-063). Washington, DC: National Center for Education Statistics. Accessed at https://nces.ed.gov/pubs2020/2020063.pdf on July 6, 2022.

Waterford.org. (2019, October 23). *Why failure is good for learning, and how it applies to your struggling students*. Accessed at www.waterford.org/education/why-failure-is-better-than-success-for-learning on December 20, 2021.

Watson, E. (2020). #Education: The potential impact of social media and hashtag ideology on the classroom. *Research in Social Sciences and Technology*, *5*(2), 40–56. https://doi.org/10.46303/ressat.05.02.3

Watson Institute. (2022). *Social skills to read body language*. Accessed at www.thewatsoninstitute.org/resource/reading-body-language on April 25, 2022.

Wattanawongwan, S., Smith, S. D., & Vannest, K. J. (2021). Cooperative learning strategies for building relationship skills in students with emotional and behavioral disorders. *Beyond Behavior*, *30*(1), 32–40. https://doi.org/10.1177/1074295621997599

We Are Teachers Staff. (2021, July 27). *What teachers need to know about restorative justice*. Accessed at www.weareteachers.com/restorative-justice on December 20, 2021.

Weisburd, D., Petrosino, A., & Fronius, T. (2014). Randomized experiments in criminology and criminal justice. In G. Bruinsma & D. Weisburd (Eds.), *Encyclopedia of criminology and criminal justice* (pp. 4283–4291). New York: Springer.

Wiggins, G., & McTighe, J. (2005). *Understanding by design* (2nd ed.). Alexandria, VA: Association for Supervision and Curriculum Development.

Wiglesworth, M., Lendrum, A., Oldfield, J., Scott, A., ten Bokkel, I., Tate, K., et al. (2016). The impact of trial stage, developer involvement and international transferability on universal social and emotional learning programme outcomes: A meta-analysis. *Cambridge Journal of Education, 46*(3), 347–376.

Willen, E. J., & Allan, C. (2021, February 11). *Understanding implicit bias, and why it affects kids.* Accessed at www.childrensmercy.org/parent-ish/2021/02/implicit-bias on April 9, 2022.

Williams, M. T. (2019, February 13). *Uncovering the trauma of racism.* Accessed at www.apa.org/pubs/highlights/spotlight/issue-128 on July 6, 2022.

Wilson, J. P., & Thomas, R. B. (2004). *Empathy in the treatment of trauma and PTSD.* New York: Brunner-Routledge.

The Write of Your L!fe. (2020, August 30). *Trauma-informed teaching strategies for remote and in-person learning.* Accessed at thewriteofyourlife.org/trauma-informed-teaching-strategies on December 20, 2021.

Xu, T. (2022, May 16). *16 unconscious bias examples and how to avoid them in the workplace.* Accessed at https://builtin.com/diversity-inclusion/unconscious-bias-examples on September 6, 2022.

York, B. N. (2014, March). *Know the child: The importance of teacher knowledge of individual students' skills (KISS)* (CEPA Working Paper). Stanford, CA: Center for Education Policy Analysis.

Youth Engaged 4 Change. (n.d.) *What does LGBT mean? Know the basics.* Accessed at https://engage.youth.gov/resources/what-does-lgbt-mean-know-basics on July 19, 2022.

Yusem, D., Curtis, D., Johnson, K., & McClung, B. (n.d.). *Restorative justice implementation guide: A whole school approach.* Oakland, CA: Oakland Unified School District. Accessed at www.ousd.org/cms/lib/CA01001176/Centricity/Domain/134/BTC-OUSD1-IG-08b-web.pdf on February 24, 2022.

Zarrabi, G. (2020, June 14). *The impacts of trauma on child development.* Accessed at https://harbormentalhealth.com/2020/06/14/the-impacts-of-trauma-on-child-development on May 8, 2022.

Zhou, L. (2021, March 5). The long history of anti-Asian hate in America, explained. *Vox.* Accessed at www.vox.com/identities/2020/4/21/21221007/anti-asian-racism-coronavirus-xenophobia on May 19, 2022.

Zimmerman, P. (2019, June 11). *How emotions are made* [Blog post]. Accessed at www.noldus.com/blog/how-emotions-are-made on December 20, 2021.

Index

D

J

K

L

M

S

W

X

Z

Solution Tree's mission is to advance the work of our authors. By working with the best researchers and educators worldwide, we strive to be the premier provider of innovative publishing, in-demand events, and inspired professional development designed to transform education to ensure that all students learn.

The International Society for Technology in Education (ISTE) is home to a passionate community of global educators who believe in the power of technology to transform teaching and learning, accelerate innovation and solve tough problems in education.

ISTE inspires the creation of solutions and connections that improve opportunities for all learners by delivering: practical guidance, evidence-based professional learning, virtual networks, thought-provoking events and the ISTE Standards. ISTE is also the leading publisher of books focused on technology in education. For more information or to become an ISTE member, visit iste.org. Subscribe to ISTE's YouTube channel and connect with ISTE on Twitter, Facebook and LinkedIn.

Change Starts With Me
Madeleine Rogin
You can make a difference in how young students see and understand race and racism. Grounded in real-world examples, this accessible, insightful guide tackles topics like White silence, the scientific origin of skin color, and societal fears of being perceived as a racist.
BKG034

The Identity-Conscious Educator
Liza A. Talusan
Learn powerful, practical strategies for creating an inclusive school community and engaging in meaningful conversations to make this work successful. *The Identity-Conscious Educator* provides a framework for building awareness and understanding of five identity categories: race, social class, gender, sexual orientation, and disability.
BKG031

Dismantling a Broken System
Zachary Wright
Become a hyperlocal activist for change and help ensure a bright future for every student. Written for educators at all levels, this resource dives into the American education system, exposing the history of discrimination and offering strategies for establishing financially and academically equitable learning environments.
BKG015

Finding Your Blind Spots
Hedreich Nichols
Author Hedreich Nichols infuses this book with a direct yet conversational style to help you identify biases that adversely affect your practice and learn how to move beyond those biases to ensure a more equitable, inclusive campus culture.
BKG022

SEL in Action: Tools to Help Students Learn and Grow
by Jorge Valenzuela (iste.org/SELJSG)

Not all educators teach in districts where training in SEL and related topics such as restorative justice, trauma-informed teaching and culturally responsive teaching is readily available. In this six-page guide, author and educator Jorge Valenzuela introduces educators to the Equity and SEL Integration Framework that will help them understand core SEL competencies and design lessons that activate SEL in their curriculum.

Closing the Gap: Digital Equity Strategies for the K–12 Classroom
by Nicol R. Howard, Sarah Thomas, and Regina Schaffer (iste.org/EquityK12)

Closing the Gap is an ISTE book series designed to reflect the contributions of multiple stakeholders seeking to ensure that digital equity is achieved on campuses, in classrooms, and throughout education. In this book, three experts on equity and technology offer concrete, evidence-based strategies for classroom teachers to move toward digital equity in K–12 settings.

Closing the Gap: Digital Equity Strategies for Teacher Prep Programs
by Nicol R. Howard, Sarah Thomas, and Regina Schaffer (iste.org/EquityTeaching)

Closing the Gap is an ISTE book series designed to reflect the contributions of multiple stakeholders seeking to ensure that digital equity is achieved on campuses, in classrooms, and throughout education. In this book, three experts on equity and technology offer research, evidence-based strategies, and examples of best practices to move toward digital equity in teacher education programs and beyond.

Creative SEL: Using Hands-on Projects to Boost Social-Emotional Learning
by Michele Haiken and Mark Gura (iste.org/CreativeSEL)

Research shows that creativity can be beneficial for mental health and can help build critical skills such as empathy and introspection, while social-emotional learning (SEL) is an integral part of education and human development. This book bridges these two ideas with a series of creative projects that foster SEL learning by promoting growth mindset, supporting mindfulness, offering ways to cope with anxiety and stress, and encouraging and guiding positive social activism.

www.ingramcontent.com/pod-product-compliance
Lightning Source LLC
Chambersburg PA
CBHW081353220125
20702CB00019BA/266

* 9 7 8 1 9 5 2 8 1 2 9 1 0 *